Defending China

GERALD SEGAL

OXFORD UNIVERSITY PRESS
1985

Oxford University Press, Walton Street, Oxford OX2 6DP

London New York Toronto
Delhi Bombay Calcutta Madras Karachi
Kuala Lumpur Singapore Hong Kong Tokyo
Nairobi Dar es Salaam Cape Town
Melbourne Auckland

and associated companies in
Beirut Berlin Ibadan Mexico City Nicosia

Oxford is a trade mark of Oxford University Press

Published in the United States
by Oxford University Press, New York

British Library Cataloguing in Publication Data

Segal, Gerald
    Defending China.
    1. China—Military policy
    I. Title
    355'.0335'51   UA835
    ISBN   0-19-827470-X .

Library of Congress Cataloging in Publication Data

Segal, Gerald, 1953–
    Defending China.

    Bibliography: p.
    Includes index.
    1. China—Military policy.   2. China—Armed Forces.
3. China—History, Military.   I. Title.
UA835.S44   1984   355'.0335'51   84–16669

ISBN 0-19-827470-X

Set by South End Typographics, India.
Printed in Great Britain by Billings and Sons Limited,
London and Worcester

For my mother

Acknowledgements

It would be most convenient to blame the shortcomings of this book on those who read the manuscript and failed to spot the errors. However, these colleagues are also friends, so I must accept full responsibility. Special debts of gratitude are owed to Ellis Joffe and David Armstrong, both of whom showed great patience in deciphering early drafts and in urging me to tone down the rhetoric. Above all, Edwina Moreton picked apart the prose in a way that only a good journalist can. If not for her, this book would have been published sooner.

January 1984   Gerald Segal

Contents

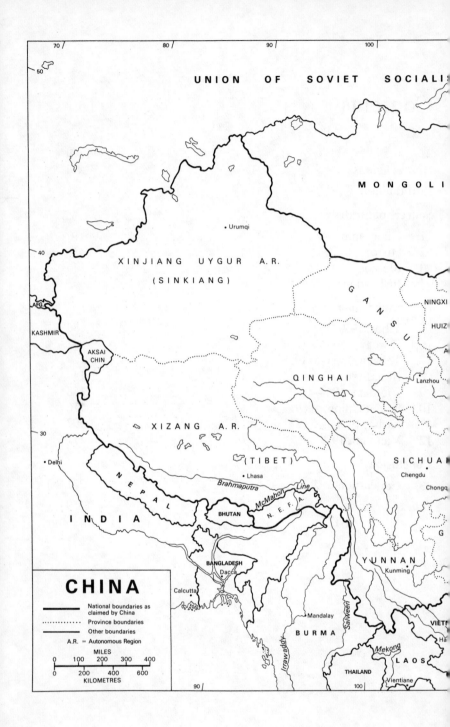

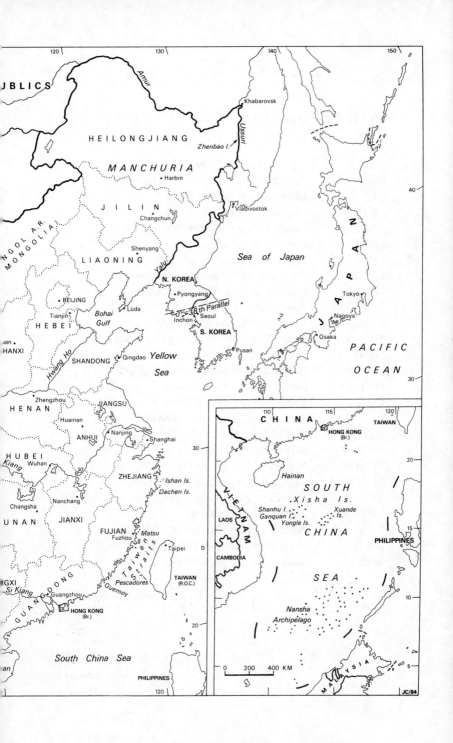

Abbreviations (For the text and notes)

AFP	Agence France Press
BBC	British Broadcasting Corporation
CCP	Chinese Communist Party
CCPCC	Chinese Communist Party Central Committee
CMC	Central Military Commission
DRV	Democratic Republic of Vietnam (North)
FBIS	Foreign Broadcast Information Service
FEER	Far Eastern Economic Review
GPD	General Political Department
JPRS	Joint Publication Research Service
MAC	Military Affairs Committee
NCNA	New China News Agency (Xinhua)
NDIC	National Defence Industrial Committee
NDIO	National Defence Industrial Office
NEFA	North East Frontier Area
PLA	People's Liberation Army
ROC	Republic of China (Taiwan)
ROK	Republic of Korea (South)
RVN	Republic of Vietnam (South)
SCMM	Survey of China Mainland Magazines
SCMP	Survey of China Mainland Press
SPRCM	Survey of PRC Magazines
SPRCP	Survey of PRC Press
SRV	Socialist Republic of Vietnam (United)
SWB	Summary of World Broadcasts (BBC)
URI	Union Research Institute

Introduction

Actually, when Comrade Mao Zedong was guiding Chinese revolutionary warfare, he never adhered to one pattern. He always adopted flexible strategic and tactical principles in the light of the political, economic and military conditions of the enemy and ourselves.

Yang Yong, 1983[1]

...we should never forget that war is a practical question...whether we'll have to fight is not decided by our subjective wishes.

Liberation Army Daily, 1979[2]

Defending China is not easy. China's long land and sea frontiers, often shared with hostile neighbours, make the demands of defence difficult. States evolve defence policy for a number of reasons, and use force in pursuit of national defence in their own special way. But how special is China's defence policy?

An answer to this question can be provided in several ways. Most attempts to explain Chinese defence policy have focused on the military system of China, or the equipment of its forces.[3] The following analysis will slice the subject in a different way. The aim is to analyse how China uses armed force in pursuit of its foreign policy. Far more comprehensive analyses have recently been undertaken of the United States's and the Soviet Union's use of force,[4] but since the Second World War China has fought more major wars and lost more men in combat than either of the superpowers.

To be sure, there have been some attempts to draw over-arching conclusions about Chinese defence policy,[5] but in only one have more than two case studies been analysed in a book-length work. What is striking however is that, to the extent that comprehensive conclusions have been drawn in the Chinese case, they have pointed to some logic or consistent calculus in how China uses force.[6] In contrast to many of the surveys of the superpowers, the majority of China analysts have claimed to see regular and coherent patterns governing the use of China's military instrument. Without giving away too much of the heart of this study, it should be clear (if only from the introductory quotations) that one conclusion of this study will be that in the main no such consistency or logic really exists.

This scepticism regarding rules of behaviour is not derived from any natural dislike of social science theorizing or synthesizing.[7] The original purpose of the present study was precisely to look at further patterns in Chinese behaviour. But in the early stages of research it became clear that the main assumption behind the approach would have to be altered.

This difference between what John Gaddis has called 'lumpers' and 'splitters'[8] is not new. Some emphasize the common—the lumpers—and others emphasize the special nature of each event—the splitters. In the study that follows, the emphasis is clearly with the splitters, but not uncritically so. Those who have drawn our attention to supposed patterns of behaviour have done us a great service, if only in focusing our attention on key questions. But after having used these structures of analysis, we should have the courage, to tear down the models if they are found to be structurally unsound.[9] That is not to say that the building process was a waste of time, for at the very least we learned a great deal about what is special about our territory.

Before outlining in detail what this study will try to do, it is perhaps useful to pre-empt some lines of potential criticism by suggesting what it will not try to do. First, this is not a study of the use of the Chinese People's Liberation Army (PLA) in domestic politics. While great attention is paid to the domestic dimension of Chinese policy making, the use of the PLA, for example in the Cultural Revolution, is only considered in its effect on Chinese foreign policy. Second, unlike the two Brookings studies of the superpowers, this study of China does not cover every incident where China used force beyond its borders. For example, there have been numerous border clashes, even where casualties were suffered, but they are ignored unless they resulted in a crisis,[10] as in 1969 with the Soviet Union, or in 1979 with Vietnam. Third, this study does not consider all cases where China may have implicitly or explicitly threatened the use of force, but never actually carried out its threat. For example, such threats were made in the 1971 Indo-Pakistan war, but nothing ever came of them.

Fourth, this study is not primarily concerned with the nuts and bolts of military deployments. While others may study the specific military equipment used by the PLA, or the details of 'the face of battle', this study is more concerned with broader implications for strategy and defence policy. In any case, superior studies of the technical dimension of Chinese defence policy already exist.[11]

Defending China

Having said what this book is not, obviously some outline must be provided of what the book more positively tries to achieve. The book's two main sections attempt to provide answers to the basic questions of why and how China uses force in its foreign policy.

The first section outlines what are said to be the four main sources of Chinese strategy. A great number of analyses have suggested various determinants of Chinese defence policy, and this section looks in depth at the most prominent ones. They relate to a wide range of topics, covering the relationship between the Party and the military, biases in military doctrine, and limitations on PLA capability. In this first section the intention is merely to sketch the most important trends. The real testing of the validity of these principles comes in the second, and larger section of the study.

The second part is composed of comparative case studies of the major incidents where China used force on, or beyond its frontiers. Before explaining precisely which aspects of these cases have been studied, some points must be made about the rationale for choosing the nine events. It can be argued that operations in Tibet, the Taiwan Straits, and Zhenbao and Xisha (Paracel) Islands were all on rightful territory of the People's Republic of China (PRC) and therefore constituted internal use of force beyond the scope of this study. However, in all those cases, sovereignty over the territory was seriously disputed and outside states became involved. This study is less concerned about legal issues of sovereignty, and more with the actual nature of the conflict. Whatever the case, all the nine incidents involved the use of PLA power beyond the line of actual Chinese political control. None of the cases involved significant foreign infringement of territory on the Chinese side of the line of control, although some border incidents did penetrate a few miles inside China's front line.

Needless to say, this study has not been primarily concerned with establishing the justification or otherwise of China's use of force, but rather with explaining why China chose to resort to violence, and how it carried out its operations. To this end, the case studies were organized around three major areas of analysis. First, what were China's objectives? Some previous analyses have concluded that China is defensive and cautious to a remarkable degree in the pursuit of foreign policy objectives. However evidence from the analyses of the use of force by the superpowers suggests that intentions are rarely so clearly pacific, and that objectives are rarely unchanging during the course of combat. More often than not, states pursue what Moltke called the 'strategy of expedients', for as the German strategist noted, 'I have always believed that there are always three courses open to the enemy—and that he usually takes the fourth'.

In fact it seems to be the consensus of military strategists that the objectives of war are far from fixed and straightforward. Strategists, from Sun Zi to Clausewitz and beyond, have argued that war is a continuation of policy, and thus objectives in war must change as general policy changes.[12] B. H. Liddell Hart wrote of the need for 'alternative objectives' as grand strategy must necessarily be complex. 'A plan, like a tree, must have branches—if it is to bear fruit'.[13] Since the object of war is 'to gain a better peace' it is difficult to be certain what the peace will look like when the war starts. It is precisely because wars are generally fought for multiple objectives that the attempts to terminate war have been plagued by such problems.[14] A prime focus of this study will be how Chinese objectives change, and the extent to which they have been realized at the end of each crisis.

The most frequently identified objective pursued by China since 1949 has been deterrence. However, even if China may have entered a particular crisis with the purpose of simple deterrence it has often found its objectives changing. Here deterrence is taken to mean the attempt by China to persuade an opponent not to undertake an action because the costs to the opponent will be too high.[15] Should the opponent persist, deterrence has failed and China may decide to engage in compellence—the attempt to force the opponent to undo his unacceptable action.[16] While deterrence and compellence are separate actions, they can both be elements of the same crisis. They can also feature in crises where China engages in more aggressive action. For example, China may choose to probe enemy intentions prior to taking offensive steps; it may try to teach lessons to an enemy, or even try to seize territory.

These objectives do not necessarily lie on a single ladder of escalation. Rather they can be pursued in various orders as crises undergo major changes of nature in the heat of battle. The absence of a single escalation ladder does not mean that this study is not concerned with the details of crisis management.[17] On the contrary, it is one of the main purposes of this study to determine how China manages crises.

The second major aspect analysed is the nature of PLA operations. Here we are concerned with two broad sub-sections. First, what was the nature of China's strategy and tactics? This central aspect to the study seeks to determine whether there is any pattern to Chinese military strategy. Obviously China faces different types of threats, but does it respond to them in the same way? This involves an analysis of both Chinese strategy—for example does China fight 'at the gates'—and Chinese tactics—for example does China regularly engage in 'human wave' operations and/or eschew positional warfare? A great deal has been taken as given about the nature of China's military doctrine, including particularly the notion of 'people's war'.

The dividing line between strategy and tactics is of course far from clear. For Liddell Hart, strategy is

the art of distributing and applying military means to fulfill the end of policy....When the application of the military instrument merges into actual fighting, the dispositions for and control of such direct action are termed 'tactics'. The two categories, although convenient for discussion, can never be truly divided into separate compartments because each not only influences, but merges into the other...It is difficult to decide exactly where a strategical movement ends and a tactical movement begins, yet in conception the two are distinct. Tactics lies in and fills the province of fighting. Strategy not only stops on the frontier, but has for its purpose the reduction of fighting to the slenderest possible proportions.[18]

In the study that follows, strategy remains a broad term, encompassing 'grand strategy' and the broad objectives of policy. Finally, strategy and indeed tactics, are considered 'arts' not subject to rigid scientific definition.[19]

The second part of the operations section deals with the role of outside powers. To what extent have powers, not directly involved in the conflict, affected China's conduct of its operations? Is there a pattern to the way China has coped with these outside pressures? It has been argued that China tends to avoid alliances more than any other great power, and that this is a distinctive aspect of Chinese foreign policy. However, while it is true that China has no open, formal alliances with other states (unlike the superpowers) this places undue emphasis on the formal meaning of alliance. Often less formal bonds are tighter and of greater significance.[20]

The third and final aspect analysed is the role of Chinese domestic politics. In other words, how do China's domestic and foreign policy interact? The issue in focus here is whether domestic politics (be it debates over policy or even agreed domestic policies) affect the conduct of foreign policy. China's use of force has been seen by some as largely a response to a sense of acute fear derived from domestic unrest. However, while it seems clear that internal politics do have an important impact on China's conduct in a crisis, Beijing's reaction is not always defensive.

Research Questions

The concluding chapter will try to pull together these numerous strands running through both main portions of the book. In order to make this task easier, as well as to help keep the reader's attention, ten of the most basic themes of the study can be stated here, and carried through the text to a review in the conclusion. These themes are in fact more questions than answers. They are designed to be fairly general, in order to provide a framework of analysis, rather than suggest neat answers. Although, this study will suggest there are few consistent patterns explaining China's use of its military instrument, this does not mean that the subject is so amorphous that it cannot be organized in some way. The following ten major questions can be outlined.

1. *In what way does China's geography determine the way in which China uses its military instrument?*

This aspect of Chinese strategy is outlined in chapter one and then assessed in each of the chapters of section two as it seems relevant. While Mackinder-like determinism for geographic factors is no longer in vogue, it is plausible that any special Chinese quality in its defence policy will be derived, at least in part, from its physical and human attributes.

2. *In what way does China's history determine the way in which China uses its military instrument?*

This aspect of Chinese strategy is outlined in chapter two and then assessed in each of the chapters of section two. It is often asserted that Chinese foreign policy has deep historical roots, while others, mimicking Henry Ford, would suggest that all 'history is bunk'. There is no doubt a more balanced perspective.

3. *In what way does China's ideology determine the way in which China uses its military instrument?*

This aspect of Chinese strategy is outlined in chapter three and then assessed in each of the chapters of section two. China, like the

Soviet Union, asserts that it follows a defence policy with a consistent ideological base, while many observers in the West suggest ideology is merely a smoke-screen for other motives. The role of ideology in fact seems to be much over-simplified, especially to the extent that it is seen to be inflexible and unchanging.

4. *In what way do China's institutions determine the way in which China uses its military instrument?*

This aspect of Chinese strategy is outlined in chapter four and then assessed in the domestic dimension of each case study. That Chinese policy is not made in a 'black-box' is now fairly clear. But the extent to which Party–Army, inter-service, or other institutional conflicts affect policy making, is far from clear.

5. *Does China pursue any consistent objectives in its use of military force?*

This question forms the bulk of the first part of chapters 5–12. The analysis is especially concerned with how and why Chinese objectives change, whether this tends to happen within the course of one crisis, or varies from one crisis to another.

6. *Is there a consistent pattern to Chinese crisis management?*

This question is tackled in the first part of chapters 5–12. In many senses this was the first question that stimulated the research for this study. Many analysts have suggested that such a consistency does exist, but the evidence in the following chapters suggests a more complex judgement.

7. *Is there a consistent Chinese military strategy?*

This question forms part of the second section of chapter 5–12. Obviously different threats require different military strategies to cope with them. On those grounds alone the assumption of any single coherent, let alone consistent, Chinese military strategy seems most dubious. What is more, the changing circumstances in which combat is waged suggest the very practical need for flexibility in strategy.

8. *Is there a set of consistent Chinese military tactics?*

This question is dealt with in the second part of the second section of chapter 5–12. It is clear that the dividing line between strategy and tactics is less than precise, but one of the purposes of this study was to assess whether PLA tactics followed any consistent pattern.

9. *Is there a pattern to the way in which outside powers determine the way in which China uses its military power?*

This question is covered in the final part of the second section of chapters 5–12. In each crisis at least one outside power has played an important role in China's calculus, but it is far from clear that China reacts to the presence of outside powers in the same way in each crisis.

10. *How important are domestic politics in the determination of how China uses its military instrument*?

This question is covered in detail in the third section of chapters 5–12. The fact that domestic debates were of varying intensity, and pitted different factions against each other, suggests only some of the difficulty in drawing persuasive patterns on this question.

Finally, to a certain extent, the splittist and critical bias of this study is in keeping with attitudes towards China that came to the fore in the early 1980s. While writers in the previous decade were working in an atmosphere where the dominant pressure was to be positive about China, there is now a greater willingness to point to hypocrisies and failings in Chinese policy. After all, the Chinese are themselves leading the way in self-criticism. Western analysts would be lax if they failed to take account of that and other changes.

NOTES

1. Guangming Ribao, 22 January 1983, in *BBC*/SWB/FE/7252/B11/7.
2. Editorial, 26 March 1979, in *BBC*/SWB/FE/6078/A3/11.
3. The study of Chinese defence policy has been surveyed in Gerald Segal, 'Chinese Defence Policy', *International Affairs*, Vol. 59 No. 3, Autumn 1983, and in Gerald Segal and William Tow, eds., *Chinese Defence Policy* (London: Macmillan, 1984).
4. The two superb Brookings studies are by Barry Blechman and Stephen Kaplan, *Force Without War* (Washington: Brookings, 1978) and Stephen Kaplan, *Diplomacy of Power* (Washington: Brookings, 1981). There have also been some excellent, but more general works on Chinese foreign policy. See Michael Yahuda, *China's Role in World Affairs* (London: Croom Helm, 1978), and David Armstrong, *Revolutionary Diplomacy* (Berkeley, University of California Press, 1977).
5. The two most comprehensive surveys are Melvin Gurtov and Byong-Moo Hwang, *China Under Threat* (Baltimore: Johns Hopkins, 1980) and Davis Bobrow, Steve Chan, John Kringen, *Understanding Foreign Policy Decisions; The Chinese Case.* (New York: The Free Press, 1979). Also, Samuel Kim, *China, the U.N. and World Order* (Princeton: Princeton University Press, 1979). Two shorter, or monograph length studies have also suggested some coherence and consistency in China's policy. Steve Chan, 'China's Conflict Calculus and Behaviour' *World Politics*, Vol. 30 No. 3. April 1978, and Jonathan Pollack, *Security, Strategy and the Logic of Chinese Foreign Policy* Research Paper No. 5, (Institute of East Asian Studies, University of California, Berkeley, 1981). The work of Allen Whiting has been left for last not because it is inferior—far from

it—but rather because from this author's point of view, Whiting's work is decidedly superior. It is notable that despite his suggestion that China may see itself as pursuing a consistent policy, it in fact rarely does so. See *China Crosses the Yalu* (New York: Macmillan, 1960) and *The Chinese Calculus of Deterrence* (Ann Arbor: University of Michigan Press, 1975).

6. Segal, 'Chinese Defence Policy' and especially Gurtov and Hwang, *China Under Threat*, and Chan, 'China's Calculus'.
7. Gerald Segal, *The Great Power Triangle* (London: Macmillan, 1982). *The China Factor* (London: Croom Helm, 1982).
8. John Lewis Gaddis, *Strategies of Containment* (London: Oxford University Press, 1982).
9. For two studies that use flexible but useful structures, the first more openly than the second, see Alexander George and Richard Smoke, *Deterrence in American Foreign Policy* (New York: Columbia University Press, 1974). Christopher Thorne, *Allies of a Kind* (London: Oxford University Press, 1978).
10. The use of the term crisis is drawn from Segal, *The Great Power Triangle*.
11. Harlan Jencks, *From Muskets to Missiles* (Boulder, Colorado: Westview Press, 1982) and service chapters in Segal and Tow eds., *Chinese Defence*.
12. On Clausewitz see Michael Howard and Peter Paret, eds. and trans., *Carl Von Clausewitz: On War* (Princeton: Princeton University Press, 1976). Also Michael Howard, *Clausewitz* (London: Oxford University Press, 1983). Michael Howard, *The Causes of War* (London: Temple Smith, 1983) especially pp. 198–207.
13. B. H. Liddell Hart, *Strategy* (New York: Signet, 1974) pp. 329–30, 338–52, Ch. 22.
14. Gordon Craig and Alexander George, *Force and Statecraft* (London: Oxford University Press, 1983) Ch. 16.
15. For a review of deterrence literature see Gerald Segal, 'Strategy and Ethnic-chic', *International Affairs*, Vol. 60 No. 1, Winter 1983–4.
16. Based loosely on Thomas Schelling, *Arms and Influence* (London: Yale University Press, 1966), pp. 69–78.
17. On crisis management see Craig and George, *Force and Statecraft*, Ch. 20. Also A. L. George, D. K. Hall, W. E. Simons, *The Limits of Coercive Diplomacy* (Boston: Little Brown, 1971). Coral Bell, *The Conventions of Crisis* (London, Martin Robertson, 1971) Phil Williams, *Crisis Management* (Oxford: Martin Robertson, 1976).
18. Liddell Hart, *Strategy*, pp. 321, 324.
19. *Ibid.*, p. 322 and Howard, *Clausewitz*.
20. Michael Brecher's important work on this relationship is developed in *Decisions in Israel's Foreign Policy* (London: Oxford University Press, 1974) and *Jerusalem Journal of International Relations*, Vol. 3. Nos. 2–3, Winter-Spring, 1978.

1

Geography

It is clearly unfashionable to suggest that geography or geopolitics are in any way useful in the analysis of Chinese defence policy. The significance of the works of Sir Halford Mackinder and Admiral Alfred Mahan is properly minimized in earlier studies of China, but this does not mean that there is no value in the issues they explored. Modern students of strategy are increasingly returning to the study of such basic elements as geopolitics and national style in an attempt to overcome the serious problem of ethnocentrism in strategic analysis.[1]

While geography does not wholly determine Chinese strategy, it is an important starting point in setting some of the possible parameters of defence policy. While it is also true that geopolitical analysis tends to build on preconceptions of what are the main problems, it can also point to some enduring facts—for example, that modern technology has reduced, but not eliminated the importance of topography.[2] In any case, one state's perception of its own geographic weakness (for example the USSR) and the strength of its opponent (Moscow's view of China) can be just as important as the reality of geography. The Chinese themselves are in little doubt about the importance of geographic factors, for Mao's comments on the connection between defence and China's special qualities, are still viewed favourably in Beijing.

At the most fundamental level of strategy it is important to explore such basic topics as what is being defended, or what is easier or harder to defend? Mackinder's 'heartland' theory tells us little about China, but it does urge us to explore the extent to which there is a 'core' China to be defended. Some of the more outlandish analyses have suggested that China's core would dominate Russia's core, while others have ascribed to Lin Biao the geopolitical strategy of engulfing the world's urban population in a sea of peasant-based people's war.[3] It is more useful to know what is contained in China's core, whether it is divided, for example, between a monsoonal south and a continental north, and whether China has any important naval interests.[4] It is therefore necessary to begin with the basics. By analysing the essentials of China's physical and human geography it will be possible to suggest some issues which are more important than others, and some relative strengths and weaknesses in Chinese defence policy.

Physical Geography

China is the third largest country in the world.[5] Its 9.6m square kilometres make it the largest country in the temperate zones, but more than half the country is more than one and a half kilometres above sea level and only 11 per cent can be classified as plains.[6] Thus defending China means defending virtually an entire continent. In physical geographic terms China certainly can lay claim to great power status. However, the question must be asked whether this geography is a strength or a weakness.

China's land boundary is 28,072.6 kilometres long, and it has an 18,000 kilometre coastline. Defence needs are therefore both land and sea oriented. By contrast Soviet defence is overwhelmingly land-based, whereas the United States has focused on sea-based defence. China's maritime interests bring it into contact essentially with three states (USSR, Korea, and Japan) in the north, and three others in the south (Vietnam, Taiwan, and the Philippines).[7] The northern sector is more difficult to defend as the coastline is relatively open and the shore generally sandy. However, the Bohai Gulf, which constitutes a large portion of this section, is nearly a Chinese lake which makes the defence of Tianjin and Luda relatively easy. The crucial port of Shanghai farther south is dangerously exposed to attack. The southern portion of the coast, on the other hand, is rocky, but dotted with over 5,000 islands making defence of all territory next to impossible. The key port of Guangzhou is less vulnerable than Shanghai but can be blockaded, especially if Macao and Hong Kong are in hostile hands. Thus in geographic terms China would appear to require urgently a large and flexible naval force capable of dealing with great varieties of conditions. Like India's, and unlike the USSR's which is land-oriented, China's defence depends to an important extent on naval power. While this sea-borne threat may be a less serious challenge to the defence of

China's core, in limited war a naval challenge could assume greater importance. The geographical legacy is therefore relevant to certain aspects of naval power.

China's main national security problems are concerned with the configurations of its land frontiers. China borders on twelve countries, and has by far the longest land frontiers in the world.[8] Unlike the Soviet Union, China has no buffer of friendly states among those neighbours, and thus border security is more crucial in geographic terms for China than for any other country. To China's geographic credit, its relatively compact shape makes it more able to deal with disparate neighbours compared with either the elongated and vulnerable Soviet Union, or the United States (with distant territory like Alaska or Hawaii). This preliminary assessment suggests greater challenges for Chinese defence. However, China probably has less to fear from threats to fundamental national security and more from separate threats from individual neighbours. The question remains: how do the facts of China's physical geography help or hinder the attempt to meet these challenges?

China's land frontiers are mostly favourable to her defence either against general attack or small scale invasions, especially as compared with the Soviet Union. While it is true that there is rarely such a thing as a natural frontier to aid defence, China does seem to have several topographical advantages.[9] In the south, China generally holds the high ground, making attack by China easier and defence certainly more simple. Few clear topographical lines are apparent, which therefore makes frontiers uncertain, but defending such territory is not as difficult as attacking it.

However, this applies primarily to the less crucial southern territory, and largely the reverse is true on the northern borders with the Soviet Union and Outer Mongolia. In this area, which is close to some of China's most crucial economic centres, the USSR holds most of the high ground. The border area is largely not clearly marked by natural features, and is therefore more subject to incursion and subversion. To a certain extent the open plains and plateaux of the north are also a Soviet vulnerability, but they are far from any crucial Soviet site. The USSR's main population centres along the Pacific coast are relatively well protected by various geographical features.

From the Chinese side the topographical features do however provide some comfort. The Great Khingan mountains in the northeast shield all but the first 200 kilometres of China, and in combination with the Lesser Khingan mountains offer an invader only two relatively vulnerable access routes into Manchuria. The Nun river to Qiqihar and the Lungani to Harbin cut gaps in these mountain ridges, but these can be easily shut, and thereby the difficulties in defending China are minimized. The plateaux and mountains of Inner Mongolia are closest to big population centres such as Beijing or Lanzhou, but are not nearly as vulnerable in a topographical sense as parts of Manchuria. Thus defending China's geographic frontiers is generally encouraging, and even in the northeast the problems are not extreme.

Among other aspects of physical geography, climate does not seem much to affect China's defence. Despite some vehement proponents of theories relating climate and policy, it is more plausible to share Adolf Hitler's view when some sought to dissuade him from invading the Soviet Union, that: 'it rains on the enemy too'.[10] (Though the rain proved to be the least of his worries.) Climate does have different effects on strategy: it makes defence marginally more effective than offence in the summer, when it rains in the south, or in the winter, when the mountains are impassable. The only time when climate might favour offence would be in the winter in the north when frozen rivers and marshland make offensive movement easier. Thus the timing of war may in part be influenced by climate, and this may affect the management of certain small-scale crises— yet it seems unlikely that the long-term defence of China is much affected.

An important long-term dimension of physical geography in defending China is that of natural resources. For example, the superpowers are largely self-sufficient in most resources, but Japan's dependence on foreign oil makes it less able to carry on a prolonged conflict. China seems to fall very clearly into the superpower category, and although this barely affects the defence of China against small-scale threats, it can be crucial in major challenges to national integrity.

China's relative supply of natural resources is roughly equal to that of the US or USSR. It is a major producer of almost all essential minerals; its world ranking, for example, in coal reserves and production is third, and fourth for iron ore production.[11] While China has some problems in extracting some of its minerals, of all the major items it is short only of copper and to a lesser extent of aluminium, nickel and chromite. These shortcomings are however hardly different from Soviet and American ones, and place China in the exclusive rank of states potentially independent of resource pressures.

The location of these minerals is also a source of security in defending China. Most energy sources, ferrous, and non-ferrous metals are inside what can be designated as core China.[12] This territory, which comprises about half China's territory and over 95 per cent of its population, possesses almost all minerals except some iron ore, and oil deposits near the Soviet border and Outer Mongolia. Important non-ferrous metals are located in China's southeast, but still inside the core. Thus China is not only less likely to become embroiled in resource disputes with its neighbours, but more importantly, in all but the most massive invasion, China's potential for self-sufficiency is unlikely to be affected.

To sum up, China's physical geography suggests that defending China, while not easy, is by no means impossible. Land invasion—the only fundamental threat to China's national security—is made difficult by aspects of topography. While China is vulnerable to certain border challenges or seaborne threats, its geography makes it easier to defend rather than attack 'core China'.

Human Geography

China has more people than any other country, but is this essential fact of human geography an asset or a liability? China's 1982 population of 1,008,175,288[13] is roughly four times that of the USSR or US making foreign occupation of the PRC next to impossible. An invading power would have to cope with a combination of population plus territory; China's density of population is 102 people per sq. km., slightly greater than that of Europe, half that of Japan, and ten times that of the USSR.[14] More accurately, core China is only half the land but has over 95 per cent of the population, thereby doubling the population density and making it comparable to Japan's peak.[15]

The near impossibility of occupying China is made even more clear if the distribution of that population is considered. Sixty six per cent of the Chinese population is in agricultural employment, twice that of the USSR or East Europe, three times that of Japan and West Europe, and twelve times that of the US and Canada.[16] Some agricultural areas such as the Yangtze valley, and parts of

Sichuan and Guangdong are very densely populated, but by and large the massive and dispersed rural population makes it most difficult to occupy and hold China.

China's urban population is about 15 per cent of the total, compared to 50 per cent in the USSR. One third of China's urban population is concentrated in twenty-one great cities, each with a population above one million. The Soviet Union has more cities over the one million mark and they contain a higher proportion of the total USSR population.[17] Thus attacking China's cities, either in a massive nuclear strike, or in a punitive raid, does proportionally less damage to China than to any other great power. While China is clearly vulnerable to attacks on its cities, it is far less so than the superpowers. To defeat China, the core must be invaded and occupied and demography renders both tasks extremely difficult.

The location of China's twenty-one largest cities adds to the difficulty of invading China.[18] None of the twenty-one are outside core China and of the seven cities with more than three million people none are within 800 km of the nearest frontier. Beijing, Tianjin and Shenyang are the closest to the Soviet frontier and Guangzhou and Shanghai are on the coast and therefore vulnerable to naval attack. While it is true that in the missile age, where both superpowers have massive overkill, such urban distribution remains vulnerable. Nevertheless, compared to the superpowers' population distribution, China is relatively better off. It is also true that these five most vulnerable cities provide targets for conventional, punitive attacks on China, but such an attack would fall short of dealing a fundamental blow to Chinese society.

From a demographic point of view a strategy based on defending core China in a people's war, makes sense. The 50 per cent of the country that is sparsely populated cannot be defended in such a way and indeed is· geographically most vulnerable. It is also the less crucial part of China. Although this does not minimize its vulnerability to limited attacks, such offensives would not be as damaging to China. In the event of strategic nuclear attack, China's defence is not so much based on the absence of useful urban targets, as on the fact that the majority of China's population live outside these obvious targets.[19] In order to subjugate China, the country must be invaded in a costly conventional fashion.

These conclusions are reinforced by consideration of China's minority population. There are fifty-six ethnic groups in China but

93 per cent of the country's population is Han. Ten of these groups number more than one million people and they are largely based in the five autonomous regions which lie almost entirely outside core China.[20] The border areas outside core China are vulnerable to cross-border subversion, but the impact on core China would be minimal. With the exception of the Zhuang population in south China and some Koreans in the northeast, core China's population is ethnically unified. The thesis about the dismemberment of China because of its ethnic vulnerability does hold for non-core areas.[21] On the other hand, if such a tactic were used, it would pose as much of a threat to the enemy (such as Vietnam or the Soviet Union) since it too has similar minorities along its side of the frontier. In any case, an attacker hoping to seize territory and set up a regime attracting support in core China, would find little help from the minorities. On China's debit side these outlying minority areas would make China's people's war very difficult to carry out, but then there would also be little room for exploitation of the population by an enemy. In sum, the presence of minorities especially in border areas may be a source of instability, but it is not a basic challenge to core China.

Agriculture

The ability of a state to feed its population is one of the most basic influences of human geography on defence policy. China has 130m hectares of arable land compared to 220m in the USSR. In relation to total size of the country they are roughly comparable, but China has a population four times the size and thus, the Soviet Union has eight times the amount of agricultural land per person.[22] Measured by total food production, China ranks second only to the US, but in proportion to population China's output is far less impressive. While it is true that China is essentially self-sufficient in food production, the margin of sufficiency is not great.

As with minerals and population, core China contains by far the greatest concentration of Chinese agriculture. This is most true of Hebei, Shandong, Henan, Jiangsu and north Anhui provinces. Unlike the USSR, which is more vulnerable to the interruptions of food supply, China cannot be realistically deprived of its 'bread-basket' without a near complete invasion of core China.

Agriculture contributes 40 per cent of China's GDP, twice that of the USSR and five times that of the US.[23] This makes China less rather than more vulnerable to attack. Destruction of agriculture is next to impossible without occupation or bacteriological war. What is more, China's level of technology employed in agriculture is very low, thereby strengthening its ability to survive an attack. For example, China has about as many tractors in use as Yugoslavia, or one tenth of the USSR and one twentieth of the US.[24]

The one area of food production that might be more vulnerable and more likely to involve external relations, is the fishing industry. China's major fishing grounds in coastal waters lie around the Shandong peninsula, Shanghai, the Taiwan straits, Guangzhou and the Gulf of Tonkin. The broad continental shelf stretching out to the Ryukyu Islands makes Japan the main coastal neighbour, but also creates potential problems with Korea, Taiwan and Vietnam. But overall the fishing industry accounts for a minor part of China's food production, and coastal operations have remained constant at about one third of total fishing. Unlike the USSR, which has a massive ocean-going fishing fleet, China's fishing industry is less likely to bring it into contact with foreigners and if it does, fish is even less likely to be seen as an issue worthy of conflict.[25]

Industry

If China's agriculture is difficult to disrupt, the same cannot be said of China's industry. Not only is industry more directly related to war potential, but it is also more vulnerable to attack.[26] The starting point for an analysis of industry is the state's energy potential and capability.

As we have already seen, China's energy resources are relatively plentiful and well placed. China is the world's fourth largest energy producer and consumer (not on a per capita basis), the fifth largest natural gas producer and tenth in oil production.[27] Therefore China does have great power potential, but how vulnerable is it to attack?

China's energy consumption, 70 per cent of which goes to industry, is based 85 per cent on coal, a resource China has in plenty and which is generally close to core China's industrial centres. China's oil resources are more vulnerably situated in areas near the USSR and to a certain extent in contested offshore waters, but most of the resources lie in relatively safe areas such as the Bohai Gulf. Far more vulnerable are the power generating plants. While the government has made repeated and to a certain extent successful attempts to diversify Chinese energy production, three major centres remain. The Manchurian system serves Beijing, Tianjin and Tangshan, the

Zhejiang area focuses on Shanghai and the third area is centred on Loyang. These co-ordinated and relatively modern grids are prime targets for an enemy seeking to cripple Chinese industry. The task would seem to be relatively easy.

The process of diversification has begun to minimize these problems. New plants, especially in Lanzhou, Xian, and Sichuan are explicitly designed to improve the flexibility in China's power industry. Paradoxically, the most positive aspect of energy production in China is that it is relatively primitive and on a small scale. The lack of centralized power generating means that 'surgical strikes' or limited invasions of China would have less effect than they would for the superpowers. While this means that China does not have backup power systems, the relatively large number of small scale stations provides greater flexibility and security.[28]

Much like China's energy production, its total GDP ranking is impressive (6th in the world), but when measured on a per capita basis the picture looks rather different. China's GDP in absolute terms is more than half the Soviet total and more than one sixth that of the US. On a per capita basis China's is less than one sixth that of the USSR and 4 per cent of the US total. China is not an economic superpower. Its steel production is one third of the US's, one quarter of the USSR's and even less on a per capita basis.[29] Thus China's ability to support a massive modern war machine is significant, but China is not in the class of the superpowers.

China's foreign trade constitutes roughly 5 per cent of her GNP, thereby ranking her among the most autarchic of states. What is more, the relative lack of modern industry is a benefit if China is attacked, for a less sophisticated society takes less time to recover its previous production levels. In addition, China's light industry makes up nearly half of the total industrial output, a figure twice that of the USSR. Not only is light industry more dispersed and therefore harder to destroy, it also provides a more diversified economic base. Chinese industry can be relatively easily attacked, but in comparison to the sophisticated economies of the first world, it would be easier to rebuild.

The location of Chinese industry is not as encouraging for defence. There has been gradual success in the diversification schemes, but three major industrial areas in China's northeast remain most vital. Tangshan, Beijing and Shanghai stand out as the most important sites, but others are centred on Harbin, Zhengchou, Lanzhou,

Changchow, Changsha, and Kunming. The spread of industry has been mainly to the centre, south and west, especially Kunming and Wuhan. Outside of core China the percentage of industry has remained around 8 per cent of the total. On a per capita basis some of the greatest concentrations of industry are in Inner Mongolia and Xinjiang, but that is misleading because of their sparse populations. The most crucial areas for industrial production in order of priority are: Shanghai, Liaoning, Jiangsu, Shandong, Hebei, Guangdong, Beijing, Heilongjiang and Sichuan. The northeastern region accounted for 42 per cent of the total in 1966, but this has now been reduced to 36 per cent.[30]

While it is true that some of the heavier industries are still relatively concentrated in the northeast, a region vulnerable to Soviet attack, the clear and successful trend is towards diversification and hence increased security. When compared to concentration of industry in the USSR, China is better off. Eighty per cent of the Soviet machine building industry is east of the Urals, in an area smaller than China's core, and this pattern is true for most sectors of the Soviet economy.

As in the Soviet case, China's nuclear production facilities are more spread out than they are in the US. However, the fewer number of targets in the relatively limited Chinese programme makes them more vulnerable. In addition, and unlike the Soviet Union, the relatively poor dispersal of China's missile force away from population sites (about half in core China) means more population damage to China if it is a victim of a counter-force attack.[31]

There can be little doubt that valuable Chinese sites exist to be targeted by an enemy, but as compared with the USSR, China's industry is less concentrated and less crucial to its national power. There is some value to be gained for an enemy in attacking certain industrial centres in China, if only because it is relatively easy to destroy the comparatively few sites. However, once these points are destroyed, the marginal utility of an attack falls off very quickly. The smaller scale Chinese light industry spread around the country, and above all the scattered rural population, means that an enemy's overkill capacity in nuclear weapons would have less impact than against the superpowers.[32] Defending China's cities and industry is not easy, but their destruction would be less catastrophic for China than for any other great power.

Transport and Communication

The final key sector of human geography relevant to a calculation of defence potential is the means of ensuring contact and communication within the state. Not surprisingly, the pattern appears to follow that of energy and industry. China's transport is based overwhelmingly on rail and water technology, with the latter making China unusual in comparison with any other great power. The total of goods and passengers carried on various types of transport is half that of the USSR when adjusted for size of the country, thereby underlining the relative under-development of China's economy.[33]

China's largely unsurfaced road network is inadequate for main heavy transport except in the northeastern part of core China. Water transport carries a great deal of freight traffic, but, especially in the north, rivers are subject to freezing in the winter. Waterborne transport is particularly unsuited to military operations as it is slow and relatively vulnerable. The backbone of the communications system is the railway network. The lines are mostly single track and provide comprehensive coverage for core China. The occasional line to outlying areas, such as the northwest one to Urumchi, is highly vulnerable to interdiction. In comparison to the concentrated and modern Soviet rail system, China's system lacks duplicate tracks which are crucial in minimizing the effects of attack. China's system is also still based in the northeast (one third of the total) with only 7 per cent in the south.[34] The main rail centres and repair points are at Changchun, Beijing, Zhengzhou, Wuhan, Shanghai, Lanzhou, Chengdu and Guangzhou, all sites vulnerable in attacks on China's population and industry. There are also few bridges across the main rivers, rendering rail communication especially vulnerable to attack.

Despite the centrality of rail links and their apparent vulnerability, four factors tend to minimize these weaknesses. First, China showed during the Vietnam war that it could maintain transport routes under heavy bombardment in a limited area. Second, as with Chinese industry and power production, the low level of development makes attacks less devastating and encourages regional independence, an approach that the Chinese economy is already better geared for. Third, unlike the USSR or US, China is relatively compact with relatively simple lines of internal communication. The long and spread out Soviet Union is especially vulnerable in this respect, and its Asian territory particularly so. Finally, despite all these weaknesses, China's transport links with its frontiers are no worse than those of its enemies. For example, the Soviets are vulnerable in their two exposed Siberian rail lines across vast distances and a paucity of road links, and India has very difficult communication with its mountain outposts. The advantage will lie with the defender unless the attacker can bring to bear a well-supported mobile force, preferably by air.[35] Defending China is therefore not as difficult as the lack of modern transport might indicate.

Communication by radio, telephone, or more sophisticated means remains rudimentary at best. The telephone service is said to be adequate and basic communication is ensured as one might expect in a society that puts a premium on ideological unity. The most effective communication pattern however, is not to be counted by the number of radio receivers,[36] for China's already well established local channels based on party control are likely to provide the best means of ensuring communication within the country. In time of war such channels are some of the most invulnerable to interdiction and are likely to ensure efficient command and control in ways that modern technology could not.

Summary and Conclusions

Without arguing in a deterministic fashion that the physical and human geography of China decree a certain way of defending China, it is still possible to outline some broad conclusions in relation to three basic types of security threats. First, there is the threat of nuclear attack on China. It is clear that China's major cities, industry, and power production can be devastated in such a strike. While this would not defeat or destroy China in nearly the same way as it would either of the superpowers, it could provide a smaller power with a viable minimum deterrence posture against China in a way not possible against the US or USSR, which have far more extensive cities and industry. The relative inability to subjugate China in a nuclear strike also suggests the relative futility for China to engage in civil defence. No amount of shelters could equal the demographic reality of a vast rural population engaged in agriculture or dispersed light industry. These geographic facts also suggest that China's own nuclear forces could be targeted on value (cities) rather than force of the enemy. Defence of Chinese cities in a nuclear war is next to impossible unless the enemy's cities can be similarly threatened and thus an attack deterred. (The USSR's Asian population for example is highly urban.) This however does not preclude some other use for Chinese counter-force nuclear weapons. Overall though, China's defence against nuclear attack is easier than it is for the superpowers, if only because there is less of value to attack. To a certain extent, geography is a main pillar of Chinese nuclear weapons' policy, and one relatively invulnerable to a superpower strike.

The second major threat, large-scale conventional invasion of China seems to be a next to impossible task if geographic factors are considered. The land-war threat is the only one that could defeat China and that would require a full-scale invasion into what we have called core China. An enemy might seize outlying territory or the northeast, but to do so would not defeat China in economic or demographic terms. People's war appears to make great sense for defeating an invasion threat. China retains the ability to absorb and survive a lengthy invasion in a way more than comparable to Russian absorption of threats from the West. Although some strategists believe that China needs massive purchases of Western arms so as to defend herself against the Soviet threat, they may well be overselling their case, and China's needs.

The third threat, that of limited war along the periphery, raises more problems for China. While it is clear that such an attack could not defeat China, there are important vulnerabilities suggested by geographic factors. It is true that there are few resources, population centres, or industrial sites outside core China, but the rest of the territory constituting one half of China is relatively vulnerable to attack for various limited-war purposes. A naval attack on islands or oil resources, let alone a 'land-grab' in the north, would be relatively hard to guard against. People's war would not be effective although the local minorities would be as much a problem for the attacker as the defender. The northern and coastal frontiers are similarly more exposed to limited attack. On the more positive side, physical geography provides relatively more protection against a limited attack in the south.

These limited threats to China seem to be the main area of strategic weakness. To the extent that the study of geography is relevant, it suggests the need to concentrate on meeting these limited threats to China and less on large scale nuclear or conventional attack. The mobile, modern, and flexible forces required for such limited tasks suggests a certain kind of Chinese policy, and one that is not necessarily the same as discussed by Western strategic analysts. Tailoring the suit to the buyer's physical geography rather than to the seller's account book, would seem to be most logical for Beijing.

These trends derived from an analysis of China's geography can only be a starting point for a study of the defence of China. Other sources must also be tapped. But geography is still crucial in many aspects of strategy, and remains therefore inextricably bound up with politics. In an age when we seem to be obsessed with weapon categories and capabilities, or the minutiae of changing political coalitions, the more important fundamentals of China's land and people are all too easily underestimated.

NOTES

1. Sir Halford Mackinder first developed the 'Heartland' theory in 1904. He suggested that the inner area of Eurasia was the pivot of world politics, and in a later refinement argued that he who controlled that pivot controlled the world. In contrast, Admiral Mahan urged the centrality of seapower. For a discussion see Saul Cohen, *Geography and Politics in a World Divided* (London: Oxford University Press, 1973, 2nd Edition). Paul Colinvaux, *The Fates of Nations* (London: Penguin, 1983) on biological determinism. Harold and Margaret Sprout, *Foundation of International Politics* (New York: D. Van Nostrand, 1962). Ken Booth, *Strategy and Ethnocentrism* (London: Croom Helm, 1978). Colin Gray, 'Strategy and National Style', *International Security*, Vol. 6 No. 2. *Fall* 1981.
2. See a discussion of these problems in Sprout, *Foundations of Politics*, and Colin Gray, *The Geopolitics of the Nuclear Era* (New York: Crane and Russak, 1977).
3. James Fairgrieve, *Geography and World Power* (London: University of London Press, 1910) on China dominating Russia. Cohen, *Geography and Politics* on Lin Biao and geopolitics.
4. Is China only a land power? Is there a useful distinction between the north of China, which grows wheat, single crops, possesses minerals, manufacturing, land transport, and a water shortage, and the south, which grows rice, multiple crops, and has water transport?
5. The USSR has 22.4m square kilometres. Canada has 9.9m, but both have huge sections locked in permafrost. *Statesman's Year Book 1980–81* (London: Macmillan, 1980).
6. Chiao-min Hsieh, *Atlas of China* (New York: McGraw Hill, 1973). C.I.A. *The World Factbook, 1982* (CR 82–11117, April 1982), p. 43.
7. *An Outline of Chinese Geography* (Peking: FLP 1978). *China: A General Survey* (Peking: FLP 1979). *United Nations Statistical Yearbook 1978* (New York: United Nations, 1979). China's coastline ranks tenth in length. Canada's is longest, USSR is 3rd, and the US is 10th. George Kurian, *The Book of International Lists* (London: Macmillan, 1981).

8. The bordering states are: North Korea, Soviet Union, Outer Mongolia, Afghanistan, Pakistan, India, Nepal, Bhutan, Burma, Laos, Vietnam, Macao, and Hong Kong. The official Chinese view omits the last two and adds Sikkim to make 12 bordering states. See article by Jie Chengzhang in *People's Daily*, 6 July 1981 in *SWB*/FE/6769/C1/1–2. The Soviet Union borders on 12, Brazil on 10, West Germany on 9. The total length of China's border is 28,072.6 km. or roughly 17,000 miles: 4,150 miles with the Soviet Union, 2,710 miles with Outer Mongolia, and 2,500 miles with India. Kurian, *International Lists*.

9. J. R. V. Prescott, *Boundaries and Frontiers* (London: Croom Helm, 1978), notes that mountains usually have more than one watershed change. Neither are rivers natural boundaries where they are part of regular transport and straddled by common ethnic groups.

10. On climate see S. F. Markham, *Climate and the Energy of Nations* (London: Oxford University Press, 1944). See also A. F. K. Organski, *World Politics* (New York: Alfred Knopf, 1968, 2nd edition).

11. Basic data on minerals are available in Kurian, *International Lists*, and US Congress, Joint Economic Committee (JEC), *China's Economy Post Mao*, 95th Cong., 2nd session (Washington, USGPO, 1978). Also J. F. Copper, *China's Global Role* (Stanford: Hoover Institution Press, 1980). *The Economist* (London), 23 April 1983, pp. 80–5.

12. This concept of a core area will be frequently used in this chapter. It comprises an area roughly similar to China in the Yuan dynasty, i.e. everything except Inner Mongolia, Xinjiang, Tibet, Qinghai, half of Heilongjiang, Ningxia, and Guanxi.

13. Official PRC figures for the mainland cited in /*SWB*/FE/7168/C/1.

14. Charles Taylor and Michael Hudson, *World Handbook of Political and Social Indicators* (New Haven: Yale Univ. Press, 1972).

15. 75 per cent of Chinese live in 15 per cent of the land. The Soviet Union's concentration can also be increased, for 70 per cent of the Soviet population resides in only the territory west of the Urals.

16. *Times Atlas of China* (London: Times Newspapers, 1974).

17. China's population in cities over 100,000 was 10 per cent of total in 1960, ranking it 76th in the world in such density. The USSR had 25 per cent in cities of that size (36th rank), and the US had 50 per cent (8th rank). China had more than 100 such cities and a further 100 with a population between 50,000–100,000. Soviet urban population even in East Siberia is 55 per cent, and in the Far East it is 70 per cent. While there are no cities above one million in those regions, there are cities of around half a million such as Krasnoyarsk, Irkutsk, and Khaborovsk. Thus the USSR is vulnerable to urban attack and perhaps even occupation more than China, especially in the proximate areas to the border. Leo Orleans, 'China's Urban Population', *China Under the Four Modernizations*, JEC, 13 Aug. 1982. Details in Taylor and Hudson, *World Handbook*; John Dewdney, *A Geography of the Soviet Union* (New York: Pergamon 1979); Paul Lydolph, *Geography of the USSR* (New York: John Wiley and Sons 1970); Robert Taafee and Robert Kingsburg, *An Atlas of Soviet Affairs* (London: Methuen 1965); J. P. Cole *Geography of the USSR* (London: Penguin 1967): Kurian, *International Lists*.

18. The cities closest to the frontier are Lanzhou and Baotou with only the former with more than one million people. The top 7 cities in order are Shanghai, Beijing, Tianjin, Guangzhou, Shenyang, Chongqing, and Wuhan. The top 21 Chinese cities are 40 per cent of China's total urban population and a mere 6 per cent of China's total: not really as effective for counter-value nuclear strikes as in the superpower's case. Orleans, 'China's Population', p. 289. Frederick Kaplan, Julian Sobin, Stephen Andors, *Encyclopaedia of China Today* (London: Macmillan 1979).

19. A US Congressional study of the effects of nuclear war estimated, *inter alia*, that in the US–USSR case there is little to distinguish between the effects of a Soviet first strike or a US second strike in its real effect on society. Thus a Chinese counter-value threat is likely to be credible, and China will be proportionally less vulnerable to such an attack. US Congress Office of Technology Assessment, *The Effects of Nuclear War* (London: Croom Helm, 1980).

20. Compared to about 50 per cent Russians in the USSR. For China's data, see Theodore Shabad, *China's Changing Map* (London: Methuen and Co., 1972), and Kaplan, Sobin, Andors, *China Today*. The largest minorities in order are: Zhuang, Uygur, Hui, Yi, Tibetan, Miao, Manchu, Bouyei, Mongol, and Korean. The five regions are: Inner Mongolia, Xinjiang, Tibet, Ningia, and Guangxi Zhuang. 1982 census data in *BBC/SWB/FE/7168/C/1*.

21. For example Victor Louis, *The Coming Decline of the Chinese Empire* (New York: Times Books 1979).

22. China has 0.13 hectares per person which is also one fifth that of the US. China ranks fourth in total agricultural area behind the USSR, US, and Australia. Taylor and Hudson, *World Handbook*.

23. Ibid.

24. *UN Statistical Yearbook 1978*. In 1977 China had 210,000 tractors in use, compared to 271,000 in India, 2,461,700 in USSR, and 4,370,000 in the US. *USSR Facts and Figures* (Moscow: Novosti, 1980).

25. Shabad *China's Map*, and Charles Dragonette 'The Dragon at Sea', *US Naval Institute Proceedings*, May 1981.

26. On war potential in general see Klaus Knorr, *The War Potential of Nations* (Princeton, New Jersey: Princeton University Press 1956), and *Military Power and Potential* (Lexington, Mass.: D. C. Heath, 1970).

27. On a per capita basis China ranks around number 50. Its gas production is one tenth that of the US and one fifth that of the USSR. Its oil production is one fifth that of the USSR and one quarter that of the US total. Copper, *China's Role*; Taylor and Hudson, *World Handbook*; *USSR Facts and Figures*; and V. Pokshishevsky, *Geography of the Soviet Union* (Moscow: Progress 1974). China's vulnerability to strategic attack is high and even in the US's case, where it will be relatively more secure, ten nuclear weapons can destroy 64 per cent of the US oil refining capacity and 73 per cent of the USSR capacity. The Soviet refineries are fewer in number but more dispersed and also further from population centres; a situation more analogous to the Chinese core. US Congress, *The Effects of Nuclear War*.

28. Data on energy based on J.E.C. 1978, and Robert M. Field and Judith A. Flynn, 'China: An Energy Constrained Model of Industrial Performance' in *China Under the Four Modernizations*, Joint Economic Committee, Part I, August 13, 1982. Also Shabad, *China's Map*. Most of Chinese power is generated in 192 stations, 126 of which are thermal and 66 are hydro. The shift to the latter, more difficult to attack system, is underway.

29. PRC figures, see note 13. See also Taylor and Hudson, *World Handbook*; Kurian, *International Lists*.

30. Data based on chapters in JEC 1978 and JEC, 1982 and US Congress, Joint Economic Committee. *China: A Reassessment of the Economy*, 94th Cong., 2nd session (Washington: USGPO, 1975).

31. Taiwan data cited in George Tan Eng Bok, 'La Strategie Nucleaire Chinoise', *Strategique* No. 3, 1980.

32. Compare for example the USSR's top 30 cities containing 15.4 per cent of the Soviet total or 27.3 per cent of the total urban population, and 25–40 per cent of total industrial capacity, with China's top 30 that are about 6 per cent of the total

population, 40 per cent of the total urban population and a comparable percentage of industrial capacity. See Dewdney, *A Geography*; and Pokshishevsky, *Geography*.

33. See note 29 for sources. China's road surface is 890,000 km., more than half of which is unsurfaced and 25,000 of which is asphalted. There are 150,000 km. of navigable waterway, of which 40,000 are suitable for ocean-going craft. Rail length is 52,000 km. compared to 141,000 in the USSR. See also, Ministry of Foreign Economic Relations and Trade, PRC, *Guide to Investment in China* (Hong Kong: Economic Information and Agency, May 1981); Albert Peterson, 'China: Transportation Developments, 1971–80' in JEC, 1982.

34. Shabad, *China's Map*.

35. China's air lines are the most limited of its transport. Based on Beijing, Wuhan, and Shanghai they carry less than 2 per cent of all domestic passenger volume. Soviet air capability is far greater, not to mention the vastly superior US network.

36. *JEC 1975*, and the JEC's Subcommittee on Priorities and Economy in Government, *Allocation of Resources in the Soviet Union and China—1981* (Washington: USGPO, 1981). *UN Statistical Yearbook 1978* reports that China ranks 7th in the world for radio receivers, but very low on a per capita basis. Also, Kurian, *International Lists*.

2

History

'Men make their own history, but they do not make it just as they please: they do not make it under circumstances chosen by themselves but under circumstances directly encountered. The tradition of all the dead generations weighs like a nightmare on the brains of the living.'

(Karl Marx, 1851)

How relevant is the study of China's military history to an analysis of contemporary Chinese defence policy? Some might suggest the significance of the fact that 225 million years ago, what we now call China was an island in the Pacific Ocean,[1] and that China retains its isolated and Sinocentric approach to this day. Others might point to the evolution in China of such crucial military technology as the crossbow, cast iron, and gunpowder as evidence of China's persistent concern with military skill and technology. In this chapter the analysis will focus on those areas where the legacy of Chinese history might have had a long lasting effect on the present. The past will not be viewed as a tyrant of the present,[2] but neither will it be dismissed entirely. While it is possible to divide this vast subject in various ways, the following three categories of potential historical influence would seem the most useful:

(1) The relationship between military and civilian authority;
(2) The role of the military in foreign affairs;
(3) The way in which military force was used in battle.

Not all the areas will be as important, but it is necessary to analyse a great number of potentially relevant historical legacies before reaching accurate conclusions as to the few that are in fact significant.

Military and Civilian Authority

The starting point for an analysis of the role of the military in politics can begin logically with an assessment of how the armed forces are treated by civilian authorities. Is the military relatively independent, and does it have a high status in society? The historical legacy on these issues is relatively clear cut; the military instrument has been strictly controlled and military skills have received relatively little approval.

Civilian Control of the Military

While it is true that the Chinese were responsible for such crucial military technology as gunpowder, they also seem to have been the first to develop a coherent system for maintaining civilian control over the armed forces. Few conclusions emerge so unambiguously from Chinese military history. Although central rule over the Chinese empire traditionally arose from the sword, horseman, or gun, it rarely rested on these supports for long.[3] The triumph of the civil (*wen*) authority over the military (*wu*) authority was a crucial underlying principle of Chinese society, certainly after the fifth century BC. Literate culture triumphed over brute force in Chinese dynasties ruled by a Confucian literati class.

Important qualifications should be added to this historical judgement, for few matters are clear cut, especially in historical perspective. First, this legacy of civil control is not unusual, as few societies can be found to have regular military rule over the length of time concerned in Chinese history. This does not invalidate the historical trend, it merely suggests that China is not unlike many empires.

Second, and perhaps more importantly, the tradition of civil control is not uniform. Some Chinese military historians, and pre-eminently Sun Zi, stress civil control, but not without pointing to important areas where the military should be allowed to get on with the job it knows best. Sun Zi wrote, 'he whose generals are able and not interfered with by the sovereign will be victorious'.[4]

Sun Zi was not arguing for military control of the civilians, for he established the need for civil control of the sword long before Clausewitz immortalized the need to pursue war as a continuation of politics. He was, however, running against the tide of Chinese history that severely circumscribed the professional portion of the military's activities. The trend was to establish a strong bureaucratic system that could cope with military as well as political problems without resort to military professionals. Unlike the Western tradition, peacetime law was rarely superseded by martial law, for the Chinese bureaucratic system was designed to cope with most situation.[5]

In the vast and formative period between the sixth and twentieth centuries, the Board of War controlled a vast array of professional military affairs including the military industries.[6] This was part of a more general process of keeping power centres in a vast continental empire as divided as possible without dissolving the structure of authority. The idea was to grant the armed forces only as much power as was required to perform limited military tasks. By dividing military commands between region and centre, between civilian and military, and between Chinese and foreign collaborators, it was hoped that no single power could emerge to challenge central authority.[7] These various tactics make it difficult to discern a single role for the military, other than one that did not involve much influence in central policy-making.

In fact it is somewhat artificial and western-centred to suggest that the Chinese were ever extremely exercised about the question of civil control. The historical tradition of seeing military pursuits as an aberration from the more normal agrarian pursuits of the peasantry, suggests that it was taken for granted that *wen* must dominate *wu*. Chuguo Liang is reported to have said in the third century, in regard to the military, 'Man's loyalty is like deep water to the fish; if the fish loses water he dies, if a man loses loyalty he will meet disaster....'[8] This concept that Mao would later make famous, is part of the more general tradition of the military as a temporary phase of normal civilian life. Standing armies were relatively unusual and in peacetime the military profession nearly disappeared entirely. This legacy of anti-professionalism needs to be explored further, for it is an important by-product of the tradition urging civil control of the military.

Disesteem of Military Professionalism

In traditional China, war was seen as an abnormal state of affairs. Calm and order were natural and if they were disturbed by conflict, then peace should be restored as soon as possible. Military professionalism was disesteemed in the predominant pacifist bias.[9] It is difficult to find war glorified and few bellicose military heroes like Alexander, Caesar, or Napoleon can be found in Chinese traditions. Even in foreign relations, notions of good conduct and proper principle were at least ideally seen as sufficient to order human affairs. As one Confucian classic said, 'War is destructive to the people, an insect that eats up the resources'.[10] Chinese society was to a large extent divided between those who were literate and those who were not, and military men fell unambiguously into the second category. The military were confined to basic battlefield tasks and were prevented from having a significant effect even on military planning.

Clearly this tradition is not uniform, as some examples can be cited favouring at least a degree of professionalism. However, the overall trend is clear and it had important implications for the development of China's military affairs. Only in times of protracted war did the military have an opportunity to develop a professional ethos. In general the armed forces were demobilised as soon as possible with only a minimum garrison retained. The military soon disappeared as a disciplined profession in times of peace.

In the all-important bureaucratic terms, the military fared no better. No academies or examination systems were established that might encourage professionalism, and permanent military command structures were just as rare. Usually the military was hurriedly assembled when the threat appeared, but other than scattered regional forces and a garrison in the capital, there was little of a permanent structure to build upon.

There are of course exceptions to the historical rule, but they are few and mainly due to peculiar circumstances.[11] The diversity of China in physical and human geographic terms often meant that regional military forces were maintained. But they tended to be *ad hoc* and subject to rapid change in their individual fortunes. Very often the 'barbarians' on the frontiers were allowed to do most of the fighting and so long as they did not join forces, China found no need for a central and permanent military organization of its own.[12] The high cost of maintaining such a force in the vast Chinese countryside was another reason for minimizing permanent military structures. Manchu generals in particular were known to love a protracted campaign because it literally kept them in business.[13] Therefore, if possible, non-military means were sought to resolve the inevitable development of military problems. (See also Section 3, below.)

These inevitable military problems never provided a uniform military response. The T'ang dynasty militia system was adopted because of the tendency towards independent regional power that resulted from using mercenary troops on the frontier. But the militia system was less professional and tied far more to side-line production tasks. The Sung dynasty tried to reduce and control regional forces with the resulting weakness to foreign threat. They also had a smaller professional force in the capital, but it was expensive and still not useful in the defence of China.[14] Thus no pattern in the type of military system is apparent in Chinese history, but what is more clear is that professional forces had virtually no long-lasting role to play.

It is also true that China produced an impressive body of technical military literature and military leaders were not always locked into a limited military career, but the overall trend remains against professionalism.[15] Sun Zi had written, 'The advance and retirement of the army can be controlled by the general in accordance with prevailing circumstances. No evil is greater than commands of the sovereign from the court',[16] but this exhortation remained more theory than practice. The long periods of peace, the lack of military administration, and above all social disesteem of the military profession, all conspired to leave an historical legacy that is critical and suspicious of professional soldiers.

The Military and Foreign Policy

In view of the historical tendency to minimize the professional military's role in defending China, the analysis of traditional Chinese defence of its territory must be broadened to include a wider look at foreign policy-making. Consequently, it is useful to analyse in detail what is perhaps the most common belief held by those comparing modern and ancient Chinese defence policy: the Sinocentrism of China.

Sinocentrism and Defending China

The history of defending China against foreign threats is generally taken to begin with the fourth century BC when an expanding China met northern tribes.[17] The view is held by many that China dealt with all foreigners in more or less the same manner, assuming a Sinocentric world view that ensued naturally from domestic Chinese society. The close connection between internal and external policy was epitomised by the phrase, 'inside disorder, and outside calamity'. The centrality of the Middle Kingdom ruled by the Son of Heaven encompassed an area called *T'ien hsia* (all under-Heaven). This Chinese area was notable for its culture, script, Confucianism, examination system and bureaucracy. When dealing with foreigners this was seen as the only system that could be properly applied to the various less civilized peoples abroad. The degree to which these other peoples were tied to China varied according to which of the various concentric circles of influence they were to be found in, but all in some important way were part of a system where they paid tribute to the Chinese emperor.[18]

This theory of Sinocentrism by necessity must be broad because many changes of fortune can be noted for Chinese imperial rule. The theory explains the rise of foreign rulers by suggesting that Sinocentrism was so strong that in the face of a superior military power, China could draw in the foreigner and assimilate him in keeping with the western adage, 'if you can't lick 'em, join 'em'.[19] Traditional China was able to exploit its great strength in size and population by swallowing invaders in the Chinese mass. Foreign invaders were also unable to find a convenient geographic or demographic dividing line for China, unlike the Roman empire.[20]

A key principle that is said to follow from Sinocentrism is the Chinese belief in the hierarchical nature of society. Since China was civilized and others were not, China , and within China its emperor, were poised at the pinnacle of a pyramid of power. Equality of states as suggested in a post-Renaissance Europe was simply not possible. The tribute system was said to be a manifestation of this world view and resulted in China not appreciating the concept of alliances. Since China was superior, alliances were superfluous. Neither were intricate ideas like balance of power understood when a Chinese dominated pyramid was accepted. According to the Sinocentric theory, national boundaries were not acknowledged because international society was merely an extension of the virtue of China itself.[21] In brief summary, this is the supposed Sinocentric world view derived from the history of defending China in foreign relations. However, this theory is open to criticism on several grounds.

It is difficult to suggest that the traditional Chinese view of the world was not Sinocentric, but it is possible to challenge the relevance of this concept in forming universally valid principles about defending China. In the first place, the Chinese never conceived of Sinocentrism or tribute as a system. Western historians and political scientists are fond of such categories, but for the Chinese it was not a question of China having a better civilization, it simply *was* civilization.[22]

The problem was that this hubris was not always justified. Ethnocentrism on the part of large empires was common to various great civilizations including ones in Europe, Egypt, and India.[23] What is perhaps most interesting is how China managed to ignore reality for so long and cling to its invalid theory. Even Chinese historians had difficulty in reconciling the repeated challenges to the assumption of Chinese superiority when China was invaded or defeated.[24] This gap between the ideological convention of Sino-centrism and the reality of inter-state politics was most evident when analysing the supposed concentric rings of Chinese control of its neighbours.

Some historians have suggested three rings of Chinese control, some have used other numbers, but it is clear that these rings of power were rarely static.[25] For example, Japan was supposed to be a key member of the first circle, but it was rarely subservient to China. Northern Vietnam, another area in the first circle, had held firmly to Chinese tribute in the tenth century, then slipped away until Ming times and then away again in the nineteenth century. Like any large power, the rings of power can be seen as spheres of influence. These spheres expand and contract depending on myriad factors including the simple strength of China.[26] While Chinese leaders may have deluded themselves into believing the reality of the tribute system, it has no more relevance than do myths in American foreign policy that the international market responds to forces of the free market. Sinocentrism and tribute were part of the Chinese ideology crucial to legitimizing domestic power and so long as it was not severely challenged, it was easiest to retain the coherent dogma.[27] This phenomenon is common to contemporary communism or most organized religions. Chinese power waxed and waned like most empires, and with these relative shifts of power, Chinese influence and social system expanded and contracted.

The kind of pattern that emerges from the practice of Chinese history is a more conventional one than the hierarchical Sinocentrism might suggest. The pattern emphasizes the need to secure the Chinese core territory, followed by unco-ordinated attempts to secure favourable states on the frontiers. Chinese tradition offers little guide as to how to achieve these ends and in this respect China is also no different from other great empires. History is not a tyrant and tradition is not uniform, even in China.

Perhaps the main reason why Sinocentrism is not applicable is that other states rarely accepted its premise in the first place. Paying tribute did not always mean an acceptance of Sinocentrism, but merely of Sino-power. Only Korea can be said to have consistently accepted the Chinese system, and this hardly constitutes proof of the historical tradition.[28] But even in the crucial realm of social policy, the rise of Buddhism by the third century meant that China could not even claim centrality of thought in how to establish social order.[29]

It is striking that these obstacles to Chinese domination simply lacked the consistent power to force China to change its Sinocentric ideology. Unlike the European empires where rivals soon emerged to engage in a balance of power, China never faced another consistently strong power with universal aspirations until the nineteenth century western challenge. China never had the problems of Egypt or Mesopotamia which could not expand without encountering others' spheres of influence. China met varied challenges in the north but the expanse of the open steppes and sparse population could never support a civilization rivalling the Chinese one for permanence. In other directions China found only isolated tribes before reaching deep seas and high mountains that marked its boundary. Until the nineteenth century China probably was superior to its immediate neighbours, and the other cultures that it knew to be equal were too far away to be a serious threat.[30]

Despite the superiority over the long term of the Chinese civilization, they were still forced to take a more *ad hoc* approach to defending China than suggested by the Sinocentric and tribute system. Historians have been quick to point out the numerous and sophisticated tactics developed by various Chinese dynasties to cope with foreign challenges. The essence of the strategy was pragmatism. When China was powerful it could enforce tribute. When China was weaker it had to engage in alliances, some of which were formal.[31] Often China could play one barbarian against the other and thereby guarantee its security. When China was weak it might even surrender territory or adopt a foreigner as a ruler. In such times tribute was still reported as being paid, even if in reality this was not so.[32] This variety of tactics casts serious doubt on those who would rigidly assert a simple Sinocentric view in Chinese tradition. Like most states, China would adopt a tactic from a different point along a continuum of force and persuasion depending on its relative ability.

Such classical realist calculations are evident in the *Romance of the Three Kingdoms* or the *Chronicle of the Warring States* and epitomized by Qin Shih Huangdi's tactics in forging unity among the warring states.[33] Realism bred a multiplicity of traditions in meeting foreign challenges with some emphasizing the need for pacification and appeasement while others used force and cunning tactics. The wide choice of strategy naturally led to domestic debate in China on how best to cope with foreign threats and so it should not be surprising that a single coherent Sinocentric policy cannot be isolated. The Qing dynasty debates on how to meet a naval threat in the east and a land threat in the west is the most recently emphasized case in point.[34] China tended to yield in practice when it met superior force and/or if it was weak at home. The strategic logic for such realism and multiplicity of traditions is evident and compelling.

Even if one is not disturbed with all these reasons why the Sinocentric hierarchical system is not a valid tool in understanding Chinese defence policy, there is even more compelling evidence in the period from the nineteenth century. Most historians have accepted that, even if Sinocentrism was valid for the past, the advent of nationalism and communism in China negated its influence. When China met the West it was not only forced to open its doors, but it adopted and modified crucial principles of nationalism. China gradually entered international relations as a sovereign state and today sets itself up as the champion of equality of states despite variations of size and power. The rise of communism with its emphasis on international relations on the basis of class and not quasi-nationalism like Sinocentrism, further eroded what might have been left of a Chinese hierarchical world view.[35] Unlike the tradition of civilian control of the military or minimization of professional military interests, the Chinese historical tradition does not suggest a unified view of how China should deal with the outside world. But if we look at more specific foreign policy problems, is the legacy any more clear?

Defending China's Frontiers

One of the most important aspects of a state's defence policy is the way in which it regards its frontiers. Crucial questions are whether the lines are rigidly fixed and whether they are permeable. It will be useful to turn now to an examination of the answers to these questions in Chinese tradition. The development of China's borders is, by comparison to Byzantine European politics, relatively simple.

By the fourth century BC China's northward expansion reached the escarpment of the Mongolian plateau where agriculture was vastly more difficult. Under emperor Qin Shih Huangdi China consolidated the northern walls into the Great Wall so as to contain China from foreign influences.[36] From that time in the north, China was to struggle with various ways of coping with a potentially permeable frontier. That China wanted a stable and fixed frontier is relatively clear from the historical evidence, although the methods for reaching this goal were diverse.[37] As already suggested, depending on China's power, it was relatively forward or passive in the face of northern encroachment. In general though, the pattern was forward defence and expansion of territory so as to create buffer zones. Often these zones were as much a result of the fact that China's rulers themselves came from Manchuria or Mongolia and therefore already controlled these northern borderlands. The closeness of the capital in Beijing (65 km from the Great Wall) was both a source of concern in defending China, as well as a symbol of the need to control the northern frontiers of Inner Asia. The Manchurian territory just north of the wall was of acute importance because it could serve as a training ground and jump-off point for a serious challenge to core China. Thus the Sinicization and control of Manchuria was a special concern. China tended to be drawn into the northern territories, rather than seeking them for colonial occupation. It was often seen as necessary to occupy territory merely so as to deny it to an enemy. However the effect was similar: frequent responsibility for non-ethnically Chinese territory in an unstable military position. These efforts were all for the essentially defensive purpose of holding a vulnerable northern frontier.[38] Implicit in this tradition is also a strong sense of national space and territorial integrity despite a more universal ideology of Sinocentrism. While China may have debated the best way to defend these nothern borderlands,[39] there is little debate in the historical record about the importance of holding a firm line and neutralizing potential threats. The Maginot line complex can be said to apply more to China than to its western formulators.

The overwhelming importance of the northern frontier for Chinese defence is clearly evident, but important related points can be made about other Chinese borders. Bounded by high mountains and deep seas, the other Chinese frontiers took somewhat longer to be reached, but were generally easier to consolidate once the population for colonization was available. Unlike in the north, natural frontiers set definite limits to China and imperial control was possible once these lines were reached.[40] This evidence for the relative impermeability and salience of China's frontiers is also reinforced by the trend to separate commerce from high policy making. Unlike the western tradition that emphasized wide-ranging trade as a tool of policy, China saw little need or desire to penetrate foreign markets.[41]

The historical tradition is equally clear on the relative importance of land and sea threats to national security. In striking contrast to the western use of sea-based travel as a mode of expansion and combat, China was distinctly unconcerned about defence from the sea. In the Ming dynasty there were seven great expeditions some of which reached Africa, but despite being symbols of the power and vitality of the regime, they were too costly and not seen as relevant to Chinese defence and security interests. They remained mere exploits, as the main focus was fixed on the northern Mongol threat.[42] In the sixteenth century the Mings had to cope with sea-based attacks on China's long undefended coast and they responded with the mentality of the Great Wall. Walled cities and forts along the coast were supplemented by coastal patrols in a passive effort to hold a coastline tightly. The attractive Chinese economic centres of Jiangsu and Zhejiang were not defended by attacks on the source of the raids and in the end the enemy was defeated by bribes and tactics of skill and cunning.[43] But in the total sweep of Chinese history, these incidents were rare. Not until the coming of western sea-power was China ever concerned with, and defeated by sea-power.[44] While it is true that the advent of modern naval forces and above all air-power with long range might challenge the assumptions of China's preoccupation with land defence, the historical legacy is clear that China's land frontiers are crucial and a clearly defined border should be defended if at all possible. Whether there is an equally clear set of strategies and tactics for this defence is another matter.

A Distinctive Military Strategy?

In a review of several thousand years of the practice of defending China can certain general trends be identified? The task is a daunting one, for virtually no other state can identify its own special tradition over such a vast time, and military affairs is a field more subject to the changes of technology than most.

It is clear from the start that the vast majority of specific military operations must be cast aside as irrelevant to anything but their own particular time. A vast portion of the historical tradition in military affairs in China is concerned with chivalry and semi-feudal activities. Sun Zi discusses in great detail the ritualized warfare of his time and the need to cast it aside. He noted the need for new armies that did not cease battle merely because an old man had fallen from his horse or the sun had set.[45] In western military thought we now no longer consider the relevance of chivalry and ceremonial war, and so in the case of China these operations are not significant.[46] Various other social changes have affected the conduct of war since feudal times, such as a shift to mass armies instead of mercenary forces which obviously had important effects on the number of casualties and the attitude of leaders and led to change in the conduct of war. But these social factors also change, and a detailed analysis of the past reveals little about modern war and the defence of China.

Change is even more rapid in military technology, thereby rendering past trends obsolete. Between the fourth and fourteenth centuries the stirrup gave horsemen a clear dominance in war and therefore enhanced the position of warriors from the northern steppes trained in such combat.[47] Equally the absence of powerful artillery to destroy heavily walled towns encouraged a certain type of defence, but was quickly outmoded when new technology of firepower became available. To discuss strategy based on cavalry charges or walled forts is hardly relevant in an era of Mach-2 aircraft and ICBMs. However, if we step back from technology and look at more general strategy, the traditions may yield more useful lessons.

Unfortunately there seems to be little pattern in the use of force to defend China. Various attempts have been made to identify various types of forces, but no pattern is valid for the vast Chinese tradition.[48] Some have suggested that there is a pervasive tradition of passive defence in Chinese history, but this is based overwhelmingly on evidence from wars where walled cities were the main focus. It was said that regions were administered from such centres and thus military strategy was obsessed with building firm walls and developing siege tactics. While it is true that this military problem lasted longer in China than it did in the West, it still did not last forever.[49] When the technology for destroying walls became available, the passive tradition disappeared.

Perhaps the most potent image in the history of China's defence is the Great Wall. But even in this case, the Wall has meant different things to different people. Numerous legends exist about its creation, with few offering consistent explanations. In reality, the Wall is many walls, built at different times and only unified briefly by emperor Qin. The Wall is both a symbol of fear (keeping the enemy out) and of the unity of China. By and large the Wall divides the northeast pasture land from the southeast arable farmland. The Wall is thus a geographic and cultural frontier, but one that was often permeated either by an expanding China or an ascendant northern neighbour. There were also times (Tang dynasty) where the wall was seen as a barrier to Chinese expanion. What is more, in AD 280 a Chinese minister warned 'trust in virtue, not in walls', thereby emphasizing that the Wall could be little more than a symbol.[50] It could only keep out an enemy for short periods, usually only when the dynasty was strong. True pacification of nomads depended on affecting their hearts and minds. But even if the Wall had provided a uniform legacy for the defence of China (which it did not) it certainly ceased to have any relevance after the seventeenth century. Manchu rule on both sides of the stones, and the coming of new military technology undercut the usefulness of the Wall. It remains a symbol of Chinese unity, but with little relevance for defence policy.

Others have suggested various patterns of a yielding strategy in Chinese defence. For example, some have argued that the judo-like strategy of using the enemy's force to your own advantage thereby stressing cunning and skill, is China's natural approach. Similarly, drawing on the Weichi model of non-linear battle where there is no front line and various interconnected struggles taking place simultaneously, it is asserted that this has resulted in a flexible military tradition. Victory remains incomplete in these wars, although they can be protracted before they are resolved.[51]

Several problems quickly emerge in trying to suggest that the yielding Weichi model is generally applicable. To begin with, it conflicts with the passive defence outlined above in that Weichi places great emphasis on keeping the initiative, even in defence. Weichi would have China ignore walled cities and concentrate on controlling the countryside. Second, it conflicts with equally persuasive theorists like Sun Zi who criticize protracted war and who seek decisive engagements with concentrated forces. It is, however, true that Sun Zi does not support total war, but he does place more emphasis on a quick if less devastating conflict that capitalizes on enemy error. What is more, Weichi is more concerned with insurgency campaigns and therefore is far more willing to yield territory in a way that is simply not applicable to a modern state behind defined frontiers. In any case, there are also other persuasive examples of a more forward strategy, for example in the sixteenth century in order to cope with threats from the north.[52] The various opposing strategies claim historical legitimacy, often quoting Sun Zi, even though the conclusions are radically different from past masters.

It seems impossible to identify continuity in military operations if only because of the vastness of Chinese experience. Military commanders require flexibility in combat, for to stick rigidly to a plan in unsuitable conditions is to court the ultimate reprimand, defeat and death in battle. Sun Zi's dictum concurs when he says 'When confronted by the enemy respond to changing circumstances and devise expedients. How can these be discussed beforehand?' In 1717 the emperor K'ang-hsi added that there is no point in studying ancient strategy because 'all one needs is an inflexible will and careful planning.'[53] Thus the premium on pragmatism was high, thereby rendering the task of synthesizing by historians next to impossible.

One crucial area of strategy has however been ignored and requires some detailed comment. There is said to be a long tradition in Chinese defence of emphasizing cunning and minimizing brute force, of stressing the quality of soldiers and minimizing the sophistication of weapons. Both of these possible conclusions would also coincide with the already noted tendency to de-emphasize the role of military professionalism and emphasize the wise civilian scholar.

Sun Zi urges the best policy of first attacking the enemy's strategy, then disrupting his alliances, then attacking his forces and finally the enemy people.[54] The emphasis on cunning stratagems does indeed appear to be an unusual emphasis in the Chinese tradition. Not that tricks and stealth do not figure in other military traditions, but it does appear to be a relatively special focus in the Chinese case. A reader of the *Romance of the Three Kingdoms* is especially aware of this emphasis.

The stress on skill rather than brute force is a natural development in a culture that did not exalt military prowess. If politics of the civilians are to take a large part in war, then it must be in part because wars can be seen to be won by natural intelligence and psychological warfare rather than some special study of the mechanics of troops and weapons. The politicization of the military put new premiums on the wise leader who could win the decisive engagement by using superior intelligence, and thereby avoid long drawn-out combat. The emphasis was naturally then placed far more on the skill of man than on the weapons at his disposal. While there are numerous examples of force defeating skill, the Chinese tradition emphasizes the latter as superior.[55] Naturally a balance is struck between man and weapons, for as one sixteenth century military writer said, quality troops with poor weapons are 'empty strength' and quality weapons and poor troops are 'waste'.[56] Thus pragmatism and flexibility continue to be central, but the Chinese more than most seemed to feel that weapons could be relatively de-emphasized in favour of superior men and skill.

Conclusions

The search for 'lessons of history' in Chinese defence policy began with many of the same handicaps that limit any analysis of a broad historical tradition. Some aspects of Chinese tradition can be identified as being distinctive, but most of those are commonsensical and do not belong to any specific national historical tradition. More seriously, however, various problems prevent sweeping generalizations being made. First, there is rarely a unified historical tradition. Revolutions occur in politics, economics, social, and military affairs which render obsolete the previous pattern, no matter how durable it was until that point.[57] Second, there is rarely an agreement at any specific time what the supposed historical traditions are, and debates rage in most ages. Politics and military affairs were dynamic, even in history. Thus it is also not surprising that there is relatively little agreement on what the historical reality was, and new vogues and biases alter the supposed firm lessons of history.

History therefore can provide some of the symbols of analysis, for example the rigidity of the Great Wall as a symbol of firmness on frontiers, but can offer few specific prescriptions, especially on military operations. History helps identify the questions to be asked of the present, for example whether a defence posture is forward or yielding, but can offer few answers. In this chapter we looked at five broad areas of potential historical relevance, and emerged with a mixed judgement.

As Michael Howard has pointed out in another context, 'historians may claim to teach lessons—history as such does not.'[58] Certainly Israeli strategists do not claim anything but occasional coincidences between their modern predicaments and the Bible or Bar Kochba.

There does seem to have been a pattern of civil control over the armed forces that was deeply rooted in Chinese history. Those in the present who would pursue a similar policy, might well find fertile ground for this approach. In addition, this civilian control extended deep into areas preserved in other societies as zones of professional military expertise. The relative denigration of military skills flowed naturally from civil control, and left a tradition where the armed forces would have to fight even for the most basic issues of recognition of their expertise in certain fields.

These relatively clear-cut traditions tended to be restricted to military institutions rather than military operations. The often cited Sinocentric world view was found to be largely irrelevant to present problems of the defence of China. Not only was the China-centred model never truly applicable in its own time, but even if it was held by the Chinese, it did not prevent a pragmatic approach to outside military forces. Concepts such as 'core China' as outlined in the previous chapter were seen to be more relevant, and the Chinese appeared to adopt normal tactics of defending their core, boundaries, and spheres of influence like any continental power. If there was a tradition in defending China, it was not an especially Chinese one, but rather based on pragmatism and flexibility in the face of changing threats. The pragmatism is best seen in the one aspect of strategy that does stand out; the tendency to use skill, cunning, and psychology rather than brute force or to rely on fancy weapons. In sum, China's very breadth of historical experience seems to be the main reason for being sceptical about drawing any specific lessons in military operation from Chinese history.[59] The past is indeed a foreign country.

NOTES

1. Quoted *Nature*, Vol. 293 p. 212, in *The Times*, 6 October 1981.

2. The phrase is borrowed from Michael Hunt, 'Chinese Foreign Relations in Historical Perspective', in Harry Harding ed., *China in Asian and Global Perspective*. On the role of history in China studies generally see: John Fairbank, *Chinabound* (New York: Harper and Row, 1982). On the role of culture in general strategy see Akira, Iriye, *Power and Culture* (Cambridge: Harvard University Press, 1981).

3. John Fairbank, 'Introduction: Varieties of the Chinese Military Experience', in Frank Kierman Jr. and John Fairbank, eds., *Chinese Ways in Warfare* (Cambridge: Harvard University Press, 1974); Edward Boylan, 'The Chinese Cultural Style of Warfare', *Comparative Strategy*, Vol. 3 No. 4, 1982; and Edward Dreyer, 'Military Continuities: The PLA and Imperial China', in William Whitson, ed., *The Military and Political Power in China in the 1970s* (New York: Praeger, 1972).

4. Samuel Griffith (trans.), *Sun Tzu, The Art of War* (London: Oxford University Press, 1963) p. 83.

5. Fairbank, 'Varieties of Experience'.

6. Dreyer, 'Military Continuities'; William McNeill, *The Pursuit of Power* (Oxford: Blackwell, 1983) Ch. 2.

7. Charles Hucker, 'Hu Tsung-hsien's Campaign Against Hsu Hai, 1556', in Kierman and Fairbank, *Chinese Ways*. Also, Edwin Reischaur and John Fairbank, *East Asia: The Great Tradition* (Boston: Houghton Mifflin Co., 1960) pp. 364–5.

8. Cited in Stanley Henning, 'Chinese Defense Strategy: A Historical Appraisal', *Military Review* Vol. LIX No. 5, May 1979.

9. Dreyer, 'Military Continuities' p. 7; and Fairbank, 'Varieties of Military Experience' p. 7.

10. Lien-sheng Yang 'Historical Notes on the Chinese World Order', in John Fairbank ed., *The Chinese World Order* (Cambridge, Mass.: Harvard University Press, 1968).

11. Dreyer, 'Military Continuities'; and Fairbank, 'Varieties of Military Experience'.

12. Frank Kierman Jr., 'Phases and Modes of Combat in Early China'; and Charles Petersen, 'Regional Defense Against the Central Power: The Huai-hsi Campaign, AD 815–17', both in Kierman and Fairbank, eds., *Chinese Ways* p. 63.

13. Reischaur and Fairbank, *East Asia* p. 391.

14. *Ibid.* pp. 190–205.

15. Dreyer, 'Military Continuities' p. 9.

16. Griffith trans., *Sun Tzu* p. 81.

17. Wolfram Eberhard, *A History of China* (London: Routledge Kegan Paul, 1977) p. 54. Hunt, 'Chinese Foreign Relations'.

18. The elaboration of the Sinocentric system is based on John Fairbank, 'A Preliminary Framework', in Fairbank, ed., *Chinese World Order*; C. P. Fitzgerald, *The Chinese View of their Place in the World* (London: Oxford University Press, 1964); Norton Ginsburg, 'On the Chinese Perception of a World Order', in Tang Tsou ed., *China in Crisis*, Vol. 2 (Chicago: University of Chicago Press, 1968); Mark Mancall, 'The Persistence of Tradition in Chinese Foreign Policy', in *The Annals of the American Academy of Political and Social Sciences*, Vol. 349, Sept. 1963; J. L. Cranmer-Byng, 'The Chinese Attitude Towards External Relations', in *International Journal* Vol. 21, Part 4, Winter 1966; Boylan, 'Chinese Style'. For a critical view shared by the author see Morris Rossabi ed., *China Among Equals* (London: University of California Press, 1983).

19. John Fairbank, 'The Early Treaty System in the Chinese World Order', in Fairbank, ed., *Chinese World Order*, p. 274.

20. Fitzgerald, 'Chinese View'.

21. Mancall, 'Persistence of Tradition', pp. 17–19; and Cranmer-Byng, 'Chinese Attitude'.

22. Mark Mancall, 'The Ch'ing Tribute System: An Interpretive Essay', in Fairbank ed., *Chinese World Order*, p. 63.
23. Benjamin Schwartz, 'The Chinese Perception of World Order: Past and Present', in Fairbank ed., *Chinese World Order*, p. 277.
24. Rossabi, *China Among Equals*. Also Wang Gungwu, 'Early Ming Relations with Southeast Asia: A Background Essay', in Fairbank ed., *Chinese World Order*.
25. Fairbank, 'A Preliminary Framework'; Theodore Herman, 'Group Values Toward the National Space: The Case of China', *Geographical Review* Vol. VLIX, 1959; Norton Ginsburg, 'Chinese Perception'.
26. Fairbank, 'A Preliminary Framework'; and Lien-sheng Yang 'Historical Notes on the Chinese World Order', in Fairbank, ed., *Chinese World Order*; Rossabi, *China Among Equals*.
27. See the penetrating critique by Albert Feuerwerker, 'Chinese History and the Foreign Relations of Contemporary China', *The Annals of the American Academy of Political and Social Sciences*, Vol. 402, July 1972.
28. Gari Ledyard, 'Yin and Yang in the China–Manchuria–Korea Triangle', in Rossabi ed., *China Among Equals*. Also Feuerwerker, 'Chinese History'; and Schwartz, 'Chinese Perception'. For another view see John Cranmer-Byng, 'The Chinese View of Their Place in the World: An Historical Perspective', *The China Quarterly*, No. 53, March–May, 1973.
29. Eberhard, *History of China*, p. 111.
30. Fitzgerald, 'Chinese View'; Feuerwerker, 'Chinese History'; Schwartz, 'Chinese Perceptions'.
31. Rossabi, *China Among Equals*. Also Frank Kierman Jr., 'Phases and Modes of Combat in Early China', in Kierman and Fairbank eds., *Chinese Ways* pp. 34–5.
32. In 1804 the Chinese recorded that George III of the UK paid tribute when he did not. Feuerwerker, 'Chinese History'.
33. Hunt, 'Chinese Foreign Relations'; and Hucker, 'Hu Tsung-hsien's Campaign'.
34. Wang Gungwu, 'Early Ming Relations'; Ssu-yu Teng and John Fairbank, *China's Response to the West* (Cambridge: Harvard University Press, 1954). On the modern debate see Gerald Segal, 'China's Strategic Debate', *Survival* Vol. 24, No. 2, March/April, 1982.
35. Schwartz, 'Chinese Perception'; Hunt, 'Chinese Foreign Relations'; Feuerwerker, 'Chinese History'.
36. Owen Lattimore, *From China Looking Outward* (Leeds: Leeds University Press, 1964) pp. 6–7.
37. Owen Lattimore, *Inner Asian Frontiers of China* (New York: American Geographical Society, 1951).
38. *Ibid.* and Herman, 'Group Values', and Fredrick Mote, 'The T'u-mu incident of 1449'; and Michael Loewe, 'The Campaign of Han wu-ti'; Reischaur and Fairbank, *East Asia*, pp. 327–47, in Kierman and Fairbank eds., *Chinese Ways*.
39. Loewe, 'Campaign of Han Wu-ti'; and Yang 'Historical Notes', pp. 29–30; Fairbank, 'Varieties of Experience', pp. 12–14.
40. Lattimore, *Inner Asian Frontiers*, pp. 470–3.
41. Fairbank, 'Varieties of Experience', p. 26.
42. Reischaur and Fairbank, *East Asia*, pp. 321–5.
43. Hucker, 'Hu Tsung-hsien's Campaign', pp. 273–6.
44. Lattimore, *From China*, and *Inner Asian Frontiers*. Fairbank, 'Varieties of Experience'.
45. Griffith (trans.), *Sun Tsu*.
46. Kierman, 'Phases and Modes'; Dreyer, 'Military Continuities'.
47. McNeill, *The Pursuit of Power*, pp. 34–60. Reischaur and Fairbank, *East Asia* pp. 248–9; and Eberhard, *History of China* e.g. p. 49.

48. Yang, 'Historical Notes', Henning, 'China's Defence Strategy'.
49. Mote, 'The T'u-mu Incident'; Dreyer, 'Military Continuities'; McNeil, *Pursuit of Power* pp. 34–5; Fairbank, 'Varieties of Experience', Petersen, 'Regional Defense'.
50. Jonathan Fryer, *The Great Wall of China* (New York: A. S. Barnes, 1975).
51. The theory is developed in Scott Boorman, *The Protracted Game* (London: Oxford University Press, 1969); and Henning, 'Chinese Defense Strategy'.
52. Henning, 'Chinese Defense Strategy'.
53. Griffith (trans.), *Sun Tzu* p. 70. Jonathan Spence, *Emperor of China: Self Portrait of K'ang-hsi* (London: Jonathan Cape, London, 1974) p. 22.
54. *Ibid.* pp. 77–8.
55. Dreyer, 'Military Continuities'; Henning 'Chinese Defense Strategy'; Kierman 'Phases and Modes', Boylan, 'Chinese Style'.
56. Cited in Henning, 'Chinese Defense Strategy'.
57. Michael Mandelbaum, *The Nuclear Revolution* (London: Cambridge University Press, 1981) Ch. 1.
58. Michael Howard's inaugural lecture as Oxford Regius Professor of Modern History, *The Listener*, 12 March 1981, p. 333.
59. This is not to minimize the potential importance of tradition in other aspects of Chinese policy. Thomas Metzger, *Escape From Predicaments* (New York: Columbia University Press, 1977).

3

Ideology

Ideology and Defending China

The potential patterns in defending China from military threat as suggested by geography and history can only be a starting point for an analysis of Chinese defence policy. Another, and perhaps more immediately relevant source must be considered in the ideas of the Chinese Communist Party's (CCP) leadership. The strategies of Mao and his colleagues are complex, but they can be usefully divided into an analysis of general principles, followed by an assessment of the main uses of military power in foreign policy.

The Military, State, and Strategy

The importance of military force for good Communists must be stated at the outset. Mao and his colleagues were engaged in revolution, and they had little doubt that it was a violent process. As Mao said, 'Every Communist must understand this truth: political power grows out of the barrel of a gun ...'[1] This is not to say that the CCP sought power for its own sake. On the contrary, the desire to change the Chinese social order lay at the heart of Mao's strategy.[2]

Mao's thought on revolutionary war was not necessarily a brilliant new intellectual insight. His view of war as a 'supreme example of conscious activity' echoed Lenin and paraphrased Clausewitz. Mao spoke of war as 'politics with bloodshed' and contrary to a great deal of traditional Chinese attitude (see Chapter Two) he did not see war as an abnormal state of affairs.[3] Courage, bravery, and other romantic military attributes were priased by Mao despite China's more pacific traditional legacy.[4]

However, the emphasis on politics and power through the gun was only part of Mao's vision. He added that, '... Our principle is that the Party commands the gun; the gun shall never be allowed to command the Party. But it is also true that with the gun at our disposal we can really build up the Party organization.'[5] Thus, like many Communist parties, the CCP had to come to terms with how much the needs of an effective Party would clash with the needs of an effective military force. The Party–Army nexus remains central.[6]

In considering the 'red' versus 'expert' continuum, it would be misleading to suggest that Mao or any other CCP strategist had a clear view of what point along the continuum was acceptable. The primacy of politics suggested a leading role for the civil/Party authority, but the dividing lines between these political and military groups were often indistinct. Mao, Zhou Enlai, Zhu De, and others were supposed to be noted for insisting on the 'leading role of the Party',[7] and one recent analysis praises Deng Xiaoping (a political commissar before 1949) for saying that 'what the political commissar says is final'.[8] In the light of the flexible guerrilla war strategy of dispersal of units, it is not surprising that Party control was of paramount importance.[9]

The absence of any unified ideological view of how much Party control was required stems from the needs of military flexibility. Even in his early writing Mao spoke of the need not to counterpose military and politics, and Zhou Enlai made clear that no 'rigid instructions' should be given to the military as 'concrete circumstances' change.[10] In the early 1960s we know that the ratio of military to political training in the PLA was roughly 60-40.[11] More recent official pronouncements on the subject speak of the need to reduce bureaucratic interference and praise for 'commanders acting promptly' when waiting for political advice would have meant too slow a reaction. Flexibility in war seems to require less Party control.[12]

Despite the ambiguity in Party–Army issues useful points can be made about the general approach to military affairs. In the first place, the general tendency to minimize the value of military professionalism provides China with a useful rationale for not emphasizing military procurement and expensive, fancy weapons. The bias in favour of the human element in war, as opposed to military hardware is by and large unchallenged in CCP ideology.[13] Thus at its most basic, China adopts a 'people's war' strategy because it is carried out by people more than machines. Excessive emphasis on equipment or decisive engagements misses the point of revolutionary warfare waged by a communist party. But despite this emphasis on the quality of soldiers, it is clearly better to have quality in quantity.

Thus it is crucial to keep in mind that Mao's military thought is also flexible. Like any successful ideology it must be able to adapt to change, and the varying needs of party or professional interests have from time to time been incorporated in Mao's military ideology and PLA practice. This pliability has given rise to frequent strategic debates[14] and has resulted in a new assessment that Mao's thought is merely the crystallization of many ancient and CCP thinkers' ideas.[15] The new slogan, attributed to Mao, of 'seeking truth from facts' is the ultimate sanction for flexibility in military affairs. Today, more than in much of the preceding twenty years, the armed forces can therefore learn what they need from disparate domestic and foreign sources, and can concentrate on training and military practice. One contemporary Chinese commentary said that Mao's military thought,

...has inherited and absorbed the quintessence of the military theory of ancient times and from abroad, attached particular importance to the summation of the practices and experiences in war according to the special feature of the Chinese revolutionary war and created something unique.[16]

Uniqueness is however difficult to discern essentially because the doctrine seems so flexible. In sum, people's war can be seen as the highest form of military strategy. Much like communist ideology, it refers to basic principles, and not operational guidance. Thus people's war requires a close relationship to local conditions, but it requires very little specific form of military force.[17] This distinction between the first principles of military science and the details of military art is already well known to students of Soviet military doctrine.

The Threat of Invasion

A military operation designed to control all China was of great concern to CCP strategists, in large measure because the Communists' campaigns against Chiang Kai-shek as well as the Japanese dealt with just such a problem. Thus it is not surprising that more than any other threat to China, the problem of general invasion is the one most comprehensively analysed. Mao made it plain that in defeating an invader, geography was China's first ally.

China is a vast country—'When the east is still dark, the west is lit up; when night falls in the south, the day breaks in the north'; hence one need not worry about whether there is room enough to move around.[18]

Mao's geography may have been poor, but the essential principle that China's vastness aids the defender and allows space to be traded for time, is an accurate one.

China's second ally is its people. At its most basic, Mao's people's war suggests the need to rely on the people to defeat an enemy; China's hostile billion souls are a formidable deterrent. Therefore the CCP urged strategists to pay attention to the psychological dimension of war, emphasizing men not weapons, surprise and deception rather than brute force, and close combat rather than distant technological war.[19]

Mao's strategic thought is however more complex than mere emphasis on geography and people. Defending China from a general invasion is seen as having three different phases. This protracted war begins with defensive operations, then shifts to a stalemate and finally a more conventional and positional offensive stage.[20] The first, defensive phase provides a major role for guerrilla war. It proceeds from the assumption that tactically the enemy is strong, but strategically he is weak. Therefore the guerrillas fight flexibly, quickly, and furtively, all the while seeking to kill the enemy and preserve themselves. The strategy is protracted but the campaigns are designed for quick decisions that destroy the enemy force.[21]

This mobile war is also fought by the leading units in this phase, the regular army. Mao does not suggest that guerrillas can replace regular forces, but they can help. In the end it is necessary to concentrate forces, 'strike with one fist' for only regular forces can 'produce a decision'. In this first stage the holding of territory is not crucial, for as Mao said in 1938, 'To gain territory is no cause for joy, and to lose territory is no cause for sorrow'.[22] When confronted by a superior force, retreat and luring the enemy in deep is the preferred strategy.

It would be an error to exaggerate the importance of this first phase in Maoist strategy, for it was never seen as anything but part of a more protracted war. In the 1930s even Mao agreed that 'In the future this guerrilla character will definitely become something to be ashamed of and to be discarded, but today it is invaluable and we must stick to it'.[23] For Mao the guerrilla phase was neither especially Chinese nor particularly modern, but it was useful under certain limited conditions. Other CCP strategists seemed to concur.[24]

Defending China from invasion has other, more positive, phases. The second phase of stalemate, epitomizes Mao's flexible strategy. This period of transition allows for a bit of everything in the strategic bag of tricks, according to requirements. Some guerrilla tactics and some positional war are suggested, but above all annihilating the enemy is the best objective. It would be misleading however to view this phase as more coherent than merely abiding by the principle of 'if it works, then use it'.

The third phase of offensive war is even less unusual in the annals of strategic studies, for it is basically conventional war of massed armies. It does however play a crucial role in Mao's conception of how to defeat the general invader of China. He called it 'the most fascinating, the most dynamic' phase when it is increasingly clear that victory can be achieved. The precise moment at which the shift into offensive war should be made is left vague, but once it comes, the bypassed cities can be captured, the enemy forces engaged in positional war and more than one place can be struck at the same time.[25] Nevertheless, the operational principles still stress mobile war that concentrates superior force in order to defeat the enemy's forces rather than to hold territory.

These phases of Mao's people's war are both flexible and logical. Thus it should come as no surprise that they continued to serve as the focus of Chinese defence against general invasion in the period after 1949, and that they were subject to elaboration and adjustment. Soviet strategy was not incorporated whole-heartedly even in the hey-day of the Soviet model, as Mao soon came to urge the military not to 'eat pre-cooked food'. Soviet strategy for the modern services (navy and air force) appeared more relevant than for the ground forces.[26] In the early 1960s people's war seemed to stress 'walking on two legs', i.e. incorporating modern aspects into China's revolutionary experience. Positional war was emphasized along with close combat. Professionalism, 'compactness and quality', and modern war were underlined by Defence Minister Lin Biao, Chief of Staff Luo Ruiqing and above all Marshall Ye Jianying.[27] They praised people's war, 'under modern conditions' and said it included combined arms operations.[28] They revized old manuals and invoked the flexibility of Mao's military strategy as sanction for the modernization. Now even cities and vital installations were to be defended in positional warfare. To be sure, the 'expert' component did not go unchallenged, for by the Cultural Revolution, the PLA was placing greater emphasis on politics and professionalism was forced into the background.

China, as an established state with borders to defend, had

somewhat different priorities than did the CCP engaged in first phase strategy. Maoism was not discarded, but the flexibility of people's war was invoked as the main principle. Mao was quoted as saying, 'Any kind of guideline rules of war technique develops in accordance with the development of history and war; there is nothing in the world that does not change.'[29]

This eclectic approach has by and large continued to the present day without any successful attempt to formulate a new strategy for defending China. To be sure, there have been temporary changes of emphasis, and debates about these changes, but the wide spectrum of strategy covered under the people's war umbrella allowed all the variations to be labelled Maoist.[30] For example, Lin Biao was accused in the mid-1970s of both military caution and adventurism in the pre-1949 campaign, indicating the absence in China of any clear, coherent Chinese doctrine.[31]

Following Mao's death, military strategy designed to cope with the threat of general invasion still did not evolve in any clear direction. Flexibility of people's war remained a main feature, including guerrilla operation and positional war. According to Su Yu, Mao 'highly valued this kind of positional warfare, which illustrated the continuous development of our tactics under new conditions and the flexible application of the various methods of fighting according to objective conditions.'[32] Ye Jianying said 'the laws for directing war vary with the changing situation of war' and declared it was time to formulate new ideas for 'people's warfare in contemporary conditions'.[33]

In the early 1980s Chinese strategists were more openly discussing the meaning of 'people's war under modern conditions'.[34] There was however no attempt to invent a coherent strategy as articles spoke openly of differing views on guerrilla war, 'active defence' combined arms operations, and positional war.[35] The dominant theme was flexibility and even Mao was said to be a silent supporter of this line. One writer in *Military Science* went further than most when he suggested that Mao would have updated his views on conventional war if he had had the chance:

It was a pity that Comrade Mao Zedong had no time to make a systematic summation of large-scale wars, especially the practice of strategic counter-offensives in this period in the same way as he had summed up the experiences in strategic defensive operations in the early period of the anti-Japanese war ...[36]

The emphasis was also placed on abandoning guerrilla war and 'building a regular and modern army for national defence'. People's war meant fighting for the people with their support, but 'modern conditions' had to be taken into account. Better logistics, equipment and tactics were needed for this new war, and it would include holding major cities and military sites. Deng Xiaoping and others were praised for fighting such a war at the end of China's war of liberation. The strategists made plain that although there were going to be changes, they were uncertain as to the precise outcome.

During the first stage of a war, we should mainly use positional defensive warfare, with powerful support and co-ordination of mobile warfare, and guerrilla warfare in order to gradually consume and annihilate the enemy's strength and bring about a change in the balance of strength between the enemy and us. Concentrating a superior force to destroy the enemy forces one by one is still the basic way for our army to fight. However, when we use this way of fighting on the battlefield, we have to study and solve a series of new problems because of development in weapons and technical equipment.[37]

In sum, China's strategy for defending itself from threats of general invasion was rarely rigid, but only now is this flexibility openly acknowledged.[38] People's war has never been a fixed doctrine, but always incorporated change. Although at times some Chinese strategists interpreted the theory in a rigid manner, and these times (mid 1960s–mid 1970s) were often prolonged, that said more about the quality of the theorists than the theory. Thus China in the 1980s can claim that its belief in people's war under modern conditions is not new in principle, although the specific nature of modern conditions is obviously new. In the final analysis China has not had to test this aspect of people's war as China has not been invaded since 1949. But threats of a less serious nature have been faced since the Communist revolution.

Limited Threats

Defending China since 1949 has arguably had more to do with limited war along the frontiers than it has with general threats of invasion. But unlike the problem of total war, there are few stated Chinese strategic ideas on how to meet the limited threats. There is a great deal of practice, from Korea in 1950 to Vietnam in 1979, of limited frontier war, but precious little strategic thinking about this complicated kind of conflict.

The paucity of analyses of limited war may well be due to the apparent reluctance to face the implications of any such strategy. Limited war necessarily involves a degree of forward deployment so as to hold certain positions. Such positional war was previously only conceived of as the third stage of a protracted war and Maoist strategy did not see it as a starting point for any strategy. Mao spoke clearly of the need not to 'engage the enemy outside the gates' because it opposes the strategy of 'letting our pots and pans be smashed' by fighting a mobile war.[39]

As is already plain, Mao did accept the need for some positional war and the practical evidence of post-1949 Chinese defence policy indicates numerous attempts to meet the enemy at the gates. So what strategy was adopted in these cases? The answer seems to lie in two implicit rather than explicit elements. First, it seemed to be accepted that China could be seen as engaged in permanent positional war since 1949 in order to defend its international frontiers (but not for threats of total invasion). Second, wars remained people's wars because they had popular support but not because they followed any specific people's war strategy. In the Korean war Mao spoke of the need to pursue positional war and emphasized the sensible policy of concentrating forces, surprise attack and keeping the initiative.[40]

As the Korean war came to an end Mao again spoke of the war as a people's war largely in the positional phase. He offered a counter to those who would not meet the enemy at the gate by saying that to allow US troops up to the Yalu River would not allow China to 'carry on production free from worry'.[41] This doctrine of extended deterrence was not taken up by post-Korean war strategists in China, although some, including Defence Minister Peng Dehuai, did support positional war. Mao made it plain in 1958 that the lessons of Korea for China's strategy had not yet been analysed.[42] In the 1970s Korea was briefly listed as an example of effective positional war and was said to have 'illustrated the continuous development of our tactics under new conditions and the flexible application of the various methods of fighting according to objective conditions.'[43]

In the 1980s, the Korean war was said to have been one where 'people's war was our magic weapon', but also 'a severe trial of strength and will'.[44] Both assessments stressed the positional war dimension of Chinese strategy and one article said there was both a positional attack and a positional defence. Mao 'put forth a series of theories, policies, principles and tactics in operations in waging an international war under modern conditions'. These included emphasis on discipline, co-ordination, use of abruptness, small encirclement operations, anti-tank training, air-drops, tunnels, tactical offensives, and establishing better rear services. In short, a sensible conventional, largely positional war beyond China's gates.

It is, however, too simple to suggest that 'defence at the gates' was in effect adopted although it was unpolitic to openly admit such deviation. In fact, it seems more apparent that the policy of positional war at the gates was a focus of strategic debate that was never fully resolved in China. In January 1961 Ye Jianying spoke of both holding strongholds and coastal positions while maintaining a second defence layer that would 'lure the enemy in deep' as postulated in Mao's first and second phases of protracted war.[45] Evidence for more significantly divided counsel was apparent in the mid-1960s.

The looming US military presence in the Vietnam war made China take a more explicit stand on whether it would meet the enemy at the gates. One strategist in 1965 spoke favourably of holding cities and fighting positional war.[46] Chief of Staff Luo Ruiqing emphasized forward defence and positional war, including the construction of permanent defensive structures in North Vietnam. Other military men, including Lin Biao, rejected the idea of meeting the enemy at the gate in favour of more passive defence in depth. Lin's 1965 tract on people's war even urged the Vietnamese to pursue strategic retreat and praised guerrilla tactics. Others, perhaps including Mao, were less extreme (or less certain of their alternatives). The resulting compromise apparently included a sizeable Chinese presence in Vietnam but a decision to avoid direct confrontation with the US.[47]

In 1969 Mao seemed to explain the compromise by suggesting that defence at the gates was only possible in a limited war. Echoing Ye Jianying's 1961 line, Mao said that this third stage of protracted war would have to be abandoned if, however, the war was on a large scale.

Others may come and attack us but we shall not fight outside our borders. We do not fight outside our borders ... but if you should come and attack us we will deal with you. It depends on whether you attack on a small scale or a large scale. If it is on a small scale we will fight on the border. If it is on a large scale then I am in favour of yielding some ground. China is no small country. If there is nothing in it for them I don't think they will come ... If they invade our territory then I think it would be more to our advantage ... They would be easy to fight because they would fall into the people's encirclement. As for things like aeroplanes, tanks and armoured cars, everywhere experience proves that they can be dealt with.[48]

Coming in the wake of the border clash with the Soviet Union, Mao seemed to indicate that short of a major Soviet strike, forward defence was best, but not to the extent of his 1953 statements on extended deterrence into a neighbouring state.

Such a differentiation according to scale of attack was not made in public in the 1970s. Meeting the enemy at the gate was called 'left opportunism' when attributed to Wang Ming by Su Yu in 1978[49] (Luo Ruiqing's was a 'rightist' error). Xu Xiangqian, in the same year also said 'Engaging the enemy outside the gates has never been a good method of fighting', but added that the enemy should not be allowed to run rampant. He should be lured to where you want him and then some positional warfare should be adopted when 'at key places we will put up a strong defence'.[50] Apparently there was still no unanimity on dealing with limited threats. In the early 1980s the new material on Chinese strategy still offered no solution to the problem, although some writers did speak positively of the need to train in positional war.[51] The issue was apparently part of a broader debate on Chinese strategy and foreign policy, for the question of whether it was wise to post forces at the gate was an important aspect of the allegorical articles in the early 1980s on strategy in the Qing dynasty.[52] Defending China against threats of limited war was a vexed issue beyond even the scope of Mao's flexible military strategy.

Nuclear Threat

China's attitude towards the nuclear threat draws many of its principles from the same Maoist sources that shaped China's attitude towards general invasion. An attack on China that does not win the people's support will fail. Nuclear war against China is therefore of limited utility because it is no substitute for occupying the entire country. Thus the enduring strategic principle, first declared by Mao, that the atom bomb is a 'paper tiger', has lost none of its relevance since it was first propounded. Mao was merely suggesting that the rules of history and political power had not changed, although the destructive power of weapons had increased.[53] Zhou

Enlai concurred when he said 'The United States can't use the atom bomb to deal with a peasant war.'[54]

The paper tiger thesis does not however mean that China does not appreciate the destructiveness of nuclear weapons.[55] Chinese strategists clearly accepted that they were powerful, but they insisted that it would still be necessary to invade China in order to defeat it. Basic deterrence of nuclear war was achieved by reliance on geography.[56] It would also be incorrect to suggest that China did not study the more specific implications of nuclear weapons. The Soviet debates of the 1950s on nuclear strategy were followed and commented upon by China.[57] Beijing was only too well aware that the US had nuclear forces threatening China and at least in order to meet these limited threats some kind of nuclear support for China was required. The great value Mao placed on the Soviet ICBM test in 1957 showed that in some respects China even took nuclear forces more seriously than the Soviet Union. Chinese shifts in step with the Soviets on various strategic issues, for example the belief that nuclear war was no longer inevitable, meant that China held less than rigid views on nuclear policy.

This Chinese concern with nuclear weapons for limited rather than general threats was more visible in the early 1960s as reliance on Soviet deterrence of the US came more into doubt. The Military Affairs Committee said in January 1961—'The physical atomic bomb is important, but the spiritual atomic bomb is more important … We must reorientate the entire work of our army towards dealing with a new world war equipped for atomic warfare …'[58] Ye Jianying echoed this view and seemed to express more concern with biological weapons. He said nuclear weapons

… can only be used to destroy centres and the economic reserves of the opponent during the strategic bombing phase. After that, they are used principally as fire power preparations for assault. However, the army and regular weapons are necessary to terminate war … (this) is to rely primarily on man … They (US) also recognize that they cannot deal with China only by using nuclear weapons, because China possesses a large territory and lots of people, plus its complicated terrain. They consider using biological weapons which are the most effective way of harming farm products. They think China would be thrown into disorder if she had no food to feed her people …[59]

In the early 1960s the possibility of dealing with tactical nuclear weapons seemed to be of greater concern for China than the massive nuclear strike.[60]

Tactical or even theatre nuclear forces for China seemed to have been a source of some disagreement. Much like the debates on conventional limited war, so limited nuclear war was the focus of debate. By 1964, at least Zhou Enlai was saying unambiguously that China would not develop tactical nuclear forces.[61] The mid-1960s was a period of much change in China's nuclear posture as the testing of China's first atom bomb in October 1964 provoked a series of explicit statements of nuclear strategy. China pledged not to be the first to use nuclear weapons (hence the opposition to tactical forces) and supported nuclear-free zones. Mao said the paper tiger thesis was only a figure of speech.[62] China generally attempted to minimize the potential danger to itself that naturally occurs in the period immediately after the first test but before the establishment of a credible second strike.[63]

China's rapid rise to a secure second-strike level, coupled with superpower caution, ensured that the Chinese could carry on developing nuclear strategy. However, it is remarkable that little seems to have changed in China's original nuclear strategy. Some articles seemed more simplistic than others, but by and large deterrence against general nuclear war was not seen as a problem[64] as strategy for such a war still relied on people's war. Su Yu said in 1978

We do not deny that nuclear weapons have great destructive power and inflict heavy casualties, but they cannot be counted on to decide the outcome of a war. The aggressors can use them to destroy a city or town, but they cannot occupy those places, still less can they win the people's hearts ... (nuclear weapons) pose a much greater threat to the imperialists and social-imperialist countries whose industries and population are highly concentrated ... Our economic construction cannot therefore be destroyed by modern weapons.[65]

China's nuclear doctrine is of course more than simply a compilation of its leaders' declared positions. The pressures of technology and institutions also help shape China's changing doctrine and cannot be fully developed in this section on ideology (see concluding chapter). But suffice it to say that Chinese views on nuclear weapons include a peculiarly Chinese notion of graduated, minimum deterrence, and acceptance of the need to tailor nuclear deterrence to changing reality.

Perhaps the most current example of flexibility in China's nuclear doctrine is in the recent alteration of its previous opposition to acquisition of tactical nuclear weapons. Since the early 1980s China has been discussing the potential usefulness of tactical nuclear forces and by 1982 China had clearly been training in a simulated tactical nuclear environment.[66] One report suggested that China itself was even considering the first use of such nuclear weapons, in flat contradiction to China's pledge not to be the first to use nuclear weapons.[67] It seems that, if invaded, China might find no need to keep to its no-first-use pledge. What is clear is that Chinese nuclear doctrine is not fixed. Like other aspects of general conventional Chinese defence policy, it seems that the closer China gets to limited conflicts, the more there is pragmatism and flexibility in its military doctrine. People's war can set general principles, but even 'people's war under modern conditions' cannot predict all future military developments.

Conclusions

China's guiding military ideology is 'people's war'—whether it be under modern conditions or not. People's war is pre-eminently a notion of military science—a concept like Communism itself that is so general as to set basic goals but not serve as a blueprint for day-to-day action. People's war has some impact on military art, but it is at this more pragmatic level that China's 'modern conditions' has a greater impact. People's war is therefore essentially the notion that war must have popular support and be suited to local conditions. In China's case this means essentially a mass army prepared to trade space for time and men for weapons.

However, these principles of people's war tell us little about the specific cases of the use of the Chinese military instrument because these have mostly been concerned with limited threats. In these limited threats the Chinese doctrine is far from consistent, with little certainty on whether to meet threats at the gate, or to wage mobile or positional war. Similarly, on the nuclear level, while China seems to have fairly clear-cut general notions of deterrence, when it comes to limited nuclear war, Chinese doctrine seems more ambiguous.

The general picture of Chinese military ideology is one of flexible basic principles and even greater pragmatism when faced with less general threats to China. Interestingly enough, this is also apparently China's view of military aid to other states and revolutionary movements. That the world at large should be encouraged to have social revolutions is not in question for China, but the revolutions should be indigenous and based on local conditions. China offers military aid for various reasons, but the only revolution it seems to export is the idea of revolution itself.[68] In only Korea and Vietnam, both neighbouring states, has China used its own military force to support revolutionary causes. But in recent years China's policy on arms transfers to friendly states has undergone a major change. By the early 1980s it was clear that China was prepared to sell arms on a large scale, even in contradiction to its stated policy.[69]

Whether it be in making or defending revolution at home, or helping revolution abroad, China's military ideology has both a set of basic principles and a flexible view of how these ideas can be implemented. A pragmatist is one who adapts his purpose to suit reality. China is more like a pragmatic ideologist, trying to mould reality in the light of its purposes.

NOTES

1. Quoted in Stuart Schram, *The Political Thought of Mao Tse Tung* (New York: Praeger, 1969) p. 290.
2. Alexander Atkinson, *Social Order and the General Theory of Strategy* (London: Routledge & Kegan Paul, 1981).
3. Stuart Schram, 'To Utopia and Back: A Cycle in the History of the Chinese Communist Party', *The China Quarterly*, No. 87, Sept.–Nov. 1981; also Ralph Powell, 'Maoist Military Doctrines', *Asian Survey*, Vol. 8, No. 4, April 1968. On Mao and Clausewitz see Mao Tse-tung, *Selected Military Writings* (Peking: Foreign Languages Press, 1967), pp. 226–7. Henceforth *SMW*
4. Stuart Schram, 'The Military Deviation of Mao Tse-tung', *Problems of Communism*, Vol. 13, No. 1, Jan.–Feb. 1964, pp. 49–50. Also *SMW* p. 66.
5. Schram, *Political Thought*.
6. The literature on Party–Army relations is vast, and without wishing to minimize its importance by ignoring the issue, please see a more detailed analysis in Gerald Segal, 'The Military as a Group in Chinese Politics', in David Goodman ed., *Groups in Chinese Politics* (Cardiff: Wales University Press, 1984).
7. On Zhu De see an article in *Fifty Years of the Chinese People's Liberation Army* (Peking: Foreign Languages Press, 1978), pp. 80–1. On Zhou Enlai see generally *Selected Works of Zhou Enlai*, Vol. I (Beijing: Foreign Languages Press, 1981)—henceforth *SWZE*—and Li Yibin, 'Zhou Enlai and the Whampoa Military Academy' in *People's Daily*, 7 September 1981 in *FBIS*-CHI-81-184-K19-22. Yu Qiuli, 26 July 1983, 'The Direction of Army Building in the New Period', *Liberation Army Daily* in *BBC*/ISWB/FE 7402/B11/4–9.
8. *People's Daily*, 5 August 1981 in *FBIS*-CHI-81-160-K11-14.
9. Mao Tse-tung, *On Guerrilla Warfare*, Samuel Griffith trans. (New York: Anchor Press, 1968), p. 43.
10. *SMW* pp. 54, 82–9. On Zhou see *SWZE* p. 48.

11. Hsiao Hua on 17 December 1960 cited in J. Chester Cheng ed., *The Politics of the Chinese Red Army* (Stanford: The Hoover Institution, 1966) p. 10.

12. *People's Daily*, 2 December 1981 in *FBIS*-CHI-81-234-K21-4 and Song Shilun, 'Mao Zedong's Military Thinking is the Guide to Our Army's Victories', *Red Flag*, No. 16, 16 August 1981; *FBIS*-CHI-81-180-K10-23, Yu, 'The Direction'; Ellis Joffe, 'Party and Army' in Gerald Segal and William Tow eds., *Chinese Defence Policy* (London: Macmillan, 1984).

13. *SMW* p. 217. Mao Tse-tung, *Basic Tactics*, Stuart Schram trans., (London: Pall Mall, 1967) Chapter I; Su Yu in *Fifty Years*, p. 44. Military Affairs Committee, January 1961 and Military Science Academy, 1961, both in Cheng, *Politics of the Army*, pp. 66–7, 732. It should be noted that any such bias is relative, and changing.

14. Powell, 'Maoist Doctrines', pp. 257–9; John Wilson Lewis, 'China's Military Doctrines and Force Posture' in Thomas Fingar ed., *China's Quest for Independence* (Boulder, Colorado: Westview, 1980). Gerald Segal, 'China's Strategic Debate', *Survival*, Vol. 24, No. 2, March–April 1982. For recent evidence see *Guangming Daily*, 23 November 1981 in *FBIS*-CHI-81-237-K9-14; Yu, 'The Direction'.

15. Song, 'Mao Zedong' K16; and Fu Zhong, 'Mao Zedong Military Science is Forever the Chinese People's Treasure', *Red Flag*, No. 15, 1 August 1981 in *FBIS*-CHI-81-162-K1.

16. Song, 'Mao Zedong' K10. On flexibility see also Fu, 'Mao Zedong' K2. NCNA 31 January 1983 in *FBIS*-CHI-83-026-K11-12. Yu, 'The Direction', *SMW* pp. 82–9. Schram, *Political Thought*, pp. 275–9. Also *SWZE* pp. 52, 78.

17. Georges Tan Eng Bok, 'Strategic Doctrine', in Gerald Segal and William Tow, eds., *Chinese Defence Policy* (London: Macmillan 1984).

18. Cited in Schram, *Political Thought*, pp. 275–9. Also *SMW* p. 78.

19. Powell, 'Maoist Doctrines', pp. 241–5. Also, Sun Tzu, *The Art of War*, Samuel Griffith trans. (London: Oxford University Press, 1971) pp. 45–54.

20. 'On Protracted War' in *SMW* p. 210.

21. Mao, *Basic Tactics*. Also *SMW* pp. 97–143, 153–184 and *Guerrilla Warfare* pp. 40–86.

22. Mao, *Basic Tactics*. Ch. 3.

23. *SMW* p. 139.

24. *SWZE* pp. 27, 46–48, 103–5.

25. *SMW* pp. 122–140, 317, 332–3. Also Powell, 'Military Doctrine', p. 253 and Schram, *Political Thought*, pp. 161–2.

26. Stuart Schram, *Mao Tse-tung Unrehearsed* (London: Penguin, 1974). 28 June 1958 speech on pp. 129–30.

27. Cheng, *Politics of the Army*, pp. 133–4, 250–3, 636–9, 650–5, 729–731. See also Alice Langley Hsieh, 'China's Secret Military Papers: Military Doctrine and Strategy', *The China Quarterly*, No. 18, 1964.

28. 'Basic Differences Between the Proletarian and Bourgeois Military Lines', *Peking Review* No. 43, 24 November 1967.

29. Cheng, *Politics of the Army*, p. 735.

30. See next section for debates on 'meeting the enemy at the gates'.

31. Harry Harding, 'The Domestic Politics of China's Global Posture, 1973–8', in Fingar, *China's Quest*. *Red Flag* No. 9, No. 11, No. 12, 1974 in *Peking Review* Vol. 17, Nos. 38, 50, 52, 20 Sept.; 13, 27 December 1974. Chan Shih-pu, *Great Victory for the Military Line of Chairman Mao Tse-tung* (Peking: Foreign Languages Press, 1976). Yu Tzu-tao, 'Lin Piao's Right Military Line', August 1974 in *SPRCM* 74–15. Also Shen Sou, 'Dissecting the Reactionary Nature of Lin Piao's "Six Tactical Principles" ', Feb. 1975 in *SPRCM* 74–11.

32. Cited in *Fifty Years*, pp. 40–1.
33. 'Developing Advanced Military Science of Chinese Proletariat', *Peking Review*, Vol. 21, No. 12, 24 March 1978. Also Hzu Hsiang-chien, 'Heighten Our Vigilance and Get Prepared to Fight a War', *Peking Review*, Vol. 21, No. 32, 11 August 1978.
34. Li Xingren in the *Guangming Daily*, 20 July 1981; *FBIS*-CHI-81-K11-17. Yang Yong in *People's Daily*, 1 August 1981 in-150-K1-4; Mao telegrams from the early period of the anti-Japanese war in *Guangming Daily*, 10 August 1981 in -162-K13-15.
35. Fu, 'Mao Zedong' and Song, 'Mao Zedong'. NCNA 31 January 1983. See note 16.
36. Song, 'Mao Zedong' p. K15.
37. *Ibid.*, p. K21.
38. Yu, 'The Direction' Yang Yong in *Guangming Daily*, 22 January 1983 in *FBIS*-CHI-83-   -K11-5. Generally, Gerald Segal, 'The Soviet Threat at China's Gates,' *Conflict Studies* No. 141, January 1983.
39. *SMW* pp. 109–118.
40. Mao Tse-tung, *Selected Works*, Vol. 5 (Peking: Foreign Languages Press, 1977) 27 October 1952, pp. 82–3. For another view of Mao's strategy see William Whitson, *The Chinese High Command* (London: Macmillan, 1972), pp. 93–6.
41. *Ibid.* 12 September 1953, pp. 115–8. See also Peng Teh-huai, 'A Report on the Chinese People's Volunteers in Korea', *People's China*, 1 October 1953.
42. Alice Langley Hsieh, *Communist China's Strategy in the Nuclear Age* (Englewood Cliffs, N.J.: Prentice-Hall, 1962), p. 140; Mao on 28 June 1958 in Schram, *Mao Unrehearsed*, p. 128.
43. Su Yu in *Fifty Years*, p. 41.
44. See note 35.
45. Cited in Cheng, *Politics of the Army*, pp. 250–2.
46. Li Tzo-peng, 'Strategically Pitting One Against Ten, Tactically Pitting Ten Against One', *Peking Review*, Vol. 8, Nos. 15 and 16; 9 and 16 April 1965.
47. Lin Biao in *Peking Review*, Vol. 8, No. 36, 3 September 1965. For Western analyses see Gerald Segal, *The Great Power Triangle* (London: Macmillan, 1982); Thomas Gottlieb, *Chinese Foreign Policy Factionalism and the Origins of the Strategic Triangle* (Santa Monica: The Rand Corp. R-1902-NA, Nov. 1977), Harry Harding and Melvin Gurtov, *The Purge of Lo Jui-ch'ing* (Santa Monica: The Rand Corp. R-548-PR, Feb. 1971); David Mozingo and Thomas Robinson, *China Takes a Second Look* (Santa Monica: The Rand Corp. RM-4814-PR, Nov. 1965).
48. 28 April 1969 cited in Schram, *Unrehearsed*, pp. 285–6.
49. *Fifty Years* p. 35.
50. Hzu, 'Heighten Our Vigilance', p. 10.
51. Zhongquo Xinwen She, 5 November 1981 in *FBIS*-CHI-81-217-K7-10; *People's Daily*, 2 December 1981 in -234-K21-4.
52. *Guangming Daily*, 23 November 1981 in *FBIS*-CHI-81-237-K9-14. See also note 38.
53. Leo Yueh-Yun Liu, *China as a Nuclear Power in World Politics* (London: Macmillan, 1972); Morton Halperin, 'Chinese Attitudes Towards the Use and Control of Nuclear Weapons' in Tang Tzou ed., *China in Crisis* Vol. 2 (Chicago: University of Chicago Press, 1968).
54. *SWZE* p. 313.
55. Hsieh, *China's Strategy*; Jonathan Pollack, 'Chinese Attitudes Towards Nuclear Weapons 1964–9', *The China Quarterly*, No. 50, April–June 1972; Harry Gelber, 'Nuclear Weapons and Chinese Policy', *Adelphi Papers* No. 99, 1973.

56. Gerald Segal, 'China's Nuclear Posture for the 1980s', *Survival*, Vol. 23, No. 1, Jan./Feb. 1981; Gerald Segal, 'Strategy and Ethnic-chic,' *International Affairs*, Vol. 60, No. 1, Winter 1983–4.

57. Hsieh, *China's Strategy*, and Mao, *Selected Works*, pp. 152–3, 310.

58. Cheng, *Politics of the Army*, pp. 67–9. See a similar view by Zhou Enlai in 1960, Edgar Snow, *Red China Today* (London: Penguin, 1970).

59. Hsieh, 'China's Secret Papers', p. 84.

60. *Ibid*. p. 87. See also Mao on 16 June 1964 taking a similar line. *Miscellany of Mao Tse-tung Thought*. (Arlington, Virginia: Joint Publication Research Service. JPRS-61269-1 and 2, Feb. 1974) pp. 356–7. Also on tactical forces see Gelber, 'Nuclear Weapons', p. 19.

61. Zhou Enlai in late 1964, Edgar Snow, *China's Long Revolution*. (London: Penguin, 1974).

62. *Ibid*. Mao in January 1965, pp. 175–6, Halperin 'Chinese Attitudes'.

63. Gelber, 'Nuclear Weapons' and Pollack, 'Chinese Attitudes'. See also, Arthur Huck, *The Security of China* (New York: Columbia University Press, 1970) Ch. 4; Alice Langley Hsieh, 'China's Nuclear-Missile Programme: Regional or Intercontinental', *The China Quarterly*, No. 45, June–August 1971.

64. Hsieh Chan, 'The Atom Bomb in a Paper Tiger', *People's Daily*, 21 June 1977. *SPRCP*-77-29. Lewis, 'China's Doctrine' pp. 152–3.

65. *Fifty Years*, p. 44. See also Fu, 'Mao Zedong', p. K5.

66. Lewis, 'China's Doctrine'; Segal, 'China's Posture'; *Liberation Army Daily*, 16 September 1979; *China Report* No. 88, JPRS 75825, 4 June 1980; Xinhua, 2 January 1982; Nanfang Ribao, 25 January 1982 in *China Report* No. 80227 p. 52; Ningxia Ribao, 29 January 1982 in No. 81432 pp. 14–6; Xinhua 20 July 1982 in *FBIS*-CHI-141-K2-4. Also Gerald Segal, 'Nuclear Forces' in Segal and Tow, *Chinese Defence Policy*.

67. Ningxia Ribao, 29 June 1982 in *FBIS*-CHI-82-149-K8.

68. Chalmers Johnson, *Autopsy on People's War* (Berkeley: University of California Press, 1973); Peter Van Ness, *Revolution and Chinese Foreign Policy* (Berkeley: University of California Press, 1971); Powell, 'Maoist Doctrines'; Hashim Behbehani, *China's Foreign Policy in the Arab World* (London: Kegan Paul International, 1981, Appendix No. 1). Miscellany of Mao p. 448. Also, Song, 'Mao Zedong', p. K13. John Coon, 'The PLA and Chinese Power Abroad', in William Whitson ed. *The Military and Political Power in China in the 1970s*. (New York: Praeger, 1972).

69. Anne Gilks and Gerald Segal *China and the Arms Trade* (London: Croom Helm, 1985). See also Yitzhak Shichor, 'The Middle East' in Segal and Tow, *Chinese Defence Policy*.

4

Institutions

An analysis of the sources of Chinese defence policy would clearly be incomplete without making reference to institutional and bureaucratic forces. Does an analysis of institutional influences tell us very much about how China defends itself? In order to answer this basic question it is necessary to focus on the problem of how much independence the military has, as well as whether specific interests or branches of the PLA has an effect on policy. Therefore it is logical to start with a general review of Party–Army relations, and then proceed to an analysis of the different types of threats to China and how the institutional dimension might add to our understanding of the problem.

The Impact of Party–Army Relations

The old American Sinologist's joke that 'the east may be red, but the west is expert', indicates a large part of the problem in analysing Party–Army relations. Neither is the east exclusively red, nor is the west exclusively expert. To conceive of Party–Army relations as if Party and Army were monolithic bodies locked in inevitable struggle is seriously to misrepresent a far more complex reality. As will hopefully become apparent below, neither the military nor the civil authority in China is a monolithic group.[1] Cleavages cut across the Party–Army division so that it is misleading to view the PLA as an individual actor, let alone an independent one.

It is true that both the historical and ideological legacy suggest in no uncertain terms that the Party controls the army on all issues. The reality is, as usual, more complex. Take for example the central problem of professionalism in the PLA and the extent to which it conflicts with civilian and ideological demands. The adoption of the Soviet model for the military in the early 1950s meant professionalism in the officer corps, establishment of military academies, and the introduction of a system of ranks. At first this modernization did not conflict with ideology because the ideology itself was deemed to be modernization. However, this mad dash to professionalism along a path towards the Soviet model soon ran into roadblocks. In the military, as in many spheres of Chinese life, professionalism came under attack for denying the validity of China's revolutionary experience. However, the emerging policy dispute should not be seen as one between a Communist Party favouring ideology and a PLA holding on to newly-won professional skills. It is far more accurate to suggest that groups within both the Party and military had different views on the need for professionalism. The debate about the Soviet model was carried on at various levels of Chinese society and not between coherent and impermeable groups in politics.[2]

Even within the PLA, various different strands of opinion on professionalism can be identified. The younger members of the military had more interest in professional skills as they had risen to prominence in the post-Korean War experiment.[3] Some military men had developed closer ties to the Soviet Union and probably saw a greater need for retaining the Soviet model's professionalism. Other elements of the PLA were more involved in political control tasks and were disturbed at the loss of their political influence in a purely professional military.

In the late 1950s Peng Dehuai was replaced by Lin Biao as Defence Minister. Both were military men; they simply had different views, and represented different elements in the armed forces. Peng fell from power for his wider challenges to Mao on domestic issues, not for being a military professional.[4] If the vast majority of the PLA stood for professionalism, then the post-Peng purge should have included a vast majority of the new officer corps. On the contrary, the purge was surgical, and barely cut out an isolated few who had challenged Mao's authority on domestic economic policy. PLA leadership changes cannot be attributed to any single factor.[5] It seems more likely that rather than looking at Party–Army debates, it is better to seek root causes in central leadership politics and economic debates.

In the 1960s the same pattern continued: military men were divided on PLA policy and joined forces with diverse political coalitions in the civil structure. The purge of Luo Ruiqing (Chief of Staff) was not merely a purge of professionals. The move was in fact part of a more complex process involving military and civilian figures on both sides of the red versus expert argument.[6] Furthermore, it is impossible to identify a unified Party or Army in the Cultural Revolution when parts of the PLA were brought into the political arena on the side of one civilian group.[7] In the early 1970s the purge of Lin Biao involved many of these cross-cutting military and civil forces in a coalition to remove the Defence Minister.

Following Lin's fall, the PLA began drifting back to the barracks from which they were ordered in the mid-1960s. Far from opposing this return to professional concerns, the Party and Army encouraged it. Just as the PLA did not seek involvement in the Cultural Revolution, so they did not oppose being sent back to military pursuits. Most of the Party and Army shared a common vision of a return to normality.[8] The post-Mao struggles to remove the 'Gang of Four' also showed the same pattern of confused Party–Army lines. The Gang had some support in the PLA although somewhat less than in society as a whole. In the late 1970s much of the PLA responded quickly to the back to the barracks campaign for they agreed with the new CCP mood of professionalism and 'seeking truth from facts'.[9] Where there were limits on professionalism, they were due to lack of funds, but not a lack of desire or the presence of policy dispute. As in the 1950s professionalism was pursued in the PLA with CCP blessing. The new emphases on military training, academies, and professional skills were mirrored in various other aspects of Chinese society. The tension, such as it was, between professional and radical ideology, was a nation-wide phenomenon and not a Party–Army issue. In sum, the general absence of a unified, let alone independent military position on most issues, makes it hard to suggest that it would be useful to pursue an institutional approach to Chinese defence policy. But what of the area where the Soviet military obtains much of its power: functional specialization?

As students of the Soviet military well know, the Soviet armed forces apparently can claim power because they are specialists in certain key fields.[10] It is clear that in the Chinese case, the PLA has few of these spheres of influence. Because of Chinese technological backwardness, the PLA has few areas where it can control the flow of information and thereby gather power. There are of course military institutions in which the functional specialization may at some future point be vested. But for the time being the tasks of the PLA are open and largely intelligible to most in the civilian decision-making hierarchy.

The complex web of powerful decision-makers in China can be traced back to the CCP structure. Under the Central Committee of the Party lies the crucial Military Affairs Committee (MAC) which makes most specific policy choices.[11] The Ministry of Defence has no such power but may be more important in the implementation of policy. The MAC is staffed by senior military professionals but takes its lead from general CCP policy. In effect the MAC mediates between conflicting military demands but the overarching range of military action has already been set by the leading members of the Central Committee.

Mediation is also achieved at the level just below the MAC where several general departments deal with more specific issues. The General Political Department (GPD) is responsible for maintaining ideology, discipline, morale, and education in the armed forces. The GPD is not always in step with CCP policy as its purges in the Cultural Revolution make plain. This can be so particularly because military and Party interests are interwoven in complex patterns at various levels. For example the GPD's task at lower levels merges with that of the chain of political commissars that extend down the line of PLA power, but at higher levels the GPD and the Party Commissars are clearly separate institutions. The chain of command is even more complex. Political commissars are present at virtually every level at which there is a military commander but the pro- fessional soldiers trace their power to the second of the general departments, the General Staff Department. Headed by the Chief of Staff, the GSD executes the military orders of the MAC. The third department is the General Rear Services Department res- ponsible for logistics mainly of the ground forces as well as some of the other services and the dispersal of foreign aid.

It is clear that military institutions are diverse and far from unified in command. Decisions and problems seem to flow both up and down the channels of authority, making it very difficult to see any clear pattern. Thus even if the PLA were to obtain further specialized functions, it is unlikely that they would be able to offer a unified policy position. The same eclectic pattern is evident when looking at the role of military industry.

The equipment for the PLA is largely produced by five Machine Industry Ministries. As with the military itself these industries are in fact under the control of the MAC. In this case, the intervening body establishing policy for the ministries is the National Defence

Industrial Committee (NDIC).[12] The NDIC is staffed primarily by military professionals who soon move on to other tasks and the Committee by and large is responsive to military needs rather than pressure from the ministries.

Since the early 1980s there has been some suggestion that the Party control—through the MAC—is less important than it used to be. The reconstituted State structure, including its own Central Military Commission (CMC) and a National Defence Industry Office (NDIO instead of NDIC), is said to have assumed control of military industry. In June 1983, further consolidation of overlapping Party and State bodies supervising military industry took place, but at the time of writing, the implications of these changes were uncertain. However, it seems that Party control has not in reality been relinquished, despite some cosmetic changes. There certainly appears to be a remarkable coincidence of membership of parallel Party and State structures like the MAC and CMC. To a certain extent these changes seem part of China's attempt to rationalize its general economy, and take firmer control of military power. Whatever the case, the military industry sector stands out as one where lines of power are complex, cutting across simple Party–Army lines.

Obviously, this overlapping structure allows for numerous policy debates and does not itself impose any recognizable pattern on policies. As Western analysts have made clear, the main determinant of policy for military industry is the general state of the economy as thrashed out in the CCP Politburo. There are strong co-ordinating links in the structure, as in the Soviet system, but debates do occur. Different ministries demand a different allocation of resources, as in the 1971 steel versus electronics debate, and policy is sorted out at the top of the Party. There are inputs from the ministries and military units concerned, but making the choices are part of the Politburo's task. Similarly, debates within ministries, for example on the need for civilian versus military ship-building, produce unity in demanding more funds, but disunity in how to allocate them. Once again the issue is resolved at higher echelons. Thus there can be little certainty as to what a policy outcome might be, without a full understanding of the complex web of cross-cutting pressures that affect the process. Furthermore, the centrality of national economic priorities, as well as the removal of military men from control of the ministries of military industry in the late 1970s, means that the PLA has minimal independent influence on the economic dimension of military policy.

National economic pressures are felt most keenly on the issue of just how much of the budget is allocated to the PLA. The military's budget has been remarkably constant.[13] While this does not necessarily mean that the PLA does not have an independent role, it is probably an indicator that if it exists, such a role is severely circumscribed. Those changes in the budget that do occur can be traced either to changes in the general state of the economy, civilian leadership politics, or short-term fluctuations due to variable costs of certain military hardware.[14] The official military budget has remained roughly constant at 10 per cent of GNP and the PLA apparently is satisfied to keep to that figure. Only general economic growth can provide funds for future military needs.

Neither is it possible to suggest that different elements in the PLA have been locked in fierce factional battles over funds, for here too there is remarkable constancy in budgets. Each of the three main services has about 20 per cent of the total funds on average and thus changes in their postures (to be discussed below) have occurred gradually and within these financial constraints. Concensus seems to be the main characteristic of the budgetary process. In sum, the PLA does not appear to be an independent actor in policy debates. Decisions affecting the PLA seem to result from complex cross-cutting cleavages on various policy problems in which the military, or part of it, is only one of several participants. But if the PLA is not a monolithic actor, than perhaps it can be more usefully studied with reference to its specific tasks. Thus we now turn to an analysis of the way in which military institutions might tell us something about meeting threats to China's security.

Institutions and General Threats

It should come as no surprise that the institution most concerned with meeting a threat of general invasion to China is the ground forces. But institutions can have different ways of coping with a threat, so it is especially important to ascertain what strategic bias, if any, is exhibited by the PLA ground forces. Assuming that there is some rational calculation in their organization (and for some that is a large assumption) the ground forces appear to be organized to fight a mobile defensive war and to defend certain key positions.

China's 11 military regions, consisting of 29 military districts, are defended by ground forces organized around regional commands. The nearly four million troops in 11 armoured and 118 infantry divisions are notionally able to be shifted anywhere in China and organized in an *ad hoc* way to meet a specific threat that may arise.[15] In reality it appears that these forces are designed to operate on a regional basis in coordination with the more explicitly regional based local and militia units.

While the 11 military regions are undoubtedly of some organizational importance in peacetime, it seems that in case of a general threat of war, the regional organization will be along the line of 5 major fronts. In the early 1980s the first front comprised the Beijing and Shenyang military regions facing the Soviet Union, Korea, and Mongolia. It contained 8 armoured divisions and 46 infantry divisions with the Shenyang region standing out as the most heavily defended sector of China. Organizationally this area is of paramount importance and reflects an apparent decision to defend crucial industrial and population centres in a positional war that surrenders only the territory closest to the frontier.

The second front comprises the Lanzhou and Urumqi military regions and faces the Soviet Union and Mongolia in the north and India, Pakistan, and Afghanistan in the south. This vast and un-populated territory is defended by one armoured and 14 infantry divisions. Apparently there is little plan to hold this territory in time of invasion and the relative absence of population makes the pursuit of people's war less than credible.

The third front based on the Chengdu military region, faces India, Nepal, Bhutan, and Burma and is sparsely manned by 9 infantry divisions. Protected by the Himalayas, this region has little reason to be accorded special organizational status, especially with the diminution of a threat from India. The fourth front on the other hand has some geographic protection, but the presence of Indo-Chinese problems means it has been accorded a higher organizational status. Comprising the Guangzhou and Kunming military regions, and facing Burma, Laos, Vietnam, and Hong Kong, this front has emphasized infantry by garrisoning 18 such divisions in its territory. Like the first front it protects crucial parts of core China, but the more favourable geography and less modern enemy has meant a different balance of military forces is needed.

The fifth front is composed of the Jinan, Nanjing, and Fuzhou military regions facing Taiwan, Japan, and Korea. The presence of two armoured and 20 infantry divisions probably has more to do with internal security needs and less with facing a threat of invasion.

Like the as yet unmentioned Wuhan military region, these forces perhaps serve as a reserve from which to reinforce threatened areas and at the same time maintain a firm grip on the majority of the Chinese population in core China. The modernization needs of these central or reserve forces are less likely to be as pressing as for those units facing identifiable military threats requiring specific military forces.

In peacetime these regional interests probably play a greater role than in wartime. It seems apparent that in times of crisis central control is strengthened and more *ad hoc* military responses are organized.[16] Nevertheless, the main institutional pressures from the PLA ground forces remain regional. Apart from the obvious local interests of the militia and local forces, the differing regional interests create different policy preferences. What is more, the regional military commanders may adopt different positions on domestic politics and develop different attitudes to their sometimes diverse regional ethnic population. One need merely look at the Lin Biao affair or the post-Mao succession to see the futility of suggesting a single military viewpoint.[17] Thus, not only are the regions different from each other, but they are also not always in agreement with central civilian or military authority.

Such wide ranging differences of opinion among the military, probably are reflected also in different assessments of how the PLA should meet a general threat of invasion. Certain regions are less interested in the creation of a professional force, some are interested in a certain kind of professionalism, some benefit from unsophisticated logistics, and some might prefer a more active military role. These and other differences of opinion make it next to impossible to ascertain the institutional impact of the PLA on policy. The very complexity of motives and needs makes it necessary to try and understand the intricacies, but also makes it plain that simple institutional judgements are not useful.

What is perhaps more clear is that the ground forces are the main focus of the general defence of China. Both the navy and air force play a far less important role. But in the areas where the navy and air force are important, they complicate rather than clarify any potential institutional role in policy making. The air force, unlike the ground forces, is centrally organized with its own communication network that bears only superficial similarity to regional troop formations.[18] The central command from Beijing is less strong in peacetime, but it seems that in time of conflict combat operations by the air force would be even more firmly run from the centre.

In any case the air force's role in meeting a general threat to China is probably minimal. Chinese aircraft are by and large designed to contest air superiority, but this is a battle unlikely to be won against the far superior Soviet air force. Most of the 400 modern airfields are in core China and this leaves vast areas of the country virtually undefended from the sky. It seems that in facing the general threat to China, the air force has the smallest role.

The navy seems to take up a position in between the air and ground forces, but once again with different organizational procedures.[19] Until recently the navy was simply designed for coastal defence in a variation of people's war adapted to the sea. Thus forces were small and fast and intended to harass the enemy, lay mines, and support ground operations. The bias was also somewhat more akin to Mao's third phase of positional war in that the navy sought to defend coastal positions and vulnerable cities along the shore. Like the ground forces the main organizational control of naval forces was regional, but the regions are not the same as those identified for the ground troops. The three fleets are notionally responsible to naval headquarters in Beijing in peacetime, but this central control is tightened during war. The northern fleet covering the Yellow Sea essentially faces Korea and comprised 500 ships of substantial size. The East Sea fleet covers the main industrial areas and the Taiwan Straits. Because it faces the main potential threats in Japanese, Taiwanese, and Soviet naval forces, it has 750 major craft. The third fleet in the South China Sea has 600 ships and faces Vietnam and the more extended Soviet naval threat.

The complex lines of control are perhaps best seen when analysing the naval air forces designed to defend surface ships and naval installations. So far these pilots have been all land-based and under the organizational control of the air force. While acknowledged as the cream of the crop in Chinese military aviation, navy pilots still basically serve air defence roles.

What then does an institutional analysis tell us about defending China from a general threat? First, China's main response is to be found in the ground forces. But this does not mean that simple judgements can be made about institutional preferences for policy. Clearly the ground forces have cleavages between centre and region, as well as between region and region. The essentially regional organization of these forces means that many of these cleavages are likely to be important, but not in any coherent way suggesting a single policy. Central control will be difficult to assert, although somewhat easier for the air and possibly naval forces.

These institutional arrangements do, however, lend credence to the view that people's war remains the central, and in many senses still the credible form of defence against the general threat of invasion. Yet the allocation of forces in specific regions tends to suggest that vast expanses of territory will, if necessary be surrendered mainly in the west while in the north and east the stress might well be on the positional war phase of people's war. Thus an examination of PLA organization does not suggest a necessarily uniform defence of China.

What is also suggested by this institutional analysis is the relative lack of concern with professional military matters. The tendency to establish *ad hoc* commands during war, the flexible regional organization, and China's selective recruitment to all services,[20] means that the non-professional element inherent in much of the people's war doctrine, continues to be crucial. Thus central political judgements become paramount. Coupled with the pattern of cross-cutting military cleavages on policy, it seems apparent that the institutional dimension to strategy for the general defence of China reveals little more than that there is no pattern. It is important to understand institutional sources of policy, but they are unlikely to provide any coherent picture. Perhaps the picture is more clear and simple when looking at the relatively less complex problem of limited war threats to China.

Institutions and Limited Threats

It can be argued that, since meeting general threats to China is so crucial, the parochialism of military institution's interests are not allowed to dominate policy discussion. More limited threats might however offer greater scope for the assertion of institutional differences. Certainly the organization of the ground forces on a regional basis seems to lend credence to this conviction.

However, such regionalism or even 'warlordism' of local commanders pursuing the interests of their 'independent kingdom' does not appear to occur to any significant degree. Perhaps because of the extreme sensitivity to the potentially disastrous effects of 'warlordism', modern China seems to have avoided any such independence. The presence of cross-cutting cleavages in the military, already outlined above, is undoubtedly an added reason for the absence of regionalism. Some analysts have suggested that independent action by a local commander may explain the 1969 Ussuri clash, but the argument is a convoluted one.[21]

It seems more likely that even in the case of limited threats to China's security, the central political leadership quickly takes control in an *ad hoc* manner and overrides any existing local institutional biases. This was clearly the case during the Korean war when no specific institutional interest can be seen as determining policy. Policy was determined by the change of commanders from Lin Biao to Peng Dehuai and the objective reality of heavy military losses, rather than by competing interests within the PLA.[22] Forces were also brought into combat from different regions, thus further complicating the picture.

In the 1962 Sino-Indian war there was evidence that only regional forces were used, but conflicts in Indo-China in the 1960s and 1979 involved less reliance on local troops. More importantly, there were debates on which forces to use in Vietnam in the mid-1960s, as part of more general discussions on how to meet the US threat. There were clearly contributions to the policy process from various diverse groups in the PLA and Party, but no simple institutional judgement is possible. In the previous chapter we have already mentioned the complex issue of whether to 'meet the enemy at the gate'. An appreciation of the complexity of institutional interests helps provide a better grasp of policy, but a simple organizational approach is not helpful.[23]

A study of the air force role also does not offer a convincing argument for the organizational perspective. Central control of the air force seems to have remained crucial, as China's political elite juggled political options. For example, as new military threats developed in the south of China, the requisite airbases were constructed in order to provide a military option.[24] The organizational structure of the air force therefore followed policy choices rather than determined them.

It is however true that the air force is more likely to play a decisive role in meeting limited war threats. Because the air force is too vulnerable in a general war and less suited to people's war, it tends to see itself as undertaking limited roles assigned by the central political elite.

The air force prefers to operate closer to home as its technical and logistical weakness is then less important. This service, unlike the ground forces, is likely to be more interested in, and more important in limited war threats, be they on Chinese soil or in neighbouring territory. This role is however likely to remain limited, especially against such modern air forces as those in the Soviet Union and Vietnam. On the other hand, the air force may find a greater role in the longer term in participating in combined arms operations. Whatever the case, the PLA institutional lines in the air force tell us little about the use of military force against limited threats.

Not surprisingly, naval forces have the same pattern of limited institutional freedom. It is clear that many potential limited threats involve naval interests. Defending coasts, islands, or offshore resources give the navy a greater interest in limited war than general threats, where its role is distinctly secondary. Like the air force, the navy's interest is in planning for limited war or 'meeting the enemy at the gate' and indeed contrasts with the more passive approach of the ground troops.

On the other hand, there are numerous limited threats in which the navy's interest is minimal. In Korea the navy merely tried to hold the line, but did not try to take on the superior US forces.[25] Similarly in the Vietnam war the navy's profile was low. Again, like the air force, the navy has little interest in many limited wars where its power counts for little. Taiwan crises, on the other hand, would naturally involve the navy to a far greater extent.

Changes may well be under way in the service, not because of any institutional determinism, but more because, like the expanding Soviet navy, the Chinese navy seems to have been given a greater role by the political leadership. Whether as a result of leadership debates or technological change,[26] the navy seems to be expanding its role in the early 1980s. Both the navy and air force were first formed out of ground force units in the early 1950s, and it is perhaps only now that they are finding their institutional feet. Given prolonged development of expertise and technological sophistication, they may well take on new roles that will make the institutional perspective on policy more productive.

In sum, evidence of debates and cross-cutting institutional lines make it plain that a full grasp of institutional preferences is needed in order to understand the sources of Chinese policy. But such an organizational perspective cannot provide a guide to policy as the complexity of the issues defies such neat categories. Institutional issues do however suggest a few general points. First, the navy and air force have a more important and independent role in meeting limited as opposed to general threats to Chinese security. Second, none of the branches of the armed forces are designed for action very much forward of the Chinese gates. However changes in this judgement may be underway. Third, the use of any PLA service seems to be on an *ad hoc* basis and to depend crucially on the outcome of central leadership politics. Institutional predilections may affect policy at this point, but they tend to be so diffuse as to undermine the possibility of their having an important or decisive impact.

Institutions and the Nuclear Threat

In the Soviet Union it is suggested that the relative independence of the strategic rocket forces gives them special influence over policy. Unlike the US where nuclear forces tend to be divided among the different services, the institutions of Soviet nuclear capability are said to exert more noticeable influence. The Chinese case seems to fit into neither model.

It must be stressed that we know very little about how China's nuclear forces are organized and commanded. Thus most speculation about the institutional impact of the nuclear forces can be little more than somewhat informed speculation. With this modest level of certainty, it can be assumed that the Chinese control of nuclear weapons combines elements of both the US and Soviet pattern. Like the Soviet Union, Chinese nuclear forces seem to be controlled by the Second Artillery, a service arm ostensibly like the navy or air force and thus responsible to the MAC and the Politburo.[27]

Unlike the Soviet Union, the Second Artillery does not appear to be just another service, but rather a special one more firmly under central control and heavily influenced by the Chinese public security apparatus and the scientific and technical community. The Second Artillery does not appear to be just another fief of the military establishment. Rather, the central political leadership seems able to keep a firm grip on these powerful forces, and especially because China does not have a large number of nuclear weapons, such central control is more efficient.[28]

The decisions on production and deployment also seem to be under similar central control with institutional roles more for security and technical experts rather than military men. The few nuclear production sites as well as missile sites may be spread out across China, but they don't seem to be subject to any significant regional influences.[29] Once again it does not seem especially useful to seek evidence on how nuclear strategy is made by tracing institutional lines, other than to say that the PLA's influence over nuclear policy seems relatively reduced.

In fact, the major reason for this simplified institutional picture is that the Chinese nuclear forces are not very sophisticated and hence lack the areas of expertise and specialization that give their Soviet counterparts more power. The probable evolution by China of tactical nuclear weapons will not necessarily increase the institutional role of the nuclear forces, and it certainly will complicate it. Confusing command and control problems will have to be sorted out, but as is the case with the superpowers, the decision to use the weapons is likely to remain with central authorities. Furthermore, the PLA does not have to contend with pressures for arms control which both superpowers have found enhance the institutional differences. There is nothing like talk of limitations or reductions in a country's armed forces to bring out clear organizational interests.

It is also likely that the nuclear forces find their policy preferences intersecting with those of the other services in a complex way. Nuclear weapons are generally a cheaper path to deterrence and defence as compared to conventional weapons. Since people's war remains valid for the general threat to China, nuclear weapons only compete for resources with conventional forces when it comes to meeting limited threats. It is here that the lower cost of nuclear forces is particularly appreciated.

But because nuclear weapons have opportunity costs for other services, the other services of Chinese defence may not appreciate the central elite's efforts to cut costs by deploying nuclear forces. But even here the judgement is a complicated one, for the more technologically advanced services like the air force and navy might well be pleased with more investment in electronics rather than steel. The problem is they then might find that the special kind of electronics needed for nuclear forces still drains resources from the air or naval forces. Clearly the picture is complex. Even if we could draw the institutional lines in greater detail, it is likely that they would again show a pattern of cross-cutting cleavages defying simple institutional analysis. It is important to understand the importance attached to central control of nuclear forces and the complex series of interests involved in developing nuclear forces, but it is hard to suggest that an analysis of military institutions leads to any inexorable conclusions for China's defence policy.

Summary and Conclusions

Those seeking insights from military institutional arrangements as to how China defends itself, will be disappointed with this chapter. There seem to be few significant lines of organizational power and influence in the PLA that are crucial in shaping Chinese defence policy. The evidence for this conclusion is drawn from several sources, but the most important one is that there are no clear lines of institutional policy in the military as a whole, or in specific services. The cleavages on policy are numerous and far from consistent in any given case. What is more, the military is not independent enough to impose its will on the party leadership even if it could formulate a single coherent one. The central policy choices seem to be taken by the central party leadership, taking into account pressures from groups within the military, but also myriad other pressure groups.

It is however true that the organizational approach is more useful in considering a few types of broader military views. For example, the voice of the PLA is relatively unified and vociferous when they feel they are not getting sufficient funds or professional latitude. But even in these two areas, it has already been noted that significant differences within the PLA exist. Thus the PLA has an important role to play in policy making, but not as an institutional actor.

The scope for important independent military action as an institution is also much reduced because of the relative lack of expertise. The absence of large or sophisticated military systems where the armed forces can jealously guard information means that a crucial source of power and leverage is lacking. It is possible that with growing sophistication in Chinese forces and expansion of technological skills, the PLA will gradually obtain more power. Then it also might be more useful to look at institutional lines of control. But for the time being the analysis of Chinese defence policy is not particularly well served by institutional analysis. The development of active and independent PLA power will follow the creation of the basic military tools, but it is unlikely to precede it.

NOTES

1. Gerald Segal, 'The PLA as a Group', in David Goodman ed., *Groups in Chinese Politics* (Cardiff: Wales University Press, 1984). Gerald Segal, 'The PLA and Chinese Foreign Policy Decision-Making', *International Affairs*, Vol. 57, No. 3, Summer 1981.
2. Ellis Joffe, *Party and Army* (Cambridge, Mass.: Harvard University Press, 1971); John Gittings, *The Role of the Chinese Army* (London: Oxford University Press, 1967).
3. Michael Yahuda, 'Political Generations in China', *The China Quarterly*, No. 80, December 1979; William Whitson, *The Chinese High Command* (London: Macmillan, 1973), Ch. 9; William Parish Jr., 'Factions in Chinese Military Politics', *The China Quarterly*, No. 56, December 1973; Ellis Joffe, 'China's Military Elites', *The China Quarterly*, No. 62, June 1975.
4. Joffe, *Party and Army*. Also Ellis Joffe, *Between Two Plenums: China's Intra-leadership Conflict, 1959–62*; Michigan Papers in Chinese Studies, No. 22, 1975; Roderick MacFarquhar, *The Origins of the Cultural Revolution*, Vol. 2 (London: Oxford University Press, 1983).
5. Lucian Pye, *The Dynamics of Factions and Concensus in Chinese Politics: A Model and Some Propositions* (Santa Monica: The Rand Corp. R-2566-AF-July 1980).
6. Ellis Joffe, 'The Chinese Army Under Lin Piao: Prelude to Political Intervention', in John Lindbeck ed., *China: Management of a Revolutionary Society* (Seattle: University of Washington Press, 1971); John Gittings, 'Army–Party Relations in the Light of the Cultural Revolution' in John Wilson Lewis ed., *Party Leadership and Revolutionary Power in China* (Cambridge: Cambridge University Press, 1970); Melvin Gurtov and Harry Harding, *The Purge of Lo Jui-Ch'ing* (Santa Monica: The Rand Corp., R-548PR, February 1971); Thomas Gottlieb, *Chinese Foreign Policy Factionalism and the Origins of the Strategic Triangle* (Santa Monica: The Rand Corp. R-1902-NA, November 1977).
7. Ellis Joffe, 'The Chinese Army After the Cultural Revolution', *The China Quarterly*, No. 55, September 1973.
8. Ellis Joffe, 'The PLA in Internal Politics', *Problems of Communism*, Vol. 24, No. 6, Nov–Dec 1975; Harry Harding, 'The Domestic Politics of China's Global Posture 1973–8' in Thomas Fingar ed., *China's Quest for Independence: Policy Evolution in the 1970's* (Boulder, Colorado: Westview Press, 1980).
9. Ellis Joffe and Gerald Segal, 'The Chinese Army and Professionalism', *Problems of Communism*, Vol. 27, No. 6, Nov–Dec 1978; Allan Liu, 'The Gang of Four and the Chinese People's Liberation Army', *Asian Survey*, Vol. 19, No. 9, September 1979; Kenneth Lieberthal, *Sino-Soviet Conflict in the 1970's* (Santa Monica: The Rand Corp., R-2342-NA, July 1978); Richard Nethercut, 'Deng and the Gun', *Asian Survey*, Vol. 22, No. 8, August 1982; Ellis Joffe, 'Party and Army', in Gerald Segal and William Tow, eds., *Chinese Defence Policy* (London: Macmillan, 1984).
10. On the Soviet case see Karl Spielmann Jr., *Analyzing Soviet Strategic Arms Decisions* (Boulder, Colorado: Westview Press, 1978); Edward Warner, *The Military in Contemporary Soviet Politics* (New York: Praeger, 1977); Arthur Alexander, 'Decision-Making in Soviet Weapons Procurement', *Adelphi Papers*, No. 147–8, Winter 1978–9.
11. Details in Harlan Jencks, *From Muskets to Missiles* (Boulder, Colorado: Westview Press, 1982) Ch. 5. Also Harvey Nelsen, *The Chinese Military System* (Boulder, Colorado: Westview Press, 1977). Also, Defence Intelligence Agency

(U.S.), *The Chinese Armed Forces Today* (London: Arms and Armour Press, 1979).

12. Jencks, *Muskets to Missiles*, Ch. 6; Sydney Jammes, 'China' in Nicole Ball and Milton Leitenberg, *The Structure of the Defence Industry* (London: Croom Helm, 1983). On Party control of the PLA in 1983 see Zhongguo Qingnian Bao, 23 July 1983 in *BBC*/SWB/FE/7398/B11/1. Harlan Jencks, 'The Chinese Military-Industrial Complex and Defence Modernisation', *Asian Survey*, Vol. 20, No. 10, October 1980; 'China's Defence Industries', *Strategic Survey*, 1979 (London: IISS, 1980); Charles Horner, 'The Production of Conventional Weapons', in William Whitson ed., *The Military and Political Power in China in the 1970's* (New York: Praeger, 1972); Jencks, *Muskets to Missiles*, Ch. 6.

13. Central Intelligence Agency, National Foreign Assessment Centre, *Chinese Defence Spending, 1965–79* (July 1980); *The Military Balance* (London: IISS, annual volumes); Ronald Mitchell, 'Chinese Defense Spending in Transition', in *China Under the Four Modernizations*, JEC, 13 August 1982.

14. CIA, *Defence Spending*, and analysis in Segal 'PLA as a Group'.

15. Data and organization from *The Military Balance*, 1981–2 (London: IISS, 1981), and Defence Intelligence, *Chinese Forces*.

16. Nelsen, *Chinese System*, pp. 121–3; William Whitson, 'Organizational Perspectives and Decision-making in the Chinese Communist High Command', in Frank Horton ed., *Comparative Defence Policy* (Baltimore: Johns Hopkins Press, 1974); Harry Harding, 'The Making of Chinese Military Policy', in Whitson, *The Military and Power*.

17. Segal, 'PLA and Foreign Policy'. Also, Joffe and Segal, 'The Army and Professionalism'; Roger Glenn Brown, 'Chinese Politics and American Policy', *Foreign Policy*, No. 23, Summer 1976; Wallace Heaton, 'The Minorities and the Military in China', *Armed Forces and Society*, Vol. 3, No. 2, Winter 1977.

18. Defence Intelligence, *Chinese Forces*. Nelsen, *Chinese System*.

19. *Ibid*.

20. Conscription in China is in effect selective service in that a relatively small portion of the eligible population is inducted. Thus the quality is generally higher than for Soviet conscripts and a useful reserve system is available in times of war. The force is still less professional than an all-volunteer military.

21. Brown, 'Chinese Politics'.

22. Whitson, *Chinese High Command*, pp. 73–6, 328–9. Nelsen, *Chinese System*, p. 122.

23. On the debates see chapter 3. See also *Ibid*, and Joseph Heinlein Jr., 'China's Force Posture: Factions in the Policy Process' in Horton, *Comparative Policy*.

24. Whitson, 'Organizational Perspective', p. 37.

25. Whitson, *Chinese High Command*, p. 247.

26. Bruce Swanson, *The Eighth Voyage of Dragon* (Annapolis: Naval Institute Press, 1982). Also Bruce Swanson, 'China's Navy and Foreign Policy', *Survival*, Vol. 21, No. 4, July–August 1979. See also Segal, 'China's Strategic Debate'.

27. Gerald Segal, 'China's Nuclear Posture for the 1980s', *Survival*, Vol. 23, No. 1, Jan/Feb 1981; Harry Gelber, 'Nuclear Weapons and Chinese Policy', *Adelphi Papers*, No. 99, Summer 1973; Defence Intelligence, *Chinese Forces*, pp. 142–3; Gerald Segal, 'Nuclear Forces'; Segal and Tow, *Chinese Defence Policy*.

28. Jencks, *Muskets to Missiles*.

29. Charles Horner, 'The Production of Nuclear Weapons' in Whitson, *The Military and Power*; George Tan Eng Bok 'La Strategie Nucleaire Chinoise' *Strategique*, 1980 (3).

5

Tibet, 1950–1951

Some might balk at the inclusion of a chapter on PLA operations in Tibet. It has been suggested that the 'liberation' of Tibet was merely part of the broader anti-Guomindang war of liberation. However, there are several reasons for arguing that the PLA campaign in Tibet was the first use of force by Communist China beyond its frontiers.

First, it will be shown that the Tibet campaign was specially planned and was not merely a continuation of civil war operations. Second, unlike the civil war, the invasion of Tibet had clear and specific foreign policy implications. Finally, there is a widely held belief that because Tibet, unlike other parts of China, was an independent, or at least quasi-independent state, therefore the 1950 invasion was an expansion of Chinese territory. Without passing judgement on the legitimacy of these claims, the Tibet operation was a special one, and can properly be treated as the first use of Chinese military power beyond its *de facto* frontiers.

Course of Events

Unlike most of the case studies in this book, the basic details on PLA operations in Tibet are not readily known. However, there can be little doubt that the communists intended to 'liberate' Tibet, for even in 1936 Mao Zedong told Edgar Snow that Tibet and Xinjiang 'will form autonomous republics attached to the Chinese federation'.[1] Following the declaration of the People's Republic of China in October 1949, official government statements made it clear that Tibet would be 'liberated'. Military preparations began in early 1950 but took on concrete shape in April when Garze in Sichuan was captured and the laying of roads began toward the Tibetan border.[2]

The arduous military preparations were taken simultaneously

with attempts at peaceful unification. In January the Dalai Lama was ordered to send a delegation to Beijing for talks and to cease attempts to obtain international support. In February a Tibetan delegation left Lhasa for India. By April, when Chinese military preparations were under way, an eight man Tibetan delegation tried to reach China via Calcutta and Hong Kong. Their attempt to fly to Hong Kong on 5 June was thwarted by Britain which did not want unification and therefore refused to grant visas for the delegation.[3]

Throughout the summer there were rumours that China had invaded Tibet, but these seem only to have been Chinese probing of border positions. On the diplomatic front, the Tibetan delegation in India planned to circumvent British roadblocks by discussing the problem with the Chinese ambassador in India who was expected to arrive there shortly. On 22 August the leading pro-Chinese 'living Buddha', Geda, was killed in Tibet perhaps foreclosing Beijing's attempt at organizing a fifth column.[4] In any case, China was also told by India in mid-August that Britain had now withdrawn its refusal to grant visas.

China's exasperation at what it viewed as the delegation's procrastination provoked a Chinese Ministry of Foreign Affairs statement to India on 31 August. The statement said that the Tibetan delegation had better arrive by mid-September as PLA plans were well under way.[5] On 9 September the Tibetan delegation began talks with the Chinese chargé d'affaires in Delhi where he reportedly told them to come to Beijing as soon as possible. The Tibetans were less than anxious to speed up the matter, for they had already told the United States secretly in August that they were only playing for time.[6] During September the talks in Delhi did not seem to progress even though the Chinese ambassador eventually arrived in September. As China said at the time, 'we hear footsteps on the staircase, but nobody ever appears'.[7]

The Delhi talks in fact seemed unconnected to the military preparations. The Indian government was again warned in mid-October of the need to have the Tibetans arrive quickly in Beijing, even though Chinese forces invaded Tibet on 7 October. On 24 October the Tibetans announced they would in fact go to Beijing, but a day later the Chinese media announced that Tibet had been invaded. On 1 November, the New China News Agency (NCNA) said the town of Qamdo was taken on 19 October after a twelve day operation.[8] Wildly exaggerated reports followed suggesting China's imminent capture of Lhasa, but, apart from minor advances, no other major engagements took place. November was dominated by the Chinese entry into the Korean war (troops entered Korea on 14 October) and to the extent that Tibet was noticed, the reports cited only the abortive attempt by El Salvador to raise the issue in the UN and Sino-Indian exchanges of letters on Tibetan history.

In the spring of 1951 several Tibetan delegations converged on Beijing to begin talks as China appeared still to prefer a peaceful solution. Military operations were arduous. In April the delegations representing the Dalai Lama, the pro-China Panchen Lama, and another pro-Chinese Tibetan group, began talks. On 23 May they signed an 'Agreement on Measures for the Peaceful Liberation of Tibet' that effectively gave China control. Unlike the military manœuvres, this political coup by China received wide domestic media coverage.[9]

On 21 July the Chinese representative sent to Tibet, Zhang Jingwu, travelled via India to Yadong where the Dalai Lama was staying after his flight from Lhasa. The two entered Lhasa on 17 August and the vanguard of PLA troops arrived from the Qamdo area on 9 September. The main forces arrived on 26 October and in February 1952 the Tibetan Military Region was formed. The regional commander, Zhang Guohua, had led the military campaign in Tibet and now embarked on a lengthy stay as the most powerful leader in the region. Thus after the brief battles of October and November 1950, Chinese power was effectively established by October 1951, and without firing a shot.

Objectives

China's objectives in using the PLA were straightforward—to gain control of Tibet. Beijing's will was stated unambiguously in numerous public declarations and there is little evidence that these objectives changed at all. Two principles were paramount in almost every declaration of intent. China sought to 'liberate the Tibetan people and defend the frontiers of China'.[10] Although the objective of liberation was stated with monotonous regularity, statements by Mao Zedong and Zhu De spoke of offering to 'help our Tibetan brothers to liberate Tibet'.[11] After the dashing of China's hopes for a fifth column in August 1950, it appeared unlikely that the PLA would receive much local assistance, and would have to give up the fiction of 'helping' the Tibetans.

The second objective of defending China's frontiers seems even less persuasive, although it was repeated often enough. Some declarations said there was a need to 'strengthen the defence' of China's western frontier, 'consolidate' western defences, or 'prevent imperialist encroachment',[12] but they all shared the belief that there was a threat to China's borders. As will be shown below, the limited concern of China's enemies with Tibet at this time casts serious doubt on the validity of this belief. Some Chinese statements even spoke of the need to 'drive out' the imperialists as an objective of the PLA action, but there is even less evidence that the 'imperialists' had ever seized Tibet.

The most likely reason for the invasion, the unification of China, was only stated explicitly after the combat had ceased, and even then it was not as consistent a theme as 'liberation and defence'. One final objective, that of 'maintaining world peace' was mentioned only once,[13] and seems largely curious in the light of the by then far more serious Korean war.

However, it would be misleading to suggest that Chinese objectives were determined by such foreign policy pressures. The goals of liberation and unification were clearly rooted in domestic policy. Where there might be an objective related to foreign policy, it is the claim that imperialists needed to be held at bay. It is significant that the Soviet Union's comments on the Tibetan operation made reference virtually exclusively to this foreign policy objective.[14] This bias is even more remarkable when compared with other Communist parties which stressed the Chinese mix of domestic and foreign objectives.[15] The Soviet line does not necessarily mean that China included foreign policy objectives in its statements on Tibet at the Soviet Union's behest. On the contrary, it seems more likely that Moscow merely picked up one strand of Beijing's line in large measure because it suited broader Soviet foreign policy goals.

The caution in China's setting of objectives in the Tibet operation is even more clear when analysing the question of whether the liberation should be peaceful or not. Almost every Chinese statement of objectives included a call for peaceful settlement. Even after force was used, this was intended only to coerce the Tibetans to talk. China's pressure was cautious and the PLA tried to use the minimum force. Chinese objectives did not change during the crisis and they were achieved, in all their varieties, fairly easily. The objectives were maximalist in that they required unification with China and the drawing of a forward defence line incorporating all of Tibet. Nevertheless, the coercion was obtained economically, and from China's point of view, undoubtedly successfully.

Military Operations

It is obvious that the military details about the PLA operations in Tibet were few and far between. Estimates of the number of Tibetan forces range between 8000 and 100,000, with the most likely figure being closer to 9000. Chinese forces were said to have numbered between 20,000 and 250,000 with the most likely figure for combat troops being around 30,000. In as much as the Tibetans were lightly armed and the terrain difficult, the scale of casualties was understandably low. In the main engagement at Qamdo, China claimed to have killed or wounded 180, and taken prisoner 898, while several thousand others are said to have surrendered.[16] Reports of Chinese casualties are sparse but one source claimed they could be as high as 30 per cent, mostly due to difficult geographic conditions, and 2000 in combat.[17] Given that all figures are no doubt exaggerated, this was hardly a bloody battle, but it was undoubtedly arduous. One NCNA report said the PLA had overcome its greatest geographical obstacle, and that progress was at 5 kilometres per hour as roads had to be laid in front of advancing troops.[18] Thirteen major mountain chains were crossed on the 1300 km journey to Lhasa. China's determination in this venture, even as the Korean war expanded, shows at least that some importance was attached to the Tibet operation.

The movement of Chinese troops into Tibet did not seem to follow any specific strategy other than that determined by geography and political pressures. Zhang Guohua said his forces used Mao's guiding principle of 'massing a force of absolutely superior number to surround the enemy and striving to annihilate him completely and not to allow him to escape.'[19] But that seems a logical enough dictum under any circumstances.

There is some speculation that Lin Biao was responsible for planning the operation, but it seems likely that the planning was in fact done by Liu Bocheng and also Deng Xiaoping, both of whom dominated the Southwest Military Region and the Second Field

Army.[20] Other leading military figures included He Long and Liu's chief of staff from the 1947 campaign, Li Da. Li wrote in 1973 that He 'personally planned and prepared for the march under the leadership of the Southwest Bureau'. The actual forces were led by Zhang Guohua's 18th Corp, supported by elements from other units in the southwest. Zhang's forces were well ensconced on the roof of the world by the end of 1951 and dominated local politics for at least fifteen years.

Aside from the formidable geographic barriers to PLA operations, the main determining factor for the course of Chinese policy was political pressures. But the main political pressures arose mainly from Sino-Tibetan relations rather than Chinese ties to any other state, great or small. China had demanded that the Tibetans send a delegation to China for talks and seemed prepared to wait for some time before using force. The Tibetans made signals in early 1950 that they were seeking international recognition, and by April the Dalai Lama also tried to send a delegation to Beijing. The Tibetans were obtaining new arms shipments from India and from July talks began with the United States on further military aid.[21]

China followed a two prong strategy with the Tibetans, on the one hand urging peaceful negotiations, and on the other preparing its military options. During the summer of 1950 further delays in the sending of the Tibetan delegation could be traced to British mischief-making and above all Tibetan machinations. Until September 1950 the Chinese were probably willing to believe that the Tibetans were acting in good faith, but after then Beijing felt the Dalai Lama was procrastinating.[22] As winter set in, the pressures for immediate action built up. Even after having used force in the Qamdo engagement, China still pursued the path of peaceful unification, and when the Tibetans finally sent their delegations, the PLA halted their drive. The agreement in May 1951 made further military operations superfluous.

The salience of Sino-Tibetan relations is obvious when compared to the relative unimportance of Chinese relations with the great powers. The Soviet Union was a very passive actor in the Tibetan events—fomenting tension with premature rumours of United States military aid to Tibet, and generally playing up the alleged involvement of 'imperialist intrigues'.[23] What is more, the Soviet Union, just as much as the rest of the world, was out of touch with the specific details of the conduct of Chinese military operations.[24]

The United States was equally out of touch. It was obviously preoccupied with the Korean war and in any case had long accepted Chinese 'suzerainty' over Tibet. President Truman refused to respond favourably to Tibetan requests for aid in 1949,[25] but from the summer of 1950 the Department of State took an active part in setting up aid in addition to that supplied by India. The United States aid was never sent, due to confusion in the Tibetan camp, and India's desire not to antagonize China. Washington did not pay a great deal of attention to Tibet, but it did try to orchestrate, via its ambassador in India, some limited efforts at keeping China from launching a full scale attack by promising to provide limited 'defensive' arms to the Tibetan.[26] It was apparently felt by some United States officials that if the Tibet issue was not given undue importance, then even if China invaded, the event could be more easily minimized.[27]

At the time of PLA operations in October, the United States was unaware of the military situation but saw no need for urgent action.[28] The United States apparently was not behind the attempt by El Salvador to raise the Tibetan issue with the United Nations, and in any case it was a half-hearted venture quietly shelved with American connivance.[29] Washington also tried a more limited strategy to undermine the May 1951 agreement by using covert methods to entice the Dalai Lama into renouncing the pact he signed in 1951 with China. These efforts were aborted by the Dalai Lama's advisers.[30] The United States role, and to a certain extent also British assistance to Tibet via India, did figure in Chinese commentaries on its objectives and on Chinese operations in Tibet, but the western involvement was largely rhetorical rather than real, and more useful for Beijing's propaganda than an important determinant of policy.

The only external power of any importance for the PLA operations was India. The Indians were crucial not merely because geography determined that communication with Tibet was most effective via India (even for Chinese delegations). India was also central because the Tibetan delegation spent a great deal of time there trying to get to China, and above all because India was seen as China's most important friendly state, especially in the tense Korean War period.

This is not to say that India influenced China's position in any significant way, but China did deem it important to keep in close touch with the Indian leadership. The exchange of notes in October and November is a case in point.[31] But in the end China had set its objectives, and obtained them, according to its own plan and with full knowledge that there would be a political price to pay in Sino-Indian relations. The deterioration in Beijing–Delhi relations was noticeable, but not catastrophic. The real damage would be done later in the 1950s when the implications of the extension of Chinese power to the Indian frontier would be fully appreciated.

In general, the Chinese had only limited success in communicating its objectives to the Tibetans. On the political level the Chinese messages were hampered by difficult geographic problems. But even so, the Tibetans did not appreciate the urgency of Chinese signs sent either in the open media or via Indian intermediaries. It was not that the messages did not get through, but rather that they were misunderstood by the receiver. Messages to other states including India and the superpowers were better understood, but then they were of less importance. China did not have to deter these outsiders, but rather it had to compel the Tibetans. Only after Chinese diplomats communicated directly with the Tibetans in Delhi did Beijing's message get through, but by then it was too late.

China then used the idiom of military action to signal Beijing's seriousness to the Tibetans. The Tibetans soon responded and negotiations were rapidly wound up when they were held face to face in April/May 1951. However this Chinese use of force was not necessarily a risky game. The military operations were of a low level and used only sparingly. The minimal foreign interest in the use of force meant that risk was also kept low, especially when compared with the simultaneous, and much larger battles, beginning in Korea. In sum, Chinese operations seemed prudent, relatively clear, and above all successful. Clearly there were risks in the PLA action, but they were controlled by cautious reactions to the changing situation on the ground. Pragmatism in seeking the Chinese objective seemed to be a successful policy.

Domestic Dimension

In 1949 there were apparently important differences of opinion in the Chinese leadership about foreign policy, but in the Korean war, less than a year later, no such divisions were apparent.[32] From a careful assessment of different Chinese leaders' statements, the Tibet operation was carried out with relative unity at the top. As has already been suggested, an analysis of Chinese objectives in Tibet reveals no major differences in emphasis. The most important policy declarations were made by Liu Bocheng, the Second Field Army commander and leading figure in the southwest; Zhu De, the dominant military figure after Mao, and Zhou Enlai, the leading figure dealing with foreign policy. No major discrepancies are evident in any of their speeches except for one statement by Zhu De, and one by Mao and Zhu, declaring that China would 'help' the Tibetans achieve liberation rather than have the PLA do it for them.[33] There was however no pattern to these differences in emphasis and both Mao and Zhu also made statements more in keeping with the general line.

If there is a need to explain some of these subtle variations of statements, the answer may be found in the division of responsibilities within the Chinese leadership. For example Zhou Enlai's 30 September speech declaring that a peaceful solution was possible, when an invasion was a week away,[34] probably indicates Zhou's leading role as a diplomat. In any case, the peaceful line was used in later declarations in the hope that China could avoid a full scale invasion. Further evidence of a division of responsibility is evident in the April/May 1951 Sino-Tibetan talks. Zhou Enlai clearly led the Chinese side, but when the politically symbolic Panchen Lama arrived in China Zhu De led the Chinese side. When an agreement was reached in May, Zhu De made the major Chinese speech but Mao was also present to place the highest seal of approval on the pact.[35]

The only area where there are perhaps some more significant policy differences is the shady area between the military operations and the diplomatic communications. It is clear that even the Chinese diplomats in Delhi did not know the date of the Chinese invasion. Some Western reports were so struck by the absence of official Chinese comment on the invasion while it was under way, that they felt the military action was due to local initiative.[36] The fact that the Chinese Ministry of Foreign Affairs offered 'no comment' on 13 October when asked whether China had invaded, may indicate nothing more than caution.[37] What seems most likely is that poor communications with the recently established Chinese embassy in Delhi was exacerbated by the Chinese desire to keep silent until the first phase of their operation was complete. No deeper significance can be assumed.

Neither is it possible to discover important differences among the Chinese military leaders. It is true that the PLA operation was dominated by Liu Bocheng's Second Field Army, and He Long was brought in earlier in 1950 from the First Field Army, but there is no evidence of policy disagreements.[38] It is however notable that He received almost no coverage in comparison to Liu Bocheng on matters relating to Tibet.[39] If there were factional splits within the PLA at the time, they did not seem to affect policy on Tibet.

Summary

China obtained all its stated objectives in Tibet. The frontiers of China were fixed where China wanted them, but only after forcing the Tibetans to capitulate. Yet it is equally clear that Chinese objectives were not met until it had used force to overcome Tibetan hesitancy, although China's will was not established entirely by force of arms. The necessity to use force was not so much due to a failure in China's communication with the Tibetans or anyone else, but rather because the Tibetans did not move swiftly enough for China's liking.

This is not to say that China had any set strategy of how to obtain its objectives. It used as much force as was required, and did so at low risk and with great caution. Not even the presence of leadership debates clouded the clarity of the objectives. But the unwillingness of the Tibetans to capitulate meant that China had to compel them to do so, even though Beijing probably wished to avoid such an option. The military operation was not a major one, but it was difficult and required a decision to proceed in hard times when a far more important engagement with the US in Korea was about to get under way. The successful use of the military instrument in unifying China might have given Chinese leaders hope that a similar pragmatic policy could be pursued for that other great irridentist cause, Taiwan. But the Korean war brought the US into the Taiwan–China equation, and meant that China would not be able to invade Taiwan as it had invaded Tibet.

NOTES

1. Edgar Snow, *Red Star Over China* (London, Penguin, 1972) p. 129.

2. John Gittings, *The Role of the Chinese Army* (London: Oxford University Press, 1967) pp. 37–8; William Whitson, *The Chinese High Command* (London: Macmillan, 1973) pp. 190–3; Tieh-Tseng Li, *Tibet: Today and Yesterday* (New York: Bookman Associates, 1960) p. 200; Chang Kuo-hua, 'Tibet Returns to the Bosom of the Motherland', *People's Daily*, 25 October 1962 in *SCMP*. No. 2854.

3. *New York Times*, 22 January, 20 April, 15 June 1950; *South China Morning Post*, 22 January, 6, 21, 23, 28 June 1950; U.S. Department of State, *Foreign Relations of the United States*, 1950 (FRUS). Embassy in Delhi to Sec. State, 9 June 1950, p. 361.

4. Chang, 'Tibet Returns', p. 3.

5. *NCNA*, 16 November 1950, and *People's Daily*, 17 November 1950 in *NCNA* (Supplement), No. 59, 21 November 1950.

6. *FRUS*, Delhi Embassy to Sec. State, 7 August 1950, pp. 424–6.

7. *Ibid*. Also *Manchester Guardian*, 9 September 1950. *The Times* (London), 3 October 1950.

8. NCNA 1 November 1950 in *BBC*/SWB/FE/81/p. 3 and 8 November in No. 82/p. 1.

9. *BBC*/SWB/FE/104–111.

10. Zhou Enlai, 30 September 1950 in *BBC*/SWB/FE/77/pp. 39–40.

11. Zhu De, 1 October 1950 in *BBC*/SWB/FE/77/p. 36 and Mao and Zhu on 11 November 1950 in No. 82/p. 3.

12. Note 10 and Liu Bocheng in August 1950 in *NCNA*, 5 August 1950, PRC Government Statement to India, 30 October 1950, 16 November 1950 and *People's Daily*, 17 November 1950, all in NCNA (supplement) No. 59, 21 November 1950. NCNA 24 October 1950 in *BBC*/SWB/FE/80/p. 39. *People's Daily*, 22 November 1950 in No. 84/p. 2. NCNA, 1 January 1951 in No. 90/p. 10.

13. *People's Daily*, 17 November 1950 in NCNA (Supplement) No. 59, 21 November 1950.

14. *BBC*/SWB/FE/80/p. 41. Also No. 81/p. 10, No. 84/p. 1, No. 91/p. 4.

15. *BBC*/SWB/FE/81/p. 10 for Vietminh and Polish comment.

16. NCNA, 8 November 1950 in Union Research Institute, *Tibet, 1950–1967*, (Hong Kong, 1961) pp. 2–5. Higher figures in Chang, 'Tibet Returns'.

17. *New York Times*, 20 January, 24 March 1951. Also Li Da, 'Comrade Ho Lung and the Southwest' in *People's Daily*, 6 July 1973 in JPRS, *China Report*. No. 73862.

18. *NCNA*, 2 November 1950, 22 November 1950.

19. Chang, 'Tibet Returns' p. 4.

20. Whitson, *Chinese Command*, pp. 190–3; Li Da, 'Comrade He Long'. Also Michel Peissel, *The Secret War in Tibet* (Boston: Little Brown, 1972).

21. *New York Times*, 22 January, 1 February, 1950. *FRUS*, Correspondence on 22 July, 7 August, 10 September, 26 October 1950, pp. 386, 424, 493–5, 540–1.

22. NCNA, 16 November in *NCNA* (Supplement) No. 59, 21 November 1950.

23. See the rumours cited in *South China Morning Post*, 15 May 1950, *New York Times*, 16 May 1950.

24. As late as 26 October the Soviet paper in Berlin thought the Chinese forces had invaded on 24 October. *New York Herald Tribune*, 27 October 1950.

25. Allen Whiting, *The Chinese Calculus of Deterrence* (Ann Arbor: University of Michigan Press, 1975) pp. 13–14.

26. Telegram between Acheson and Henderson in Delhi, 20 January, 1 March, 8 March, 19 April, pp. 284, 314, 317–8, 331.

27. *FRUS*, Embassy in London to Acheson, 20 June 1950, p. 365.

28. *New York Times*, 25, 26 October 1950. *New York Herald Tribune*, 2 November 1950. US Ambassador to India, Henderson in *BBC*/SWB/FE/83/p. 5. *FRUS* telegrams dated 13 October, 26 October, 31 October 1950, pp. 531, 540, 546.

29. Li, *Tibet*, pp. 203–6.
30. Whiting, *Chinese Calculus*, pp. 13–14. George Patterson, *Tragic Destiny* (London: Faber and Faber, 1959) Ch. 8–9.
31. *NCNA* (Supplement) No. 59, 21 November 1950.
32. On the late 1940's see Dorothy Borg and Waldo Heinrichs eds., *Uncertain Years* (New York: Columbia University Press, 1980). Also Kenneth Lieberthal, 'Mao Versus Liu: Policy Towards Industry and Commerce 1946–49', *The China Quarterly*, No. 47, July–September 1971.
33. See note 11.
34. *BBC*/SWB/FE/77/pp. 39–40.
35. *BBC*/SWB/FE/106/p. 4. No. 107/p. 4. No. 11/pp. 1–11.
36. *New York Times*, 8, 28 October 1950. *Sunday Times*, (London) 15 October, 1950.
37. *Statesman* (Delhi), 17 October 1950.
38. Whitson, *Chinese Command*, pp. 191–3.
39. For a different view of He's role see Chang, 'Tibet Returns' and Li, 'Comrade Ho Lung'.

6

Korea, 1950–1953

> Water shapes its course according to the ground over which it flows; the soldier works out his victory in relation to the foe whom he is facing. Therefore, just as water retains no constant shape, so in warfare there are no constant conditions.
>
> Sun Zi

No war was as important to the People's Republic of China as the Korean war. The significance derives not only from the unprecedented casualties, but also from the fact that it was the only war in which Chinese troops were forced to retreat and the only war in which all three Chinese armed services took part. Most importantly, the Korean war was also China's only prolonged conflict with a superpower, and coming as it did in the first year of the People's Republic of China, helped establish basic elements of Chinese defence and foreign policy. Thus it is undoubtedly central to a study of Chinese defence policy to analyse how and why China used military force in Korea. Previous analyses have often been superb in assessing the first phase which drew China into a war that had been going on for at least three months. But it is also important for our purposes to assess the way in which China used military force in the following thirty months of combat. Both phases cast important light on the principles of Chinese defence policy. Without prejudging the account that follows, the major conclusion is that far from pursuing a coherent military and political strategy, China was forced to react pragmatically to the changing fortunes of war.

The Course of the Korean War

The reasons for the outbreak of the Korean war on 25 June 1950 have been the subject of much public and academic debate.[1] Most probably the North Korean attack 'jumped the gun', in a conflict that could have just as easily begun for other reasons. While it is reasonable to assume that China was aware of an imminent attack, it seems far less certain that Beijing's leaders approved of the venture. Even if China had given the North Koreans and the Soviet Union a silent nod of assent, it must have been in the hope that the victory would be swift and the US would cut its losses and not respond. But both hopes were soon dashed. Washington rallied its allies to respond militarily to the North Korean action, and what is worse for China, President Truman ordered the 7th Fleet to patrol the Taiwan Straits. This last act was particularly disturbing to Beijing as it delayed the final stages of the civil war—the taking of Taiwan.

The other Chinese hope—that of a swift victory—did not materialize. By late June China began moving some troops from the Taiwan front to staging areas close to the Sino-Korean frontier. By the end of July China also began speaking of 'a prolonged war'.[2] The mounting apprehension in Beijing really began in August when the US turned the military tide and Chinese commentaries began speaking less optimistically about the military prognosis. On 25 August China alleged US strafing of Chinese villages on the Yalu river and Chinese warnings to the US increased in parallel.

If China was trying to deter the US at this stage, it was failing miserably. On 15 September US troops landed at Inchon behind Communist lines and a counter-offensive began in the south, out of the Pusan perimeter. China increased its level of concern and its warnings to the US but the advance on North Korea by MacArthur's troops was swift and unchecked. Clearly the US and China had communication problems, but more importantly there was little the US could do to convince China that it was not a target. Nor was there much that China could do to convince the US not to cross the old dividing line in Korea at the 38th parallel.

Foreign Minister Zhou Enlai summoned Indian Ambassador Pannikar in the now legendary midnight meeting to warn the US of China's intent to intervene to prevent a US threat to China's Northeast. But Washington was not in a mood to heed such calls, especially from the Indians. On 7–8 October the US forces crossed the 38th parallel. On 8 October Mao Zedong ordered Chinese 'volunteers' to support North Korea, and Chinese troops crossed the Yalu on 14–16 October. Achieving complete tactical surprise they first engaged US troops on 25 October and then suddenly disengaged on 7 November. For close to three weeks China paused to see if the US would now pull back. But once again the two sides' motives were so fundamentally at odds that such a simple solution was not feasible. On 24 November the US resumed its 'end the war offensive' and two days later Chinese forces counter-attacked in force, forcing the US into its longest retreat.[3]

The Chinese military campaign achieved notable success early on and PLA forces entered Seoul on 4 January 1951. But US forces soon regrouped and the war became more of a slog and slaughter. Sometime around late February or early March the commander of the Chinese troops, Lin Biao was removed under circumstances still uncertain. His replacement, Peng Dehuai achieved less than Lin Biao on the military front, but his retreat in combat (including Seoul on 14 March), inflicted heavy casualties on the Americans. MacArthur was relieved of command on 10 April. Peng responded, perhaps in the mistaken belief that MacArthur's 'purge' was a sign of weakness, and launched a fruitless assault on 22 April. The US line held and thousands died on both sides. Another offensive in May collapsed even more swiftly. American troops did not pursue the Chinese forces as they had decided to hold the line, roughly at the 38th parallel. China's objectives might have been inflated after rapid victories in the early stages of the war, but now they had to settle for a static war along the original dividing line in Korea.

On 23 June the Soviet Ambassador in the UN offered a truce and the first serious talks began on 10 July. Now both sides negotiated, while sporadic heavy fighting took place and the two opposing armies dug into sophisticated fortifications. From October 1951 the Chinese began rapid modernization of their forces under fire including special emphasis on improvements in the air, and artillery power as well as logistics. Most notable was the 'great wall' built by China to protect its forces along the parallel.

It is hard to be sure what the remainder of the Korean war achieved. From January 1952 to the armistice on 8 June 1953, neither side gained any territory of consequence and both suffered continuous casualties. From 1952 the main excuse for deadlock seemed to be China's refusal to allow POWs to choose whether or not they wished to be repatriated. It seems more likely that China saw the benefit of limited combat behind relatively safe and static fortifications, while the US 'bled' and its position in Asia was undermined.

Following Stalin's death in early March 1953, China essentially capitulated to US demands on the POW issue and the way was open for an armistice. Last-minute obstruction from South Korea was overcome by a Chinese offensive and US political pressure. Despite occasional brief crises in Korea, little has changed since then. But if the war seems such a fruitless waste of lives, it offers revealing insights into Chinese military policy.

Objectives

If the first three months of the three year war are analysed—the period from the outbreak of war to the Chinese intervention—the objectives of Beijing's leaders seem clear cut. But a broader analysis of the war soon reveals a multiplicity of Chinese objectives, and ones that are ever-changing in response to different conditions. To suggest fixed Chinese objectives, is to engage in what Mao called 'mechanicalism'. Mao was quoted in September 1950 as having said, 'Different war situations determine the different guiding laws of war according to the differences in time, locality and character ... War and the guiding laws are developmental'.[4] By looking at the full three years war, rather than the first three months, the changing Chinese objectives and strategy become apparent.

Excellent and extensive analysis of the first phase of Chinese objectives, covering the three months from the outbreak of war to Chinese intervention, has already been done.[5] Several objectives are commonly agreed. First, China was preoccupied with national unity and therefore was initially concerned to pursue the liberation of Taiwan. Also problems of economic reconstruction at home made China shy away from becoming entangled in military ventures in Korea. But these objectives did not necessarily preclude moral support for North Korea's objectives of reunification, so long as they could be achieved swiftly and with minimal US response. Beijing supported gains for the communist world, but not if they required China to abandon its primary objective of national unity and reconstruction.

This first objective was clearly not attained. US involvement in the defence of Taiwan, the much reduced chance of a seat in the UN and above all the firm response of US forces to Pyongyang's adventure, meant that the unification with Taiwan was prevented. Nor did North Korea gain an easy victory. At this stage, the failure of Chinese objectives was serious, but not yet critical. It must have seemed as if risks were miscalculated, but not yet that China itself was under threat. A missed opportunity that went wrong (the loss of a window for taking Taiwan), was not as bad as the necessity to take active defence measures in the face of a direct American threat to China.

This brings us to the second Chinese objective, deterrence and the defence of China from a US threat as American troops approached the Chinese border. Some analysts suggest China's objectives changed, in recognition of the impending military difficulties, as early as 5 July, while others suggest it was later in August, or indeed on 15 September after the Inchon landing by the American forces.[6] What is clear is that China's position did change, even if specific transition points are in dispute. The objective military situation was changing and in order to avoid 'mechanicalism' in strategy, Chinese policy changed as well.

But like China's first objective in this period, this second one also failed. The graduated deterrence which in retrospect seems so clear and obvious, never really had a chance to work. Zhou Enlai's nocturnal warning delivered via Pannikar was only the most salient signal in a process that in many respects was doomed to fail. The sense of inevitability is derived from fundamentally irreconcilable objectives on the part of the US and China.[7] The lack of reliable Sino-American channels of communication was of course a contributory problem, but the main cause was the US's failure to understand the Chinese frame of reference. US troops crossing the 38th parallel, no matter how much it was accompanied by soothing words of honourable intentions towards Chinese sovereignty, could not be tolerated in Beijing.[8] Such a policy would inevitably have drawn Chinese intervention.

That Chinese deterrence of the United States threat failed, was then largely beyond China's ability to remedy. In many respects, Beijing's policy was too clever by half. For example, the initial engagement of United States troops after having stealthily placed fifteen divisions in ambush, and then the sudden disengagement to give Washington the chance to reconsider its approach to the Chinese frontier, was perhaps too subtle for MacArthur and United States policy.[9] Open troop movements and explicit declarations of intent might have just managed to persuade Truman to rein back his troops. The brief Chinese engagement was seen in Washington only as reinforcing the view that China was merely protecting its Manchurian frontier, and did not wish to intervene in Korea on a large scale.

Given the failure of Chinese deterrence and China's continuing desire to defend its northeast, the third phase of Chinese strategy began. From the 26 November military offensive, China began a strategy of compellence designed to ensure a United States withdrawal, the defence of China, and the viability of the North Korean regime. But in the same way that China's objectives before intervention were changed by the altering fortunes on the battlefield, so Chinese military objectives expanded as China's leaders became too dizzy with success.

The 26 November Chinese attack was strikingly successful not so much because of Chinese military prowess in this third phase, but more because the United States forces pulled back very rapidly to more defensible lines after the second phase.[10] A month later, Chinese troops had caught up with the retreating United States forces, now dug in at the 38th parallel, and in a further offensive, forced them to retreat a little further. Thus the events of December rapidly became a classic case of success on the battlefield determining the pace of political positions. Zhou Enlai on 11 December asked 'What do the Americans want?' and proceeded to enlarge the Chinese objectives in the war by declaring the unimportance of the 38th parallel line.[11] In early October Zhou had declared the parallel as almost a sacred trip wire not to be crossed by the Americans, but in December he too was prepared to ignore the line. China's disdain for the line was to be as much of a mistake as was MacArthur's two months earlier.

In February US forces pushed the Chinese back and in March Seoul was recaptured. Lin Biao surrendered the command of Chinese troops to Peng Dehuai and both sides began to sustain high casualties in relatively fruitless military offensives. The removal of MacArthur and the ensuing Chinese offensive on 22 April may have given Beijing some hope that the 38th parallel could be breached, but once again there was little movement and great casualties. The final Chinese push, in May, was an even swifter failure and Beijing must have been struck that the US refused to follow up possibilities of counter-attack on both occasions. The US forces had settled for the 38th parallel and now China was doing the same. Once again the objectives changed in the face of new facts on the battlefield.

The decision by US forces not to pursue the Chinese in defeat was a reliable signal that the war could be kept limited.[12] Thus the Chinese· objective of merely defending itself and the territorial integrity of North Korea was successfully accomplished. However, the most recent Chinese objective of victory which had developed as a result of early Chinese triumphs in December, was not accomplished. The transition to scaled down objectives was not immediate, but by June its logic was becoming persuasive to Beijing's leaders.

The Malik proposal of 23 June for a ceasefire at first seemed to take the Chinese by surprise. But China needed little encouragement to see that it had to settle for its minimum objectives of security for itself and Pyongyang.[13] From the summer of 1951, but especially from October 1951, the Chinese settled down to fight a war of attrition. The objective of wearing down the US was designed not only to weaken American power in general, but also to strengthen Chinese power in Asia. It is not necessary to postulate the conspiracy theory of Soviet pressure on China to stay in the war, to explain Beijing's continuing military operations. So long as casualties could be minimized, it was possible to see a Chinese interest in draining US power.

The objective of attrition certainly figured prominently in Chinese statements.[14] Official declarations also spoke of 'keeping the initiative' both in battle (even when retreating) as well as in political negotiations at Panmunjom.[15] It was however very difficult to see any initiative being taken by either side. The war was fading from both American and Chinese front pages as both sides developed ways of keeping down casualties by limited action and impressive fortifications. Both military machines also pursued narrower objectives as they learned something about modern war. For the US it was the lesson of limited war, but for China it was a time to modernize and 'learn from the Soviet Union' (see next section).

This final phase of attrition, where the very pursuit of combat was more crucial than the actual outcome, could of course not last indefinitely. By August 1952 Mao Zedong had made it plain to colleagues that a truce was inevitable and China could be proud of its achievements although they fell short of total victory.[16] He reiterated the strategy of attrition and acknowledged that in any case the US was now more interested in the politics of Europe than Asia.

The truce came about in stages. Early steps were aborted by US raids into Manchuria or an unfavourable political climate in Beijing or Panmunjom.[17] The election of Eisenhower in November 1952 made it plain that there would be no substantial change in US policy and China could not hope for a better future in Korea. More crucially, the death of Stalin in March 1953 opened the floodgates of change in the communist world. One need not believe the conspiracy theorists' suggestions that Stalin kept China in the war against its will, to be struck by the change of policy after Stalin's death. It is just as plausible that the new more moderate Soviet lead in foreign policy was thrust upon China. In addition, the complex factional politics in both the Soviet Union and China may well have opened such doors of policy change.[18] Whatever the case, upon his return from Stalin's funeral, Zhou Enlai broke the diplomatic log jam over the POW issue and in effect accepted voluntary repatriation. Even if the Soviet Union had to buy Chinese acquiescence with further economic aid, the resulting end of hostilities also generally suited Chinese objectives.

In this final phase, and as Mao noted in September 1953, China could be pleased with events. The US was forced to extend itself (although not as much as Mao thought); the US was seen as less frightening than some thought; China gained valuable military experience and equipment; and China's reputation for steadfastness was enhanced.[19] But Mao's self-satisfied judgement belied the crooked path that had to be traversed in the three years of war. Chinese objectives and successes were by no means clear or un-changing. In the first phase, hopes for swift victory by North Korea were just as swiftly proven false. In the second phase Chinese deterrence of US encroachment to the Yalu was an equal failure. The third phase of defence by crossing the Yalu was rapidly trans-formed into delusions of victory. Defence was indeed ensured by July 1951, but victory was unobtainable. The final phase of attrition was a success in that the risks and costs were contained. But it was a failure in that it was China that finally capitulated at Panmunjom and US power remained in Asia and on the Korean peninsula. In the end, the only clear Chinese strategy was the strategy of expe-diency, and the only verdict on success or failure was a mixture of the two.

Military Operations

If the political objectives were in large measure determined by expediency, then what of China's military objectives? As already noted, Mao (and Sun Zi) had warned against mechanicalism in military strategy, but Western (and some Chinese) analysts have suggested that China pursued a unified military strategy in Korea. After thirty months of combat and more than half a million casualties, it seems clear that Chinese military strategy (like Sun Zi's image of water) retained no constant shape.

The first phase of military operations was one in which Chinese troops took no part. Indeed the PLA was being demobilized and reorganized after the civil war, and only the Tibet and Taiwan operations commanded any military resources for combat.[20] Between May and July 1950 there was a shift of 60,000 PLA men to Northeast China, but it is likely that the transfer was part of a reorganization of local forces after the dislocation of the civil war, and not early planning for military action in Korea.

This is not to argue that the PLA was imprudent during the early stages of the Korean war. By early July 30,000 troops of the Third Field Army joined a similar number of Fourth Field Army troops in Shandong and, unlike the earlier transfer, these new troops were neither local to Shandong, nor engaged in civilian labour on arrival.[21] A month later a further 50,000 Fourth Field Army troops designated for the Taiwan front were shifted to the Northeast.[22]

It seems that from July China was planning on some use of military force in Korea, if only as a symbol of its intent to defend Manchuria. The US was clearly aware of these moves, but as with most failures of intelligence, the lacunae were in interpretation rather than gathering of information.[23] The specific manner in which the PLA would be used was of course still undecided. While China tried desperately to deter US encroachment to the Yalu, there were few specific references as to how China would use military force if deterrence failed.

China's strategy of people's war was a prominent feature of Beijing's comments, as was the view of such strategy as being eminently flexible. As has already been noted, Mao's rejection of mechanicalism in strategy, quoted in September 1950, seemed to be a clear signal that China would use the military instrument as it was best suited to the specific needs of the Korean war. The guiding doctrine would continue to be people's war, but that was defined as little more than a war with popular support.[24] Later in September the acting Chief of Staff, Nie Rongzhen took up the same theme when discussing atomic weapons and the Korean war. Nie said, 'After all, China lives on the farms. What can atom bombs do there?'[25] and went on to make clear that it was the US ground threat that counted most. China's denigration of the atom bomb as not decisive was no doubt accurate given that the US was fighting a limited war in Korea, but China had clearly not thought through the broader strategic problems of atomic war.[26] Nevertheless, China was prepared to fight the US military power deployed in Korea, and it was planning to do so with few strategic straight jackets.

Indeed the very decision by China to intervene before the US crossed the Yalu represented a major change for China. This forward defence policy beyond China's gates was unprecedented in Mao's military thought. It was a clear sign, if any was needed, that China had indeed 'stood up', and would defend its national interest, even beyond its own territory.

When the 300,000 Chinese forces crossed the Yalu in mid to late October, they achieved textbook surprise.[27] Their first engagements were fierce and largely effective. However, the Chinese had to act sooner than they wanted because the North Korean forces had collapsed so suddenly. The first jet aircraft battles, at the end of October, also did not go China's way. Nevertheless, when China broke off combat to give the US a chance to retreat, Beijing's military commanders could be well pleased with their results.

It is notable that these first engagements, and indeed the combat during the rest of 1950, was not guerrilla war. However, the military operations were very much a people's war and, in keeping with the flexible definition of that term, there were both continuities and discontinuities with previous Chinese military action.

The continuities were most apparent in the successful use of relatively untrained and under-armed soldiers against a militarily more sophisticated enemy. By using impressive deception and stealth the Chinese overcame technological inferiority. By using remarkable mobility, mostly by foot over rough terrain, the Chinese overcame logistical inferiority.[28]

There were however disturbing signs of military weakness even in these early successes. Not that China resorted to human wave tactics, but there were signs that the strategy of ambush and luring in deep, had its limits against a more modern and mobile force than Chiang Kai-shek's forces. US troops soon found that Chinese forces could not fight lengthy continuous battles without having to stop for supplies and new instructions to get to the front. The swift US withdrawal to the 38th parallel far outstripped the pace that the less flexible Chinese command and logistics system was designed to handle. China's initial victories were not so much due to any special characteristic of the people's war they used, as to the age-old ally—surprise. By taking the initial decision to intervene with a forward defence, the Chinese had broken with much of their previous strategy but then the Korean war was a new type of problem, refusing adaptations. It remained to be seen if they could adapt on the battlefield and make such a strategy hold on to the gains won by surprise.

The early campaigns of 1951 at first suggested that China had indeed adapted well to Korean conditions. However, China's early optimism soon faded as the implications of fighting a linear war (basically along the 38th parallel) with non-linear tactics became appreciated in Beijing. It did not take long before US forces learned to cope with Chinese strategy and Beijing soon was forced to fight the linear war for which it was ill-equipped. Chinese strategy was forced to change by military realities, for to fail to do so would have meant being driven back to the Yalu. US troops took advantage of the fact that the Korean war was a major war fought in a small area. The absence of much room for manoeuvre meant that defence in depth could thwart Chinese attempts to infiltrate and ambush. By rolling with the punches—giving some ground, holding the defence line straight, and then surging back when the PLA ran out of steam—the US forces inflicted costly defeats on China. Superior US firepower from land, sea, and above all air, coupled with superior communciations and logistics, meant that Chinese forces were denied any substantial breakthrough.[29]

It is difficult to say whether China fully appreciated its military weakness in these early defeats. To be sure the Chinese had accurately dismissed atomic weapons as not applicable to the limited Korean war.[30] But it also seems likely that the misunderstanding of modern weapons applied also to superior conventional force. The delusion no doubt ensued from the perception of sweeping victories in December, and vivid memories of trouncing the US-backed Chiang Kai-shek forces. But it soon became apparent to the PLA leadership that the carnage could not go on indefinitely. Lin Biao was replaced by Peng Dehuai but still offensives in the old style were tried and failed. By July 1951, when talks began, Beijing was resigned to more important changes in military strategy than merely shifting commanders. A nineteenth century army could not hope to win a twentieth century war against a twentieth century foe.

Although Chinese strategy was forced to change under fire, it is difficult to find contemporary Chinese comment admitting the failures of strategy. China spoke of 'taking the initiative in retreat', but only rarely of difficulties in military operations.[31] Indications of major changes were only apparent when China later spoke of 'improvements' in its military operations. Mao was explicit, more than a year after the changes began in July 1951, that China had to alter its military disposition.[32] The first change was an improvement of PLA equipment in order to match an enemy 'rich in metal'. Soviet military aid emphasized artillery and air force equipment, as well as more modern personal weapons. This modernization under fire was swift, and even though not all of it was used to its full extent (the air force was more for training than combat) it did allow for a more equal contest.

This shift from denigrating superior weapons, to acquiring the weapons themselves, did not necessarily mean China pursued an anti-Maoist military strategy. Mao's anti-mechanicalism line could rightly claim to encompass such modernization if that was what was needed. To stress the superiority of man over weapons is not to say that man is superior to any weapon, but rather than morale counts for a great deal in war. Thus Mao's doctrine was not so much altered, as emphasis was placed on different aspects of an already flexible approach.

Nowhere was this flexibility more apparent than in the new emphasis on fortifications and linear defence. While it is true that Mao rarely stressed this kind of defence in previous wars, he did mention it as useful. Undoubtedly China's military strategy adapted in the Korean war to place greater stress on fortifications, but it was a change that Mao's doctrine could incorporate. Mao spoke of the strategy of 'digging tunnels' and indeed the Chinese built an impressive great wall along their defence lines to protect their men. The linear defence curled in a horseshoe shape up the coasts of Korea to guard against another Inchon-type landing.[33]

The third major change came in the morale of the Chinese forces. The poor logistics resulting in inadequate clothing and above all poor food, coupled with repeated military set-backs, had caused PLA morale to plummet. Chinese forces were not well prepared for the war, and apparently political training had not caught up to the fast moving events and the North Korean defeat.

From July and especially October 1951 the transformation in the PLA was dramatic. Mao would later call it 'a big school for large-scale military exercises'.[34] One of the most crucial threads running through this modernization was a growing emphasis on Soviet military aid and doctrine. To be sure Mao's strategy still received top billing, even as it was being modified for modern conditions.[35] At first, until early 1952, China gave scant mention to Soviet aid and emphasized the changes occurring as objective necessities modern war. Stress was placed on combined arms operations, new equipment, better logistics, improved fire-power, and above all flexibility of doctrine.[36] But by early 1952 many of these discussions began to include specific reference to Soviet aid and doctrine.

Both modernization and 'modern military technique' were said to be crucial, and both could be learned, at least in part, from the Soviet Union.[37] Some Chinese leaders mentioned both Maoist and Soviet military thought while others did not (see next section). Zhu De said on 1 August 1952 that the PLA should learn from Mao and 'Soviet military science', while pursuing a great study campaign.[38] It would however be misleading to suggest that Maoist and Soviet military thought shared no common ground. Clearly changes were already under way in PLA doctrine and equipment before Soviet approval was claimed. Indeed it is more logical to suppose that the Soviet gloss was being added to, rather than replacing, Mao's emphasis on modern war. The great influx of Soviet aid after 1952 no doubt made the praise of Soviet doctrine more sensible, but the new campaign was not achieved at the expense of Maoist doctrine.

All these changes were hardly tested in battle, not for fear of their success, but rather because the war had settled into a more static and less devastating form. China claimed that its modernization of forces and doctrine had altered the balance of power,[39] but in reality little had changed on the battlefield. Mao would later claim that China had won the war because it had fought a people's war,[40] but what is more interesting is not the fatuous claim of victory, but the factors that he saw as crucial.

Mao admitted that the modernization of equipment and strategy in the light of modern conditions after July 1951, was necessary. Other benefits of the war, such as military training, were also noted by Mao. Just as China's political objectives, had changed so military strategy also needed to be flexible during the Korean war. Mao's doctrine was flexible enough to cope with the changes from non-linear to linear war, and from nineteenth century equipment to twentieth century technology, without needing to be entirely cast aside. The Soviet gloss was added to, but did not supplant Maoist ideas. In sum, China's, and Mao's military strategy were flexible.

Domestic Politics

It would be expecting a great deal of any political leadership to engage in a bloody and costly war for thirty months and not have some domestic debate on the issue. Yet it has been the conventional wisdom that Chinese leaders had no serious disagreements on the Korean war. It now appears that there were some important differences of opinion, although it apparently remains true that none of these debates on its own explains any particular policy shift. The debates may have contributed to compromises or helped tip the balance on certain decisions, but none seemed to have been decisive. Perhaps the main reason why these domestic debates were not decisive for the conduct of the war, was that there existed many different policy divisions, not all of which pitted the same leaders against each other. As in most political processes, the policy cleavages were cross-cutting.

The cleavage between those who wanted to get on with the economic reconstruction of China and those who saw the need to defend China's security at the gate, was probably the deepest. While obviously not an open fight, let alone one fought to the finish, this debate seemed to surface before the decision to intervene, as well as during the course of the war of attrition. As with all these policy debates it is hard to identify specific factions, let alone factional leaders, but some sort of debate did take place. The dark shroud draped over these debates was no doubt the result of basic unity derived from the recently completed civil war struggle, and the concern with the looming US threat in Asia.

It has already been established that China did not want a war in Korea if it was likely to drag on, and drag in its neighbours. China's eyes were set firmly on economic reconstruction and the liberation of Taiwan.[41] The hoped for swift North Korean victory would have avoided a choice between intervention for national security reasons, and abstention for reasons of economic reconstruction. In the end the choice had to be faced, and later Chinese commentary suggests that some leaders opposed the decision to intervene. Cultural Revolution sources claimed leaders like Chen Yun, in charge of economic reconstruction, opposed intervention.[42] There is even some evidence that Liu Shaoqi was to be counted among those most concerned about shifting expenditure to the military from economic reconstruction. It is also reasonable to surmise that regional economic czars, such as Gao Gang in Manchuria, would have favoured reconstruction, but also action to defend the Northeast frontier. Obviously factional lines could not have been simple. But what is clear is that some debate took place.

Peng Dehuai's memoirs speak explictly of Mao having been opposed on his decision to enter the war. Indeed Peng himself says he was initially among Mao's opponents but soon was persuaded by the Chairman's logic.[43] Other, more esoteric evidence from 1950 indicates that there was at least some kind of policy disagreement. An article in August 1950 spoke of some people taking a 'fence-sitting attitude'.[44] Later on in the war Mao seemed to go out of his way to stress that economic reconstruction could not be carried on free from worry unless the US was held at the 38th parallel. He also emphasized the reduction in war costs as a result of the post-July 1951 military strategy.[45] Western sources have made it plain that PLA soldiers were more doubtful about the purpose of the war during the attrition phase and others talk of the heavy economic burden imposed by the war.[46]

The influence of these factors and perhaps even factions is hard to gauge. They may well have helped modify Chinese military strategy or temper political objectives in the stalemate phase. They apparently did not have a decisive impact on the conduct of the war, but this may well have been because the cross-cutting cleavages reduced the impact of any single set of complaints. Economic reconstruction argued for non-intervention, but it also suggested intervention if the Northeast economic base was under threat.

The evidence of disagreement over military strategy is much more circumstantial. There are various dimensions to this issue, but one of the most crucial was perhaps whether the war in Korea should have been allowed to take precedence over retaking Taiwan. Some opposition to placing Taiwan on the back-burner appeared in a Beijing journal late in 1950 when an article spoke of 'some people' who did not appreciate that 'to let the enemy accomplish the first step of his strategy—overcoming Korea, our difficulties in liberating Taiwan across the ocean will be increased. It is therefore our urgent task to aid Korea.'[47] Certainly China was loath to move troops from the Taiwan front to Korea.[48] The difficulty in ascertaining the importance of this possible 'Taiwan first' group, is not only the lack of evidence, but also the fact that it was probably only one part of a more complex argument. No doubt some of those favouring the Taiwan option were only doing so to undercut the case for Korean intervention on the ground of national security.

Another possible cleavage, between Party and Army, does not appear to have been at all relevant to the Korean question. The absence of rigid career specialization so soon after the civil war was probably the main reason.[49] On the other hand, disputes within the military might have been more important than those between Party and Army. The reason for the replacement of Lin Biao by Peng Dehuai is still shrouded in mystery but the two were apparently involved on opposite sides of political fences later in the 1950s and again during the Cultural Revolution. They were no doubt rivals for influence in the military hierarchy, but it is not possible to suggest any specific area in which this rivalry had an impact.[50] Even in military strategy Peng seemed to pursue a course similar to that of Lin, although Peng would later shift to the linear defence. Similarly it is possible to argue that splits between Field Armies may have been crucial in the war, but once again no clear pattern emerges. Lin's Fourth Field Army and Chen Yi's Third Field Army made up the bulk of the intervention force, with the Fourth featuring more prominently at the start.[51] It is also possible to explain the centrality of, and changes between, these Field Armies more in terms of their superiority among PLA units and their heavy casualties during certain phases of the war.

The final possible area for important policy disagreements concerns the role of the Soviet Union. While it should not be suggested that there were pro-Soviet factions in the Chinese leadership, it seems more plausible that some did lean more to reliance on the Soviet Union. We certainly know of such leanings on foreign policy debates in 1949 and the pro-Soviet proclivities of Gao Gang in Manchuria have often been cited. It seems most likely that some leaders saw greater benefits than others in co-operation with the Soviet Union. This pattern of 'coincidence of interests' is most apparent when analysing the question of Chinese differences on Soviet military aid.

It is apparent that military strategy was a topic of some debate in China. It is equally apparent that Soviet military ideas did assume a greater role in China by 1952. But the two events are not necessarily linked by cause and effect. The discussions about military doctrine appeared to be heading towards a resolution before Soviet aid was taken on any great scale and Soviet equipment was used to allow China to make its adjustments in Mao's doctrine. Soviet aid complemented the changes agreed in China, and indeed allowed those changes to be made. However, this is a far cry from suggesting that Soviet military aid and doctrine replaced Chinese ideas on military policy.

There can be little doubt that some sort of debate on military strategy had taken place. Cultural Revolution sources suggest that the first three battles of the Korean war (until April 1951) were fought according to Mao's 'operational plan' urging active attack instead of 'taking a rest'. Mao then reportedly said Chinese forces should pull back to the 38th parallel to 'lure the enemy in deep', but Peng refused. What is worse, in the May campaign, Peng committed 'leftist' errors by launching a further attack and against American troops instead of only South Korean troops as Mao desired.[52] Chinese losses were tremendous, including the death of Mao's eldest son. Peng's reported desire for a further offensive was blocked by Mao in favour of 'protracted fighting and positive defence'. Obviously much of this assessment must be suspect, coming as it did at the height of the anti-Peng campaign in 1967. Nevertheless, it does suggest that military set-backs did encourage pragmatism and strategic debate.

On Army Day in 1951, He Long spoke openly of debates, supposedly taking place in 1927 about whether to capitulate to military pressure or to organize resistance.[53] He noted also that once combat was agreed, some also opposed Mao's decision to endure heavy casualties. He Long spoke openly of the fact that military strategy was still being evolved, but he praised Mao for his guiding role in military affairs. It seems possible that opposition to Mao came not only from those who opposed the use of military force, but also from critics on the right who argued for a more forthright strategy of attacking the 'strongholds'.

The complexity of the debate no doubt made it easier to reach a compromise military strategy that involved fortifications manned by soldiers who would make forays out in mobile strikes. The agreed emphasis was placed on pragmatic responses to specific military problems, and there was a frank of acknowledgement of the changing nature of the military problem.[54] It was an agreement for the strategy of expediency.

The discussions of strategy never seemed to end entirely, as each major change in fortunes triggered some questioning of policy. The war of attrition in particular provoked the question as to whether China should be optimstic about holding out against US power.[55] But what almost everyone agreed on was the need to modernize the strategy and arms of the PLA. Despite earlier denigration of Western military equipment, it was decided to seek the nearest equivalent for China's own forces. To this end only the Soviet Union could be of assistance and Soviet aid was added to the changes under way in the PLA.

It seems apparent that some Chinese leaders were more enthusiastic about reliance on the Soviet Union than others. Some military professionals, pre-eminently Peng Dehuai seemed more willing to praise Soviet aid and ideas than did other Chinese leaders.[56] But the differences, such as they were, were of degree. For example, Zhu De praised Soviet aid and military science in *Pravda* in 1952, but also praised Mao's contribution. In an era when Soviet models were deemed applicable to many aspects of Chinese society, praise for Soviet military science was not unusual. Soviet military aid was an addition to the already evolving Chinese modifications in doctrine.

The Soviet Union had apparently been involved in Chinese military strategy from the earliest days of the Korean war. But to admit such co-ordination is not to argue that Moscow dictated terms to Beijing. Just as it has been argued that Soviet influence was a contributory rather than a determining factor in the Chinese decision to intervene in Korea in 1950, so the Soviet Union was at most a contributory factor in the modernization of Chinese military strategy. In neither case should it be argued that China lost direct control of its policy. Thus if there were discussions of military strategy in China (and the evidence suggests there probably were) and there were some Chinese leaders more willing to seek Soviet assistance (and there probably were), then an understading of leadership politics is important in understanding the use of military force by China.

However, it should also be apparent that as much as there were policy disagreements in China—over the decision to intervene, military strategy, and perhaps even the degree of reliance on the Soviet Union—they did not *determine* the outcome of Chinese policy. The divisions of opinion in China did not form into coherent and relatively unified factions, so as to change policy in any specific way. What seems to have been most crucial to the choice of policy was the pressure of military contingencies and changing international political pressures. China's pragmatism may well have been assisted by the need to reach political compromises at home, but the main motive for the strategy of expediency seems to have come from insistent external pressures, be they from military defeat or super-power foreign policy.

Conclusions

The Korean war was costly to China. But when the threat of hostile US power came to its frontiers China responded resolutely, fighting an at times impressive campaign against a modern enemy. However, China made mistakes and suffered losses. Hence at times policy had to be changed.

China's political objectives changed several times, from hopes for victory, to deterrence, to defence, to victory again, and then finally to settling for stalemate. China may well have entered the war with preconceived ideas of the best policy, but these changed either because they were seen to be wrong or because China saw a chance for greater gains. Similarly, China's military strategy changed several times, from mobile war to static war with inferior equipment, to static war with more modern equipment. The pressures of war forced fundamental changes in what were viewed as hallowed concepts of Chinese doctrine, for example in fighting mobile war or relying on inferior equipment.

These changes, in both political and military strategy, were not necessarily wrenching choices for China. In military strategy there was already Mao's stated opposition to mechanicalism which urged pragmatic reactions to the changing nature of war. Under this broad guiding principle, and while maintaining certain elements of a people's war, many changes could be made with relative ease.

Most of these changes seem to have been accompanied by domestic debate, but none appear to have been determined by these debates. What is most crucial about these changes in strategy is that they cast serious doubt on the existence of any coherent Chinese military doctrine. If a doctrine presupposes a coherent set of unchanging basic beliefs, then China did not have such a doctrine. But if doctrine is taken to allow some changes as different elements are emphasized, then Mao's thought remained relevant.

Of course certain basic political objectives did not change during the war. The determination to defend China's sovereignty was unchanging and pursued with success. But beyond that objective, no other political objective seems to have been sacred and certainly no military objective seems to have been unchangeable. Some influence on military doctrine ensued from such basics as geography and the willingness to use large numbers to overcome a weakness in technology or economy or China's inability to produce modern arms. But even here, when changes became possible, they were made. Soviet aid allowed the expensive shift away from taking heavy casualties to using modern equipment and building extensive fortifications. Chinese military doctrine may have seemed coherent and unchanging during peacetime, when it was untested, or in wartime against an opponent like Chiang Kai-shek who foght on similar terms. But in the crucible of combat when changes of fortune and strategy are rapid, military doctrine, even Chinese military doctrine, must change or fail. China is no exception to this rule of strategy.

NOTES

1. Allen Whiting, *China Crosses the Yalu* (Stanford: Stanford University Press, 1960); Robert Simmons, *The Strained Alliance* (New York: Free Press, 1975); William Stueck, 'The Soviet Union and the Origins of the Korean War', *World Politics*, Vol. 28 No. 4, July 1976; Geoffrey Warner, 'The Korean War', *International Affairs*, Vol. 56 No. 1, January 1980; Mineo Nakajima, 'The Sino-Soviet Confrontation: Its Roots in the International Background of the Korean War', *Australian Journal of Chinese Affairs*, No. 1, January 1979.
2. The chronology up to the Chinese intervention depends heavily on Whiting, *China Crosses* and Simmons, *Strained Alliance*.
3. Details on the post-intervention phase are drawn from Roy Appleman, *South to Naktong, North to the Yalu* (Washington: USGPO, 1961); Walter Hermes, *Truce Tent and Fighting Front* (Washington: USGPO, 1966); James Schnabel, *Policy and Direction: The First Year* (Washington: USGPO, 1972); William Whitson, *The Chinese High Command* (London: Macmillan, 1973), pp. 93–7.
4. Shuang Yun, 'A Marxist Military Line', *People's China* 1 September 1950, pp. 28–9.
5. See note 2 and Melvin Gurtov and Byoong-Moo Hwang, *China Under Threat* (London: Johns Hopkins, 1980).
6. Simmons, *Strained Alliance* p. 150. David Rees, *Korea: The Unlimited War* (London: Macmillan, 1964), pp. 109–13. On the significance of Inchon see Strobe Talbott, ed., *Khrushchev Remembers* (London: Andre Deutsch, 1971), pp. 371–2.
7. Alexander George and Richard Smoke, *Deterrence in American Foreign Policy* (New York: Columbia University Press, 1974), pp. 187–213. Rees, *Korea*, pp. 110–13.
8. Numerous references to this sensitive issue are apparent and catalogued in the secondary sources. See also K. M. Pannikar, *In Two Chinas* (George Allen and

Unwin, 1955), pp. 108, 109–10; Mao Tse-tung, *Selected Works* Vol. 5. (Peking: Foreign Languages Press, 1977), p. 43. Other less urgent dimensions of Chinese strategy are discussed in Jonathan Pollack, *Security, Strategy and the Logic of Chinese Foreign Policy* (Berkeley, California: University of California— Research Papers and Policy Studies No. 5, 1981), p. 17. The role of the Soviet Union was assessed by Whiting, *China Crosses* as 'contributing, rather than a determining factor', p. 152.

9. Whiting, *China Crosses*, p. 111; Appleman, *South to Naktong*, pp. 673–756.
10. Schnabel, *Policy and Direction*, pp. 274–309; Alexander George, *The Chinese Communist Army in Action* (New York: Columbia University Press, 1967), pp. 6–17.
11. Pannikar, *In Two Chinas*, p. 118. Hsu Chih, 'Volunteers Armed with Thought'; *People's China*, 1 February 1951, p. 11.
12. Pollack, *Security, Strategy*, pp. 18–19.
13. John Gittings, *The World and China* (London: Eyre and Methuen, 1974), p. 185 and Simmons, *Strained Alliance*, pp. 198–9.
14. For example, *People's Daily*, 25 June 1951 in *People's China*, 16 July 1951. Also Chen Yee in 16 September 1951; Kuo Mo-jo in 16 October 1951; and Editorial, 16 June 1952.
15. For example, NCNA 21 June 1951 in *BBC*/SWB/FE/114/, p. 4, or NCNA 2 August 1951 in No. 120/p. 5; NCNA 27 June 1952 in No. 168/p. 14; Spokesman of headquarters, 24 October 1952 in No. 195/pp. 12–13.
16. 4 August 1952 in Mao, *Selected Works (5)*, pp. 78–80. Also *People's China*, 1 November 1952, pp. 3–5.
17. Gittings, *The World and China*, pp. 190–3; Simmons, *Strained Alliance*, pp. 216–38.
18. See domestic section below and Gerald Segal, 'The Soviet Connection and Chinese Politics', *The Jerusalem Journal of International Relations*, Vol. 2 No. 1, Fall 1976.
19. 12 September 1953 in Mao, *Selected Works (5)*, pp. 115–19.
20. Whiting, *China Crosses*, pp. 16–22.
21. *Ibid*, pp. 64–5.
22. Gurtov and Hwang, *China Under Threat*, p. 49; Whitson, *Chinese Command*, p. 94.
23. Rees, *Korea*, p. 104: Appleman, *South to Naktong*, p. 756.
24. *People's Daily*, 6 July 1950 in *BBC*/SWB/FE/64/pp. 26–7; Teng Chao in 'World Culture', 31 October 1950 in No. 81/p. 12.
25. Pannikar, *In Two Chinas*, p. 108.
26. *Peking Radio*'s 27 October 1950 commentary seriously underestimated the destructive impact of atomic weapons, *BBC*/SWB/FE/81/p. 21.
27. Whiting, *China Crosses*, pp. 118–139; Appleman, *South to Naktong*, pp. 717–767; George, *Chinese Army*, pp. 5–6; Whitson, *Chinese High Command*, p. 94; Gittings, *The Role of the Chinese Army*, p. 75.
28. George, *Chinese Army*, pp. 2–17; Rees, *Korea*, pp. 138–9, 156, 171.
29. Details from *Ibid*, and Whitson, *Chinese High Command*, pp. 94–7; Schnabel, *Policy and Direction*, pp. 275–340.
30. *People's Daily*, 11 November 1950 took a more realistic line on the effect of atomic weapons accepting their ability to destroy, but not as part of tactical operations. Whiting, *China Crosses*, p. 142.
31. For example, NCNA 21 June 1951 in *BBC*/SWB/FE/114/p. 4 and NCNA 2 August 1951 in No. 120/p. 5; *People's China*, 1 February, 1951 p. 11.
32. Mao, 4 August 1952, *Selected Works (5)*, pp. 78–80.

33. NCNA 27 June 1952 in *BBC*/SWB/FE/168/p. 14; Spokesman of PLA head-quarters, 24 October 1952 in No. 195/pp. 12–13; *Peking Home Service*, 13 January 1953 in No. 217 pp. 13, No. 219/p. 11; *Peking Home Service*, 26 February 1953 in No. 230/p. 6. Also, Mao, *Ibid*; George, *Chinese Army*, pp. 176–200; Whitson, *Chinese High Command*, pp. 95–7; Gittings, *The Role of the Chinese Army*, p. 121; Hermes, *Truce Tent*, pp. 283–9, 367.

34. See note 32.

35. Hsiao Hua, *People's China*, 1 August 1951, pp. 5–8; Ho Lung in *People's Daily*, 1 August 1951 in *BBC*/SWB/FE/120/pp. 14–15; Chen Yi, 31 July 1951 in No. 121/pp. 6–7.

36. Chu Teh, 31 July 1951; Ho Lung in *People's Daily* 1 August 1951; Peng Dehuai, 31 July all in *BBC*/SWB/FE/120. Also Chen Yi, 31 July in No. 121/pp. 6–7; Chen Yee in *People's China*, 16 September 1951.

37. Nieh Jung-chen, *People's Daily*, 23 February 1952 in *BBC*/SWB/FE/150/pp. 6–8; Hsiao Hua, 1 August in No. 173/p. 24; Peng Dehuai, 25 October 1952 in No. 195/p. 10 and Tu Ping on p. 11; Chu Teh, 22 February 1953 in No. 229/p. 4.

38. Chu Teh in *Pravda*, 1 August; *People's China*. 16 August 1952, pp. 10, 15.

39. Tu Ping, *People's Daily*, 3 January 1953 in *People's China*, 1 February 1953, pp. 4–5.

40. 12 September 1953 in *Selected Works (5)*, pp. 115–19.

41. Gurtov and Hwang, *China Under Threat*, pp. 26–7; Gittings, *The World and China*, p. 183; Whiting, *China Crosses*, pp. 16–19.

42. Gurtov and Hwang, *China Under Threat*, p. 55. See also Mao on 28 June 1958 in Stuart Schram ed., *Mao Tse-tung Unrehearsed* (London: Penguin, 1974) p. 128. Also *Collected Works of Liu Shao-chi* (Hong Kong: Union Research Institute, 1969); Liu on 29 April 1950 talking about the Hainan operation.

43. *FBIS*-PRC, 16 April 1982. P. K6.

44. Whiting, *China Crosses*, pp. 82–3, 151–2.

45. Mao, *Selected Works (5)*, 4 August 1952, pp. 78–9 and especially 12 September 1953 pp. 117–19.

46. George, *Chinese Army*, pp. 176–8; Simmons, *Strained Alliance*, p. 212.

47. Gurtov and Hwang, *China Under Threat*, p. 56.

48. Whiting, *China Crosses the Yalu*.

49. George, *Chinese Army*, Ch. 3; Gurtov and Hwang, *China Under Threat*, pp. 59–60.

50. Roderick MacFarquhar, *The Origins of the Cultural Revolution* Vol. 1 (London: Oxford University Press, 1974).

51. Whitson, *Chinese High Command*, pp. 93–7, 193, 248, 327, 329, 355–6.

52. Union Research Institute, *The Case of Peng Teh-huai* (Hong Kong: URI, 1968), pp. 119, 153–4, 195–7.

53. *People's Daily*, 1 August 1951, *BBC*/SWB/FE/120/pp. 14–16.

54. *Ibid*, and Chen Yi, 31 July in No. 121/pp. 6–7; Hsiao Hua, 1 August in No. 173/p. 24.

55. For example Tu Ping in October 1952 cited in *BBC*/SWB/FE/195/p. 11, and Chu Teh in *People's China*, 16 August 1951, pp. 5–6.

56. Peng on 31 July 1951 in *BBC*/SWB/FE/120/pp. 16–17, and 25 October 1952 in No. 195/p. 10. See also Nieh Jung-chen on 23 February 1952 in No. 150/pp. 6–8. See also Chu Teh and Hsiao Hua on 1 August 1952 in No. 173/pp. 3, 24, and Chu in *People's China*, 16 August 1952 pp. 10, 15.

7

Taiwan, 1954–1955, 1958

'Strategically, we must utterly despise US imperialism. Tactically, we must take it seriously. In struggling against it, we must take each battle, each encounter seriously.'

Mao Zedong, 14 July 1956.

Mao's ability to distinguish between strategy and tactics is akin to his ability to distinguish between political and military aspects of a struggle. The two Taiwan Straits crises are important for the light they cast on how China distinguishes between the pursuit of military and political objectives in crisis. Both crises are notable for absence of a direct link between the evolution of the political and military crises. The twin crises are also comparable in that, of all the times that China has used military force since 1949, the Taiwan examples reveal the least about China's conception of military strategy. Both crises were pre-eminently political events in which military force was in large part incidental to the main action.

For these basic reasons, and despite other obvious differences between the two crises, this chapter treats both events at the same time. The two crises are in fact quite similar. Chinese objectives in both cannot be explained by a simple listing of offensive or defensive rationales. Rather they can both be seen as Chinese probing of US intentions and reactions in times of regional or international instability. Both crises again illustrate China's flexible strategy in pursuit of both military and political objectives.

Course of Events

In many senses it is difficult to see the 1954–5 Taiwan Straits events as a crisis. Normal components of crisis seem to have been missing. There was indeed some military action, in fact it was one of the few times when China seized and held territory. But at no time did China appear to see a sense of urgency or threat. In fact, if studied carefully, the sense of crisis seems to be one sided—on the part of Taiwan and the US—and hardly serious at that.[1]

The Chinese civil war never truly ended in 1949 despite the obvious rout of Chiang Kai-shek's forces on the mainland. The island of Hainan was only 'liberated' in April 1950 and numerous other offshore islands, including Taiwan remained occupied by Chiang's troops. Sporadic incidents took place for more than four years with most of the period over-shadowed by the combat in Korea.[2] In 1954 China continued to respond to the anomaly of the unfinished civil war by periodic military manoeuvres against enemy-held islands and by equally frequent statements of intent to regain Taiwan and its assorted islands. In February 1954 China, apparently without any real provocation, began more aggressive naval patrols near the Dachen Islands.

Some analysts have suggested that August 1954 marked a turning point, with heightened tension over the fate of Taiwan and the islands. To be sure there were some added reasons for concern, but these hardly amounted to a crisis. Most of the tension seemed to result from the United States decision to throw up containment walls against the Sino-Soviet bloc: and in September 1954, the Southeast Asia Treaty Organization (SEATO) was formally consti-tuted. That China objected to the SEATO pact is indisputable. On 3 September when the first SEATO meeting convened, China shelled the offshore island of Quemoy.[3] However, neither the shelling nor the atmosphere in September was particularly unusual. The atmosphere was neither especially calm nor dangerous.

Only in early December did tension rise seriously. On 2 December the US signed a mutual defence pact with the Republic of China on Taiwan (ROC) and on 8 December Zhou Enlai issued a strong statement warning the US about intervention in the Chinese civil war. At some point at the turn of the year China apparently decided to take some of the offshore islands by force (others had been taken in previous years) but, as a statement by Zhou on 21 December makes clear, there was no sense of special tension, even at this time.

The United Nations Secretary General visited China from 5–11 January to discuss the release of US military personnel held since the Korean war. Just after Hammarskjold's departure, China dropped leaflets on the offshore islands of Dachen and Ishan urging surrender and warning of an imminent attack. Coupled with a nationwide campaign about Taiwan since the US–ROC pact, it was clear that China intended some military action. However, the action was less a real attempt to seize territory, and more a signal of displeasure with the December treaty.

On 18 and 20 January China seized tiny islands north of Dachen with brief, but apparently fierce combat. The US called for a ceasefire which China refused. Military success apparently encouraged China to see what else it could take and the crisis, such as it was, began to reach a peak. On 25 January the US House of Representatives adopted the Formosa Resolution offering US protection to Taiwan and the Pescadores, and assistance for the protection of Quemoy and Matsu. On 29 January the Resolution had passed through both Houses of Congress and President Eisenhower signed the document.

Faced with on the one hand a sense of threat, in the US–ROC pact and the Formosa Resolution, and on the other hand a military opportunity, in the 5 February decision by the ROC to quit the militarily indefensible Dachen island, China occupied Dachen and other islands on 13 February. This was hardly a crisis, as the US had urged the withdrawal of ROC troops, but it was a convenient opportunity for China to probe the limits of US military and political commitment after the creation of SEATO and the recent Taiwan declarations. It was also a convenient occasion for China to state its own position by seizing territory it considered its own, when the risks of doing so were reduced.

As if to signal a desire to keep events under control, on 18 February China offered support for a 4 February Soviet call for discussions on the Taiwan tensions. Although the conference idea had previously been rejected by the US, China's statement signalled peaceful intent. It was, however, noticeable that political events were largely unconnected with military operations. On 26 February China seized another offshore island and sporadic military engagements continued well into 1955. The so-called crisis ended as mysteriously as it had began, with desultory military action and continuing political uncertainties, but with China having tested the limits of US resolve and having made its point that Taiwan was still a part of China.

The 1958 crisis, like its 1954–5 predecessor, had no clear start or finish and little sense of threat that it might escalate *into* a real crisis. Once again, perceived from the Chinese or Taiwan–US side, the pattern appears very different. It is especially difficult to combine these two views to produce a simple picture of escalation and decline of the crisis.[4]

It is hard to know what triggered the tensions of the autumn of 1958. Certainly there were continuing military engagements between Chinese and Taiwanese forces, but these were not especially severe or urgent. Certainly there was no gradual build-up to tension, but rather sporadic and sudden brief campaigns that quickly blew over. China appears to have taken a conscious decision, at some point in mid-July, to probe US intentions in continuing to support Taiwan. Following crises in the Lebanon and Jordan, China's rising exuberance over the potential success of the Great Leap Forward, and confidence that the 'east wind prevails over the west wind', Mao Zedong saw some purpose in probing to see whether the US commitment to Taiwan was still firm. No doubt the dynamic state of Sino-Soviet relations and debates over the degree of revolutionary zeal to be applied to international politics, also played a role in China's calculations.

Thus on 22 July China opened a nine day political campaign pledging 'heightened vigilance' over Taiwan and determination to unify all China. The campaign had no particular trigger, and reflected no particular sense of threat or imminent offensive intentions against Taiwan. Just as suddenly, Khrushchev led a delegation on short notice to China from 31 July to 3 August. The meeting apparently did not discuss Taiwan but focused on broader aspects of Sino-Soviet disagreement. The communique revealed these differences only in vague terms, but no mention was made of Taiwan.

Nor did China resume its Taiwan propaganda campaign after Khruschev's arrival or his departure. Sporadic reports of tension in the Taiwan Straits area, attributed to US and Taiwanese intrigues, appeared in the Chinese media. But the relaxed mood was personified by Mao and Liu Shaoqi who went on inspection tours of the countryside in early to mid August. Then as suddenly as the 22 July propaganda campaign had begun, so on 22 August China began military operations against Quemoy.

One might expect the crisis to begin from the date of the Chinese shelling but this was not the case. Certainly from the Chinese point of view little fuss was made. On 28 August, local radio stations broadcast a warning of 'imminent landing' on Quemoy but this hardly official and salient warning only raised alarm bells in the non-communist world. From China's perspective this use of military force was seen as a minor event, staying off the pages of the national media. On 4 September China declared a twelve mile territorial water limit for all its coasts but still with no sense of crisis.

If there was a crisis atmosphere in China, it only followed a 4 September warning from US Secretary of State Dulles that the US would use force if necessary to keep Quemoy from falling to a Chinese blockade. On 6 September China opened a major public campaign on Taiwan. Zhou Enlai kicked off the drive in a major speech that day, and also put a damper on events that were apparently perceived as getting too dangerous, by proposing the resumption of ambassadorial talks in Warsaw with the US. This crafty manoeuvre once again brought events back into China's control by reducing the dangers of escalation, while allowing for continuing military pressure on Quemoy and a useful morale raising campaign at home.

Chinese troops had ceased firing on Quemoy from 4–8 September but resumed after it was clear that the wider tensions were under control, Soviet support was still forthcoming, and there was still some hope that the offshore island would surrender without undue risk. China's blockade of Quemoy appeared to be successful but from 14–21 September the military balance shifted in Taiwan's favour and from then on the blockade could be regularly broken. In late September, new military equipment allowed Taiwanese forces to inflict heavy casualties on Chinese forces, epecially when Sidewinder missiles took a devastating toll of MIG aircraft. On 5 October China was forced to propose a *de facto* ceasefire and wind down the military dimension of the crisis. China proposed a one-week ceasefire so long as the US would cease convoying Taiwanese ships to Quemoy. The US agreed and although on 25 October China resumed shelling on even days of the calendar, there was no doubt that the military dimension of this low key crisis was clearly controllable. The alternate-day shelling epitomized both the essential political nature of the use of the military instrument, as well as the lack of necessary connection between military force and political crisis. These two aspects were common to both Taiwan crises, and despite occasional sudden rises in tension after 1958,[5] little changed in the Taiwan Straits untill the era of Sino-American detente.

Chinese Objectives

As in the Korean war, Chinese objectives in both Taiwan Straits crises were neither simple nor unchanging. In the first phase of the

1954–5 crisis, from 11 August through to the end of November, China appeared to be merely trying to express displeasure with US policy in Asia. In the Chinese perspective, American policy was being militarized and formalized in the SEATO pact in a way that Beijing opposed, but felt it could do little about except by expressing displeasure.[6] This expression took various forms, including military action. Numerous Chinese statements were issued denouncing US policy around the world, in Asia and especially in the Taiwan area. In addition, Taiwanese political and military action came in for equally harsh criticism.[7]

Military force was also used to demonstrate Beijing's displeasure. For example, on 3 September when the SEATO conference opened, China shelled Quemoy. But at least at this stage China did not seem to see the military instrument as anything but a useful tool for political signalling. The 3 September shelling was by no means the only military incident at that time and it took place against a background of general uncertainity in the Taiwan Straits and continuing military clashes.[8] The situation was fluid but there was no sense of crisis requiring urgent action.

A greater degree of urgency in China's expression of opposition to US moves came only by early December. This second phase was apparently triggered by American attempts to extend SEATO type containment pacts to Taiwan and China's objectives were now aimed more specifically at probing US intentions. To what extent had the US altered its policy on Taiwan? On 2 December the US signed a mutual defence pact with Taiwan and China responded with more vigorous opposition. The risks of passivity for Beijing were greater, for to do nothing would encourage the US to believe that China was not concerned.[9] It was apparently at this stage that China began to introduce the military option—to seize some territory and lessen the Taiwanese blockade of China's coast, and not merely as a graphic signal of political opposition.

China's new political campaign was kicked off by Zhou Enlai who decalred on 8 December that the treaty 'is a grave warlike provocation' and the US must quit the area or else 'take upon itself all the grave consequences'.[10] However, there was no attempt by China to fabricate a major crisis. Later in December Zhou would speak of the trend towards 'the relaxation of tension' and the visit by the UN Secretary General in early January offered further opportunity for soft-line statements. China had raised up a notch its expressions of concern, but concrete action would have to await further developments.[11]

The third phase of the crisis came when Chinese objectives shifted to include a military option—the seizure of offshore islands. The US–Taiwan pact was sent to the US Senate on 7 January and US Secretary General Hammarskjold left China on the 11th. The pact did not cover the offshore islands and thus China might have felt that the risk could be kept low, while at least symbolically some territory was liberated.

The risks were lowered by China's decision to try to take some of the Dachen islands and not the more heavily fortified (and more symbolically potent) Quemoy or Matsu islands. On 11 January China dropped leaflets on these less powerful bases and the landing on Yikiangshan occurred on 18 January. It is hard to suggest that China had any clear military objectives beyond this operation, and further use of the military instrument seemed to be determined by circumstance.

The most relevant circumstance was US and Taiwan policy in general, and their decision to evacuate certain indefensible positions on the Dachens in particular. Although China continued to shell offshore islands throughout the rest of January, its eventual seizure of the Dachens was not the result of a military success. In a pragmatic and cautious policy following their first military success, China paused to see how matters would develop. The initial objective of probing US intentions was still not complete. The military objective of taking some islands was a success but whether there would be more success was still unclear.

Clarification of the extent to which Chinese objectives could be pursued, came following the Yikiangshan operation. The US extension of a limited military guarantee to Quemoy and Matsu (despite the vague wording of the US–Taiwan defence pact) came in the 24 January proposal by Eisenhower that the US Congress adopt the Formosa Resolution. By 29 January the resolution was signed by the President and on 5 February the US decided to cover the Taiwanese withdrawal from the Dachens. The US had drawn the containment line more clearly.

Thus China now had a clearer sense of US intentions and the main objectives of the crisis were achieved. However the military operations were not yet over. The next phase of Chinese objectives became the clarification of the military situation. From 11–13 February China allowed the US to cover the Taiwanese withdrawal from the Dachens and on 14 February China occupied the islands unopposed. It was perfectly clear by mid-February that whatever tension had been built up in the Taiwan Straits, was now dissipating. On 18 February China accepted a 4 February Soviet proposal for a conference on the crisis, thereby putting an official seal on what had already been clear for days: the crisis had ended.[12] On 26 February China took, unopposed, yet another of the tiny offshore islands, but by then China was clear as to what it could or could not safely occupy.

Thus the use of military force *per se* was not necessarily a signal of Beijing's seriousness. Indeed, this crisis had been through several phases where military and political policies were pursued in a closely intertwined fashion. By the very nature of China's objectives to at first signal disapproval, and then probe US intentions, it was likely that there would be no confidence about the outcome of crisis management. A probe is pragmatic, avowedly awaiting responses before further policy can be set. Thus Chinese objectives in 1954–5 were fluid and changing in response to international reactions. Similarly, military objectives were set flexibly, allowing for pragmatic responses such as the Dachen operation, after the enemy had opened new possibilities. It is extremely doubtful that Chinese military objectives, as with its political objectives, were either pre-set or pursued with a clear end in mind.

In the 1958 Taiwan Straits crisis the pattern of political objectives, and to a certain extent military objectives as well, seemed to be similar to that of the 1954–5 crisis. Both crises began with minimal Chinese objectives of merely expressing opposition to what China saw as destabilizing US policy changes in the area. In the 1958 crisis, this first phase had several distinct sub-phases, but none included military operations.

China was undoubtedly concerned with the 15 July US intervention in the Lebanon and especially the way in which the tension was transferred to Asia with the placement of the 7th Fleet on alert. But it is misleading to suggest that China was acting out of defensive motives by launching a nine day propaganda campaign on the Taiwan issue on 22 July. There had been no special sense of tension in the Taiwan area and there was no significant build up of military power or frequency of military incidents. China seemed to decide, no doubt some time after the opening of the 17 August Politburo meeting, to place the US on notice that the Taiwan problem could not be subject to Lebanon-like treatment. In the heady atmosphere of growing radicalism in the Great Leap Forward and the recently emphasized assertion by Mao that the US was a 'paper tiger', such a statement was logical, safe and far from likely to create a crisis.[13] The US had failed to respond to China's 30 June call to resume ambassadorial talks in Warsaw, despite an extension of the offer again on 15 July. Therefore the political signal of a propaganda campaign could safely achieve the minimal Chinese objective of declaring Beijing's position.

There then followed an interlude, when the Taiwan issue faded from sight almost as suddenly as it had appeared. As with the 1954–5 crisis, this first phase is in many senses distinct from the real crisis that would follow. In 1958, the division between the objective of declaring intent, and probing US policy, was sharper. The sudden visit by Soviet Premier Khrushchev from 31 July to 3 August seemed to bring an equally sudden end to the Chinese propaganda campaign, but the precise connection between the visit and the Taiwan events is unclear.

Strange as it may seem, it appears that Mao and Khrushchev did not discuss Taiwan in their meetings.[14] Apparently Taiwan was not yet an important enough international event, and the real purpose of the meeting may well have been more concerned with events in the Middle East, the impending Berlin crisis, or more probably, developing problems in Sino-Soviet relations.[15] Whatever the case, China's objectives regarding Taiwan did not seem to be affected. Indeed, the Taiwan issue remained virtually non-existent in the Chinese media untill the next phase beginning on 22 August. There had been some upgrading of Chinese defence capability in Fujian in early August, but this was far from a dramatic build up let alone an offensive marshalling of troops.[16] If there was a purpose to this limited deployment, it was in preparation for the second phase of Chinese objectives.

This second phase began on 22 August with Chinese military operations against Quemoy. From 23 August to 4 September China regularly shelled the islands in what seemed to be the pursuit of both political and military objectives. As an article in *Red Flag* put it, 'There is only one way to deal with madmen—to expose and fight them.'[17] China's attempt at exposing US intentions, the first objective, was more swiftly acheived than in the 1954–5 crisis. By concentrating only on the Quemoy Islands and by having reinforced its local military superiority by new artillery emplacements, China could control the level of crisis to a remarkable extent. Much like Soviet pressure on a surrounded Berlin, so China's physical presence gave it an ability to turn the tap of pressure off and on whenever it so chose.[18] The second objective, a military seizure of Quemoy by blockade, was no doubt something that China might have hoped for, but was unlikely to have expected. Certainly Beijing's military deployment did not indicate any serious attempt at capturing the islands by anything but a blockade.[19] Much like the 1948 Berlin crisis, the US would have to escalate, or overcome the blockade by technical ingenuity (as they later did), or else capitulate to the communist side.

The pursuit of both these objectives, as in the 1954–5 crisis, was eminently pragmatic, leaving open options of lowering risk and controlling conflict. As in the previous Taiwan crisis, it took the US a short while to clarify its position in response to the Chinese probe, but once it was done, China was able to carry on with limited military objectives in the hope that some minor gains might be possible. Unlike the 1954–5 crisis, the US and Taiwan held firm and ceded no further territory. On 27 August the US began moving new ships into the Taiwan Straits and, especially after the local Fujian radio warned the Quemoy garrison of 'imminent' capture, the US awoke to the serious possibility of Chinese military gains.[20] China's careful calibration of the crisis at this stage included no wide coverage of the shelling and its implications.[21] Furthermore, Soviet statements at the time mirrored Chinese concerns and hopes for keeping the crisis limited.[22] China's military objectives remained flexible, with broadcasts suggesting various goals from 'punishment' to 'liberation'. Clearly China was trying to keep its options open, but not at any level of risk. As Mao said in the course of the crisis, 'ships are especially for the water; they cannot come ashore'.[23] For China, naval threats are not nearly as serious as land threats, and therefore are more subject to 'management' in crisis management.

By 4 September the US had clearly decided to 'hold upright its row of dominoes' and support Taiwan. China's military action paused and the crisis entered a third phase where once again Beijing's objectives changed in response to the new conditions. Now there was no doubt as to the thrust of US policy and China's concern shifted to reducing the level of tension, and hence potential threat to China. This objective did not however mean the end of the military option. In this third phase, after a day of reassessment on

6 September Zhou Enlai set the tone of Chinese objectives in a major speech. While declaring that US reaction in defence of Taiwan was a 'grave war provocation' and 'a serious menace to the peace of the Far East and the world', he also proposed resumption of ambassadorial talks with the US. Zhou thereby indicated a desire to keep the conflict controlled, but as Zhou added 'the dangers of war created by the USA in China's Taiwan area has not been reduced thereby'.[24] Thus the crisis was far from over, but it did shrink back from dangerous war, and towards more controlled crisis management. Chinese objectives were now more military—the hope that the blockade would bring Quemoy's surrender—but the more basic objective of probing US intentions was by and large resolved. Beijing could still hope that Quemoy would capitulate, but China's leaders could have little doubt of the strength of the continuing US commitment.

The necessity for a recalculation of objectives was clear to China from 4 September. The following day Mao told the Supreme State Conference that 'I simply did not calculate that the world would become so disturbed and turbulent'. He also confessed surprise that 'firing a few shots' would stir up such a fuss.[25] Mao said that war was neither desired nor likely, but he did speak rather loosely about the continuing danger of nuclear war. Despite these admissions of miscalculation, Mao insisted that the crisis remained under control and in keeping with the principle of 'despise the enemy strategically, respect him tactically'. Mao still asserted that the US was more afraid to fight than was China. As it turned out, Mao was right that the crisis was controlled, but was mistaken in the belief that the US would not frustrate Chinese objectives, even of the more limited kind after 4 September.

The US response to Beijing's challenge to America's policy of deterrence of threats to Taiwan was more than equal to the two-pronged military and political challenges. Dulles's acceptance of Zhou's proposal to resume ambassadorial talks and thereby control the conflict, was matched by equally strong military responses. On 7 September the US despatched its first convoy to within three miles of Quemoy to help break the blockade. After a week's work, and technical ingenuity, (including new techniques of convoying and off-loading) the Chinese blockade was breached and by 21 September it was apparent that the advantages of local control (as in the Berlin crisis) were defeated by superior technical adaptation. Chinese forces then began to suffer heavy casualties, especially in the air, when newly acquired Sidewinder missiles allowed the Taiwanese to wreak alarming damage on Chinese forces.[26] Thus Chinese objectives once again were forced to change, this time as a result of the changing fortunes of war. There were times when Mao's belief in the superiority of men over weapons proved patently false, and Chinese policy was forced to change. Mao admitted as much in speeches after 7 September and made it plain that the United States was less likely to collapse in the near future.[27]

The failure of China's military initiative no doubt dawned gradually on Beijing's leaders. In the first week after Zhou's 6 September statement there was a full blown propaganda campaign in China including mass rallies.[28] But as the breaching of the blockade became apparent, China toned down the campaign and no doubt also lowered its expectations. To a certain extent the Taiwan campaign may have also served domestic purposes at this time, especially in terms of gathering support for the Great Leap Forward and the campaign to organize a militia. Mao said in November 1958 that 'it was good for Taiwan to fire artillery shots, for otherwise the militia could not have been organized so quickly'.[29] But this was more a *post facto* rationalization of Mao's miscalculation of US policy, rather than an original objective of the shelling.

With the exception of the declining media coverage of Taiwan events, it is difficult to see China's attitude towards the crisis changing before 5 October. Chinese warnings to the US were pitched at a high level and even Soviet supporting statements assumed the same exaggerated tone, even though it was apparent that China would do nothing to bolster its failing military option.[30] The rhetorical flourishes did little to inspire confidence in the meaning of Chinese statements during crisis.

On 5 October the 1958 crisis entered its final phase with China climbing down in the face of a wasteful military campaign. With a huge and well-publicized convoy about to embark for Quemoy, Chinese Defence Minister Peng Dehuai magnanimously announced a one-week ceasefire to allow resupply of Quemoy. Peng suggested to the Taiwanese that all along China's objective was just 'to call your attention' to the fact that Taiwan and the islands are Chinese.[31] This minimal objective was no doubt part of the purpose of the previous crisis, but it understated China's more optimistic hopes that had emerged in the course of the changing fortunes of the crisis.

In the following months China would emphasize its long term strategy (despising strategically) while recognizing the difficulty of dealing with the US in the short term (taking seriously tactically).[32] This policy emerged in response to Beijing's failure to unhinge US protection of Taiwan, and the evident strength of the US commitment in Asia. The more specific Chinese military objective also failed in that unlike the 1954–5 crisis, China could not overcome, nor was it allowed to occupy unopposed, any further offshore islands. The great beauty of Mao's dictum of despising the enemy strategically while respecting him tactically, was that it allowed for Chinese gains, losses, or as in 1958, a stalemate. It was the strategy of expedience.

The Operation

It is absurd to suggest that there was any kind of sophisticated military strategy governing PLA operations against the offshore islands in 1954–5. The sporadic bombardment did involve all three services, but none of the attacks involved anything like the co-ordination necessary in the Korean war. It was however notable that the November 1954 sinking of a Taiwanese destroyer was acheived by small Chinese craft hiding among junks—proclaimed as guerrilla war at sea. Only one operation in 1954–5 was of any significant scale, and that was the two hour battle for Yikiangshan on 18 January. Four thousand PLA men defeated 1000 Taiwanese irregulars, capturing 550 prisoners, and two howitzers and one large field gun. Nevertheless, it was a co-ordinated amphibious operation requiring some skill and sophistication. The seizure of islands later in February was unopposed although more equipment was taken at that time.[33]

The pattern of Chinese military operations did not appear to be determined by anything other than an expedient calculation of changing military and political conditions. Having chosen limited objectives, the scope for military action was already greatly limited as well. There was not much sophisticated military strategy that could be applied in the narrow confines of barren offshore islands supplied by convoy. The precise outcome of the crisis could not have been predicted from the start. In the end it resulted from the choice of limited objectives, geographic proximity of the islands to the mainland, and above all the way in which the US chose to respond to the Chinese challenge. For example, it was the US decision to evacuate the Dachens that determined China's ability to occupy them, not the strength or strategy of the Chinese military.

It would be convenient to suggest that the strategy of military expedience, applied during the 1954–5 crisis, was the result of a clear policy choice in Beijing. However, it appears that even if China could have pre-planned detailed military operations in the straits, there was little concensus on military policy in China at the time. On Army Day in 1954 military leaders spoke of the need to modernize and improve the PLA's technical performance, but others warned against adopting the 'purely military viewpoint'. According to the Chinese at the time, one of the most crucial services in the brief combat, the air force, was undergoing further study and development.[34] China's attitude towards nuclear weapons was also changing in response to evolving Soviet strategy after Stalin's death. The changes in Chinese doctrine did not, however, result from the Taiwan crisis, nor did nuclear weapons figure in any important way in the 1954–5 events.[35] China professed no fear of United States nuclear power, in part because demographic factors or rendered the western world's greater concentration of population and industry more vulnerable to such weapons than peasant China.[36] But in general it was apparent that China did not come to appreciate the meaning of the nuclear revolution in military strategy until after the Taiwan crisis. In January 1955 Mao appeared to lack appreciation of the destructiveness of atomic weapons, although his assertion that 'planes plus the A-bomb' of the US were inferior to China's 'millet plus rifles', was merely part of the by now familiar process of suggesting the limited utility of nuclear weapons in crises.[37]

China's lack of concern with nuclear war in the crisis was part of its more general view that it could cope with what it saw as a very limited crisis with the US. This essentially bilateral crisis excluded nearly all other states from an active role. The UN was shunned as a participant, even in arranging a ceasefire, because it was seen as hostile and pro-Taiwan. Even the Soviet Union did not play an active role, but this had more to do with internal Soviet leadership politics (Malenkov's removal was announced on 8 February 1955) and China's confidence in its own crisis management.

Soviet support for China was proffered at various times, but its generally low key approach was not necessarily a sign of any Sino-Soviet disagreement on the issues at stake. On 30 September 1954

Khrushchev declared that the PLA was guarantee enough for China's security, but he also said that the Soviet Union 'deeply sympathizes' with and 'supports' China.[38] Khrushchev may well have been preferred by the Chinese to Malenkov and his greater support for peaceful coexistence. All the same China did not seem to request any Soviet aid. On 19 January 1955 Beijing radio spoke favourably of Soviet non-intervention in Korea because 'it had deemed it unnecessary to kill a chicken with a butcher's knife'.[39] In February durng the celebrations of the Sino-Soviet treaty anniversary, warm praises were exchanged, especially about co-operation in the military field. On 12 February the Chinese endorsed an official Soviet line on the Taiwan events, and the 18 February *People's Daily*'s acceptance of the Soviet offer to arrange a conference on Taiwan indicated at most a different sense of timing for a ceasefire, but not a disagreement on the heart of policy.[40]

During this first Taiwan crisis China had great confidence in keeping control. Indeed it hardly caused a hiccup in Chinese foreign policy as the US responded to China's probe and by February a new *status quo* was arranged. But the nature of the unresolved crisis, and pre-eminently the continuing Taiwanese ability to hold US prestige hostage just several miles off the coast of China meant that, when it felt like another probe of US intentions, Beijing could resume the shelling and the military pressure. This was not a sophisticated strategy.

The 1958 Taiwan Straits crisis, as with the 1954–5 crisis, can be seen in the context of Mao's concept of despising the US strategically but taking the Americans seriously in a tactical sense. Yet such a pragmatic concept offers no guide to the military strategy adopted in 1958. Various policy options developed during the course of the conflict that allowed for more shifts between offensive or defensive action. As with the 1954–5 crisis, what determined China's use of military force was Beijing's limited objectives, the geographic location of Quemoy just a few miles off the Chinese coast, the nature of the US response, and finally the superiority of Western military technology and improvization.

In fact the 1958 crisis demonstrated an even less sophisticated Chinese strategy as compared with 1954–5. Chinese air and sea power were hardly used at all in 1958, and the blockade was imposed entirely by artillery fire.[41] These tactics helped keep the crisis controlled, but made for a rather predictable military engagement.

All the US and Taiwanese forces had to do was to arrange a breach of the blockade without escalation by, for example US strikes on Chinese artillery positions on the mainland.

Like the 1954–5 crisis, the 1958 shelling had a large political component. The policy of alternate-day shelling by October 1958 was a prime example of the military instrument serving political purposes. At times this use of military power turned into a misuse. In late August, when China threatened an 'imminent' landing on Quemoy and when it was evident that the amphibious force for such a task was not available, this only served to undermine the Chinese reputation for 'meaning what they say'. Such bravado also under-mined future Chinese efforts at deterrence.

In 1958, as in 1954–5, China did not use military force out of any defensive motive, but rather out of confidence that US intentions could be safely probed. In keeping with the 1958 Great Leap Forward rhetoric of confidence, China expressed strong belief that the US could not threaten China, and Mao apparently felt confident in his ability to control the tension.[42] Similarly, Mao was not concerned with US nuclear power as a threat during the crisis.[43] Although there was some discussion of nuclear threats in the Western press, the Chinese only took up the issue after 7 September and then only to disparage its utility in limited crises.

It is of course possible that there was a less unanimous view in China of aspects of military strategy (see next section), but it is hard to find any example of how such disagreements affected specific policy. This was a time of great change in Chinese military doctrine with the emergence of a more Chinese and less Soviet-dominated military doctrine.[44] Mao warned about eating the 'pre-cooked food' of Soviet strategy and numerous statements at the time indicated a clear shift away from doctrinaire and slavish study of Soviet military theory.[45]

As important as these changes were for the Chinese military, they did not seem to have any noticeable effect on the Taiwan crisis. Even Lin Biao, in criticizing those who learn excessively from the Soviet military, said that the Soviet doctrine still worth learning 'consists of the use of naval and air forces and the co-ordination of the services'.[46] Second, as we have already suggested, the Taiwan crisis was essentially a case of military force used for political purposes. Military strategy, or changes within a given doctrine, were not nearly as crucial as the guiding political doctrine or changes in political relationships.

Therefore it is suggested that if there was a problem with the Soviet Union during the 1958 crisis, it was not with Soviet military strategy as much as it was with the level of Soviet support offered during the crisis. However, even in this area it seems that, contrary to some previous analysis of the crisis, the Soviet Union and China had no differences that materially affected the course of the Taiwan events.[47] To be sure there were Sino-Soviet differences at this time, but apparently not on the 1958 Taiwan Straits crisis.

The assessment of the Soviet Union as a poor ally depends on the view that China demanded Soviet support in 1958 and did not get it. However, on his 31 July visit to Beijing apparently Khrushchev did not discuss Taiwan although other issues of international politics, including bilateral differences on other topics, were the subject of haggling.[48] It seems most likely that Mao and Khrushchev agreed that any challenge to the US would have to be carefully calibrated (after all Khrushchev had his own little probe in Berlin in November 1958). If China could probe the US and place the onus of escalation on Washington, then the Soviet Union could safely deter the American response. This seemed to coincide with Mao's own view that tension could be kept to a minimum.

During the August shelling, the Soviet statements of support for the national security of China were unambigious. More uncertain was Soviet support if, for example, China had chosen an amphibious landing. But then it appears that no such plans were laid. The crucial factor was that the Chinese themselves were trying to keep the crisis on a low key, and thus any more forceful Soviet statements would be undesired in Beijing.[49] In any case, according to one report, Soviet Foreign Minister Gromyko was sent to Beijing to sit in on the 5–6 September Chinese deliberations on the crisis.[50] While probably a sign of Soviet uncertainty about China, Gromyko's presence ensured that no major Sino-Soviet misunderstanding would take place this time. On 5 September an authoritative Observer article in *Pravda* said the Soviet Union could not 'sit idly by' in the face of US threats to China, and as with previous major Soviet statements, the article was reprinted in full the following day in the *People's Daily*.

Khrushchev's letter to Eisenhower of 6 September warning of the Soviet commitment to defend China came in conjunction with Zhou Enlai's effort to tone down the crisis but retain the military option. Khrushchev's letter also came before the first US convoy to break the Chinese blockade set sail and thus before the military dimension of the crisis subsided. Indeed Soviet support for China in the following week was warmly received in the Chinese press and mirrored the new level of tension that had recently appeared in the Chinese media. Further letters by Khrushchev and official Soviet statements matched the tone of the Chinese line.[51] On 8 September Mao admitted that Khrushchev 'basically' was united with China over the crisis although the Soviet leader stressed the need for a peaceful settlement of the Taiwan question.[52]

When the crisis was over, Song Qingling wrote in *Pravda* thanking Khrushchev for having 'immediately and resolutely warned the US government that any attack on the CPR would be an attack on the Soviet government and the Soviet people'.[53] While it is true that in the course of later Sino-Soviet polemics the Chinese would accuse the Soviet Union of having failed to support China in 1958, that was certainly not the Chinese line during the crisis. Indeed, the guarded nature of Chinese criticism of Soviet policy, and only in respect of the Soviet's supposed nuclear guarantee, was half-hearted considering the exaggerated rhetoric of the Sino-Soviet polemics on other issues.

It should also be noted that in September 1958, as opposed to a year earlier when China obtained a Soviet promise for assistance in developing nuclear weapons, or in 1959 when the alleged deal was abbrogated, China and the Soviet Union did not disagree on nuclear weapons co-operation. While Mao and others in China were shifting away from the Soviet model on other aspects of defence policy, on the nuclear question Mao had little cause to be displeased with the Soviet Union.[54]

China and the Soviet Union of course did have important differences on many topics, but it is not necessary to read back enmity to all issues in order to justify the reality of the Sino-Soviet split. The reason why no important Sino-Soviet differences emerged over the 1958 Taiwan Straits crisis was that, as with the 1954–5 crisis, China was confident that it could control its probe of US intentions. This confidence was well placed, and was shared by Khrushchev in his similar application of pressure to Berlin. China did not ask the Soviet Union for anything more than deterrence of US escalation, and this seemed to have been provided. In the event, the US did not need to escalate the crisis, but was able to circumvent the blockade, and China's challenge, by superior tactics and technology. That

China failed to acheive any military objectives in 1958, whereas it did in 1954–5, has more to do with the differing US response in the two crises, and emphasizes the point that both crises were essentially only between China and the United States. Passing blame to the Soviet Union should not disguise China's own responsibility for initiating and largely failing in the 1958 Taiwan Straits crisis.

The Domestic Dimension

While the 1954–5 and 1958 Taiwan Straits crises may have had a number of similarities in objectives and strategy, they seemed to differ significantly in the extent to which the domestic dimension of Chinese politics affected the course of the crises. The 1955 crisis is striking in the near complete absence of any important domestic dimension.

The decision to probe US intentions, and indeed the conduct of the crisis as well, seems to have been unaffected by any aspect of Chinese internal politics. To be sure, in March 1955 just after the crisis regional party leaders Gao Gang and Rao Shuzhi were purged, but without any doubt the reasons for their fall were to be found in domestic politics. Foreign policy did not figure in any way in the public accusation against them, and in later criticism, the only foreign policy deviation alleged involved Soviet aid for Gao Gang.[55]

The conduct of the brief crisis also did not seem to be affected by domestic politics. Peng Dehuai had returned from Korea to take up his post as the first Minister of Defence in September 1954. But despite some simultaneous adjustment in Chinese military strategy, there seemed to be no major debate on the subject.[56] While there may have been some differences of opinion, at this early stage, barely five years after the establishment of the PRC, leadership debates seemed well controlled. Neither were there differences apparent among the PLA services as all three took part in the military operations led by Zhang Aiping.[57] The partial military success no doubt helped to avoid any recrimination caused by failure that seemed to have played a part in the 1958 crisis.

Finally, neither did there appear to be any significant link to the very real power struggle taking place in the Soviet Union during the 1954–5 Taiwan crisis. Soviet aid was not required, nor apparently sought during the crisis and while the outcome of the Soviet struggle may well have had longer term importance for Sino-Soviet relations, the specific events in the Taiwan Straits seemed unaffected.

This picture of domestic tranquillity in China is in sharp contrast with the scene set for the 1958 Taiwan crisis. This is not to suggest that in 1958 China was racked by internal dissension on the Taiwan crisis, but rather that domestic politics in China were turbulent at the time, and some instability may well have affected policy making on Taiwan.

Various remarks by Chinese leaders and statements in the official media indicated some difference of opinion, pre-eminently on the question of whether the US paper tiger should be challenged. On 3 August the *People's Daily* noted that 'some people regard efforts for peace as pacifism, which paralyzes the people's will to struggle and causes them to be panic-stricken in a tense situation'.[58] Five days later the same paper spoke of 'some soft-hearted advocates of peace'.[59] On 6 September it was noted that the Supreme State Council's endorsement of Zhou Enlai's statement on Taiwan only followed an exchange of opinion on the subject.[60] On 8 September Mao acknowledged that not all Chinese leaders saw the crisis as beneficial.[61] On 14 September *Red Flag* noted that 'some people' still failed to see that the US was basically weak and in November Mao complained that 'both inside and outside the Party there are many persons who do not understand the paper tiger problem. There are people who say, "since it is a paper tiger, why do we not attack Taiwan?" '.[62]

Clearly there were diverse opinions on the decision to challenge the US, but it is equally clear that not all the differences were of the same sort. But more importantly, it is even less clear what effect these differences of nuance had on actual Chinese policy in the crisis. During the Cultural Revolution it was suggested by Red Guard sources that Peng Dehuai colluded with Khrushchev and that Mao had to overcome both conspirators and launch the Quemoy shelling to defeat their capitulationist line.[63] While it is possible that the Soviet Union might have preferred a less dangerous Chinese probe, as has already been suggested, Sino-Soviet policy did not differ materially on the 1958 crisis. What is more, as with a great many accusations from Cultural Revolution polemics, this one-off statement seems to have no basis in fact.

It is undoubtedly true that Peng was purged in 1959 but it is impossible to find a link between his views or actions during the Taiwan crisis and his fall from Mao's grace. Peng tumbled because of a complex web of disagreements with Mao and other leaders on the course of domestic politics, and especially radical aspects of the Great Leap Forward.[64] During the Taiwan crisis itself there is no evidence that Peng's line was any different from that of Mao or any other leader.[65] It seems clear that there must have been some debate on the Taiwan events, but it is unclear who took what position. What is more, differences of opinion need not always result in a purge, and in this case they seemed to be subsumed as part of a larger and more important debate on domestic policy.

Another reason why it seems impossible to identify clear factional lines on the Taiwan issue is that it is probable that there were cross-cutting cleavages of opinion. The crisis took place against a background of intense changes in internal Chinese politics during the Great Leap. Within the military the changes included such important ones as the establishment of the militia (a challenge to professional interests), the 'officers to the ranks' movement (a further challenge to professionals) and above all a revision of military doctrine away from heavy reliance on the Soviet model.[66] What is more, the Chief of Staff, Su Yu was replaced by Huang Kecheng on 12 October although he had apparently fallen from grace as early as July 1958. But Su Yu's removal, as with the other wide-ranging changes in the PLA, was not tied specifically to the Taiwan events. Su's removal seemed more involved with the changes in the status of professional officers[67] (of which he was said to be a leading advocate) and indeed this issue seemed to be resolved at the July Military Affairs Commission meeting before the Taiwan crisis got underway.

It is possible that some military officers opposed the Taiwan operation, but if so the opposition hardly seemed to carry much weight. Not only was the Taiwan operation essentially a political and non-military exercise, but it also appears that there was no coherence of views within the PLA. Su Yu's replacement, Huang Kecheng, was in turn to fall with Peng Dehuai for obviously different reasons and the new Defence Minister Lin Biao, no doubt represented yet another strand of opinion within the PLA. In May 1958 Lin had been raised up in the Politburo above Peng Dehuai and, given the rivalry between the two, Peng's wings were clearly being clipped. This took place no doubt as part of the shift from the Soviet model in defence to a more Maoist one.[68] Lin, along with Zhu De, He Long and Liu Yabou were backing the Maoist line when Peng and other professionals in the PLA wanted to hold onto the Soviet model. However, the true significance of the leadership changes and the policy adjustments lies not in the Taiwan events, but in the more far-reaching Great Leap transformation. The anti-Soviet model mood was clearly part of this broader Great Leap change.

However, despite the importance of the Great Leap in explaining such changes, it is not possible to argue persuasively that the Great Leap caused the Taiwan tensions as a distraction from internal instability. As we have already suggested, Taiwan events were later claimed by Chinese leaders to have been useful in gathering support for the domestic movement, but this was no doubt a rationalization, especially after the failure of the foreign policy challenge to the US. Domestic events in China were clearly important to an overall understanding of the background to the Taiwan events, and indeed they may help explain some signs of difference in Chinese policy, but at no time did these domestic factors have a decisive bearing on the course or outcome of the crisis.

Neither was there a direct link to Soviet policy at the time. As we have already suggested, there was no important difference of opinion between China and the Soviet Union on the Taiwan events. Neither was there a real link between Peng Dehuai and the Soviet leadership. Even if there was some coincidence of opinion betwen the two on the utility of the Soviet model for China, this topic did not seem to be a point of debate during the course of the Taiwan events.[69]

In sum, in neither of the Taiwan crises was the course or outcome determined by domestic debates. Only in the 1958 crisis is it possible to see clear signs of domestic disagreement, but these differences followed no clear pattern. What is more, the 1958 crisis (as with the 1954–5 crisis) was not a real subject of military debate. The crisis was essentially a political probe of US intentions that did not involve any sophisticated military strategy. What determined the outcome of the crises was the limited set of Chinese objectives, the geographic realities, and the nature of the US response. In the end, if China failed to achieve as much as it had hoped in either crisis, the responsibility lies in its failure to manipulate these factors. Domestic debates offer no clear indication of the course or content of the crisis.

Conclusions

In both Taiwan crises the Chinese objectives changed in response to new circumstances. This should not have been surprising inasmuch as the main reason for China's actions was to ascertain US policy in fluid regional and international conditions. Both crises also shared a basic framework in that China began by merely issuing a statement opposing US action, then moved to a probe of US intentions and finally attempted to make some military gains.

But military force was not used in the same way in both crises. In 1955 China clearly intended to take some territory and did achieve some limited success. In 1958 the Chinese shelling of Quemoy was only intended to have possible military purposes in the later phase. Despite vacuous threats of imminent landing, the use of force was more political than military. In both cases the attainment of military objectives was determined primarily by the level of the US response. In 1955 the US decided to vacate the Dachens but in 1958 the US defeated the Chinese blockade of Quemoy with superior technique and technology. In neither case did China pursue a simple strategy. By the very nature of its probe, Beijing kept its objectives and strategy flexible in order to respond to the US response. Mao's dictum of despising the enemy strategically while taking him seriously tactically was the epitome of the flexible strategy, but it offered no coherent guide to action.

In both crises the Chinese kept their aims, and propensity to take risks, under close control. All the while the military instrument was strictly subordinate to the essential political goals of the Chinese probe and whatever military gains were made seemed almost incidental. Similarly, domestic politics did not seem to have any important effect on the conduct of Chinese policy, nor did the Soviet Union play a determining role in the crisis. The Taiwan events remained overwhelmingly a bilateral US–China crisis as Beijing probed American intentions. Washington held firm even in its policy of extended deterrence of China to within two miles of its coast. But China lacked both the military power and the political will to overcome this US policy. So China settled for long term goals where it could hope to encourage the decline of US power and/or will. This strategy of 'despising the US strategically' was the epitome of the strategy of expediency, and made good sense under the circumstances.

NOTES

1. The only detailed study of this crisis is J. H. Kalicki, *The Pattern of Sino-American Crisis* (London: Cambridge University Press, 1975), and Alexander

George and Richard Smoke, *Deterrence in American Foreign Policy* (New York: Columbia University Press, 1974). The analysis that follows relies heavily on *BBC*/SWB/FE/No. 373–438.

2. For example in October 1952, Taiwan forces attacked an island off Fujian and held it for 3 days, killing 250 PLA men and capturing 720. In May 1953 PLA forces took two islands near the Dachens. Bruce Swanson, *Eighth Voyage of the Dragon* (Annapolis: Naval Institute Press, 1982), pp. 186–9.

3. The Quemoy Islands lie two miles off the Chinese port of Amoy. The Matsu Islands are 10 miles off Fuzhou and the Dachens off the Zhejiang coast.

4. Detailed studies of this crisis are in Kalicki, *Pattern of Crisis*; Melvin Gurtov and Byong-Moo Hwang, *China Under Threat* (Baltimore: Johns Hopkins University Press, 1980), Ch. 3; Kenneth Young, *Negotiating with the Chinese Communists* (New York: McGraw Hill, 1968); Donald Zagoria, *The Sino-Soviet Conflict, 1956–61* (New York: Athenaeum, 1964); Morton Halperin and Tang Tsou, 'The 1958 Quemoy Crisis', in Morton Halperin ed., *Sino-Soviet Relations and Arms Control* (Cambridge: MIT Press, 1967). The analysis that follows also is based on *BBC*/SWB/FE/Nos. 788–810.

5. This chapter does not discuss the June 1962 Taiwan Straits crisis because it was a spurious crisis. Tension was raised but no military force was used, or probably even deployed in a threatening manner. For a brief analysis see Gerald Segal, *The Great Power Triangle* (London: Macmillan, 1982) Ch. 2. On a November 1965 clash near Quemoy see Swanson, *Eighth Voyage*, pp. 234–5.

6. Alice Langley Hsieh, *China's Strategy in the Nuclear Age* (Englewood Cliffs, New Jersey: Prentice Hall, 1962) p. 15; George and Smoke, *Deterrence* pp. 270–6.

7. For example, *People's Daily*, 16 July 1954 in *BBC*/SWB/FE/376/pp. 5–6. Also No. 385/p. 1 and *People's Daily*, 26 August p. 6; *People's Daily*, 20 November in No. 409/5–6; *People's China*, 1 September 1954, pp. 3–6.

8. For example *People's Daily*, 28 July 1954 in *BBC*/SWB/FE/376/16–17. Zhu De called the note 'the most recent' series of attacks on 1 August in No. 378/20–21. Also NCNA 31 July on p. 24. No. 385/4; NCNA 10 Sept in No. 389/4–5; NCNA 9 October in No. 397/8–9; NCNA 29 October in No. 403/4–5; NCNA 14 November in No. 408/11.

9. George and Smoke, *Deterrence*, pp. 271–4.

10. *BBC*/SWB/FE/414/9–12.

11. NCNA 17 December in *BBC*/SWB/FE/417/5, NCNA 26 December in No. 419/11–12. NCNA 6 January 1955 in No. 422/3–4.

12. For the US and Taiwan, the crisis was said to have lasted through until April, but for China it was clearly not the case. This gap in perception only reinforces the point that this was hardly a serious crisis. You can't have a crisis with only one participant, let alone one with clearly identifiable segments. See George and Smoke, *Deterrence* pp. 280–292; *People's Daily*, 18 February 1955 in *BBC*/SWB/FE/434/5. Also *People's Daily*, 5 March in No. 438/7 on the lack of any sense of crisis, even while the US was less sure.

13. For various aspects of the issue see Hsieh, *China's Strategy*, pp. 118–19; Kalicki, *Pattern of Crisis*, pp. 173–4; Gurtov and Hwang, *China Under Threat*, pp. 76–7.

14. Mao said in November that the issue was not discussed. See *Miscellany of Mao Tse-tung Thought*, JPRS-61269-1, February 1974, p. 135. See also Halperin and Tsou, 'Quemoy Crisis'; Gurtov and Hwang, *China Under Threat*, pp. 89–90. See also the cryptic note by Allen Whiting in *The China Quarterly*, No. 63, September 1975, p. 611.

15. Roderick MacFarquhar, *The Origins of the Cultural Revolution* Vol. 2 (London: Oxford University Press, 1983), pp. 94–5.

16. Halperin and Tsou, 'Quemoy Crisis', p. 274 and Allen Whiting, 'New Light on

Mao: Quemoy 1958', *The China Quarterly* No. 62, June 1975; Swanson, *Eighth Voyage*, p. 213.

17. 16 August 1958 in *BBC*/SWB/FE/795/15.
18. George and Smoke, *Deterrence* pp. 370–375. On Berlin see Hannes Adomeit, *Soviet Risk-Taking and Crisis Behaviour* (London: George Allen and Unwin, 1982).
19. For one thing China brought in no amphibious landing equipment and the shelling began just prior to the typhoon season. Zagoria, *Sino-Soviet Conflict*, p. 208.
20. These broadcasts were not reproduced for the mainland, thereby keeping the crisis limited. See MacFarquhar, *Origins (2)* p. 97; George and Smoke, *Deterrence*; Kalicki, *Pattern of Crisis*, pp. 187–190.
21. *BBC*/SWB/FE/797–799.
22. Especially 31 August. Observer in *Pravda* reprinted in full in *People's Daily* on 1 September; Halperin and Tsou, 'Quemoy Crisis', pp. 281–2.
23. Cited in Whiting, 'New Light', p. 267.
24. *BBC*/SWB/FE/801/1–3.
25. Whiting, 'New Light', and Gurtov and Hwang, *China Under Threat*, p. 92.
26. George and Smoke, *Deterrence*, p. 383. Halperin and Tsou, 'Quemoy Crisis', p. 275; Young, *Negotiating*, pp. 155–177; Kalicki, *Pattern of Crisis*, pp. 191–3.
27. MacFarquhar, *Origins (2)*, pp. 99–100.
28. *BBC*/SWB/FE/801–803.
29. *Miscellany of Mao*, p. 136. Whiting, 'New Light' pp. 265, 269.
30. *People's Daily* Observer, 18 September 1958 in *BBC*/SWB/FE/804/4–5; Chen Yi, 20 September in 805/7–8. See also the series of 'serious warnings' to the US that carried on past 5 October in Nos. 806–10.
31. *BBC*/SWB/FE/809/2.
32. Hsieh, *China's Strategy*, pp. 130–5.
33. NCNA 18 January 1955 in *BBC*/SWB/FE/425/12–13; NCNA 20 January in No. 426/6; NCNA 13 February in No. 433/23. See also Swanson, *Eighth Voyage*, pp. 189–190; Kalicki, *Pattern of Crisis*, pp. 133, 135, 142; Geoge and Smoke, *Deterrence*, p. 285.
34. Zhu De on 1 August 1954, and Su Yu on 31 July, both in *BBC*/SWB/FE/378/20–24; John Gittings, *The Role of the Chinese Army* (London: Oxford University Press, 1967), p. 139.
35. Hsieh, *China's Strategy*, pp. 33–4.
36. NCNA 6 January 1955 in *BBC*/SWB/FE/422/3–4; Kuo Mo-jo 12 February in No. 432/6–8.
37. Mao Tse-tung, *Selected Works* Vol. 5. (Peking: Foreign Languages Press, 1977), pp. 152–3.
38. *People's China* Supplement, 16 October 1954, pp. 11–12.
39. *BBC*/SWB/FE/426/7.
40. *BBC*/SWB/FE/433/16–21 and No. 432/4 on the Supreme Soviet statement of 9 February. Also No. 434/5.
41. Swanson, *Eighth Voyage*, p. 213.
42. See also note 29 and *People's Daily*, 25 July 1958, *Liberation Army Daily*, 25 July; Naval Conference in Shanghai, 27 July, all in *BBC*/SWB/FE/789–9–11. Also No. 790/8 and the Army Day statement by Chang Tsung-hsun in No. 791/18–22 and the *Liberation Army Daily* on the same day, p. 23.
43. Hsieh, *China's Strategy*, p. 123. Whiting, 'New Light', p. 268. *Miscellany of Mao*, p. 108.
44. Ellis Joffe, *Party and Army* (Cambridge: Harvard University Press, 1967); Hsieh, *China's Strategy*; Gurtov and Hwang, *China Under Threat*.

45. Stuart Schram ed., *Mao Tse-tung Unrehearsed* (London: Penguin, 1974) pp. 126–9 on Mao in March and June 1958. Also Chang Tsung-hsun on 1 August 1958 in *BBC*/SWB/FE/791/18–22.
46. Schram ed., *Mao Tse-tung*, p. 129.
47. The dominant view of Soviet perfidy in letting down its Chinese ally is expressed especially well by Zagoria, *Sino-Soviet Conflict*; Hsieh, *China's Strategy*; and Kalicki, *Pattern of Crisis*. The opposing view is ably put by Halperin and Tsou, 'Quemoy Crisis'. Useful proponents of a middle ground favoured by this author, include George and Smoke, *Deterrence*; Young, *Negotiating*; and Gurtov and Hwang, *China Under Threat*. The analysis that follows draws on all these sources.
48. MacFarquhar, *Origins (2)*, pp. 93–7.
49. Based on *BBC*/SWB/FE/798–801.
50. Doak Barnett, 'Peking and the Asian Balance of Power', *Problems of Communism*, July–August 1976 pp. 38–9.
51. *BBC*/SWB/FE/802–809.
52. Cited in MacFarquhar, *Origins (2)*, p. 99.
53. Halperin and Tsou, 'Quemoy Crisis', p. 286.
54. MacFarquhar, *Origins (2)*, pp. 64–70. Problems on this question that arose in May 1958 were in part resolved in July, pp. 69–94.
55. On the Gao Gang affair see Roy Grow, 'The Politics of Industrial Development in China and the Soviet Union'. Unpublished PhD. Dissertation, University of Michigan, 1973. Also, Gerald Segal, 'Chinese Politics and the Soviet Connection', *Jerusalem Journal of International Relations*, Vol. 2 No. 1. Fall 1976.
56. Su Yu on 31 July 1954 in *BBC*/SWB/FE/378/22–3; P'eng Teh-huai on 1 October in No. 395/17–18; Peng on 22 February 1955; and Ho Long 23 February in No. 435/13–15. See also Hsieh, *China's Strategy*, pp. 18–21.
57. Bruce Swanson, 'Naval Forces' in Gerald Segal and William Tow eds., *Chinese Defence Policy* (London: Macmillan, 1984).
58. *BBC*/SWB/FE/791/4–5.
59. Cited in Zagoria, *Sino-Soviet Conflict*, p. 204.
60. *BBC*/SWB/FE/801/42.
61. MacFarquhar, *Origins (2)*, p. 99.
62. *BBC*/SWB/FE/803/10 and Mao cited in Whiting, 'New Light', pp. 266–7.
63. Union Research Institute, *The Case of Peng Teh-huai* (Hong Kong: URI, 1968), p. 202; MacFarquhar, *Origins (2)*.
64. Ellis Joffe, 'Between Two Plenums: China's Intra-leadership Conflict, 1959–1962' *Michigan Papers in Chinese Studies*, No. 22, 1975.
65. Peng on 22 September 1958 in *BBC*/SWB/FE/805/10–15, and 1 October in No. 808/25.
66. Hsieh, *China's Strategy*, pp. 142–150; Gurtov and Hwang, *China Under Threat*, pp. 66–71; Mao on 10 March and 28 June 1958 in Schram, *Mao Unrehearsed*, pp. 96, 126–9. Ho Long, 1 August 1958 in *Current Background*, No. 514, pp. 5–6; Chang Tsung-hsun on 1 August in *BBC*/SWB/FE/791/18–22.
67. Hsieh, *China's Strategy*, p. 117, and Joffe, *Party and Army*.
68. Joffe, *Party and Army*; MacFarquhar, *Origins (2)*, pp. 64–70.
69. Segal, 'Soviet Connection'.

8

India, 1962

Plainly China had no grounds whatever for fearing an Indian attack; but she had every reason to expect it.[1]

The 1962 Sino-Indian border war was a classic, of sorts. Neither side wanted war. The old nemeses of rational foreign policy makers—misperception and miscalculation—conspired to make the 1962 war a sad mistake. India, having yanked the tail of the tiger, was surprised and horrified to see the cat slash back. China behaved more like a reluctant older fighter who in the end relished the chance to throw a knock-out punch.

The miscalculations by China and India have already been superbly documented by previous analysts.[2] Thus this was a relatively straightforward case study to prepare, despite the complexity of the participants' motives. Chinese policy in particular appears superficially simple in its belated, but eventually brutal, response to Indian provocation. However, the ease with which the military instrument was wielded should not mask the fact that there was a tortuous road to travel before the decision was taken. What is more, the military instrument remained firmly in the service of political motives, and thus it is to the complexity of the political process that this analysis must turn.

Course of Events

Despite the early 1950s atmosphere in Sino-Indian relations created by the 'five principles of peaceful coexistence', disputed border problems remained unresolved. Talks on the issue had been held, but no solution found. On this background of uncertainty, Tibet, China's province bordering on India, flared into rebellion in 1959. This coupled with deteriorating economic conditions in the rest of China, and a worsening split with the Soviet Union, meant that Beijing's confidence in handling problems on its southwest frontier was shakier than it might have been.[3]

In August 1959 India and China had fought a brief but bloody clash over parts of the disputed territory. In the summer of 1961 Indian reconnaissance discovered that in the Aksai Chin area of China's western border, claimed by India, China had constructed a road linking Xinjiang and Tibet. Towards the end of 1961 India formulated a 'forward policy' in the border area to give substance to Indian territorial claims. But the Himalayan winter soon terminated any movement for the moment. On 26 February 1962 China protested about the forward policy but it was not until late April that China resumed patrols in this western sector.[4]

Shooting incidents were reported in May with ambiguous Chinese signalling in an attempt to deter Indian encroachment. To make matters more confusing, in June China ignored the border problem and focused on the brief crisis over the Taiwan Straits. Early in July Chinese attention was yanked back to the Aksai Chin as a Chinese post at Galwan was cut off by the establishment of an Indian position. China responded by surrounding the Indian troops but not eliminating them. Chinese deterrance signals increased, especially after a clash later in July resulted in casualties.

The next month was quiet as India indicated that there was still some room for talks on border issues. The lull ended on 22 August when India indicated far less willingness to negotiate and China resumed reporting border incidents. In early September Beijing clearly moved into another gear, on the one hand setting a firm date for talks (15 October) and on the other responding more forcefully to Indian posts established in territory claimed by China. In June India had established a post at Dhola across the disputed MacMahon Line in the North East Frontier Area (NEFA). But in September China began applying pressure to the position. At first India seemed to respond to this pressure and on 19 September agreed to some sort of talks as China requested.

These already dim hopes were darkened still further on 20 September when a border clash, apparently instigated by China, resulted in relatively heavy casualties. The Chinese policy on the crisis was less than consistent and Beijing did not reply to the 19 September Indian statement until 3 October. On 6 October the atmosphere had clearly deteriorated; India finally made clear that talks were no longer possible. Chinese attempts at deterrence of India had all but failed. On 10 October an Indian patrol advanced to cut off a Chinese position near Dhola and the PLA initiated combat with a brief but swift victory. India ignored this last attempt at a forceful deterrence message and on 12 October Nehru reportedly ordered the Chinese to be evicted from the NEFA. It was apparently at this point, after the passing of the 15 October deadline for talks, that China decided to 'teach India a lesson'.

Chinese compellence of India to withdraw from its forward policy was begun ruthlessly on 20 October. Indian troops withdrew swiftly, but in the three week lull after the PLA offensive, India made it plain that it was bloodied but not bowed. It was also at this stage that the superpowers, having emerged distinctly shaken from the Cuban missile crisis, took an interest in the Himalayan events.

India sought a second round of conflict with China and a local offensive was launched on 14 November. It was easily rebuffed by China and Beijing moved to deliver the final crushing part of its military lesson. By 18 November PLA forces broke through Indian lines again. With the Indians in panic, China declared a unilateral ceasefire and withdrew its forces to the lines it had originally proposed. India never formally accepted the Chinese ceasefire, but at no time did India violate the Chinese terms. On the surface it appeared to be a successful surgical strike—a model of calculated and calibrated use of force. Was it really that impressive?

Objectives

Chinese objectives in the Sino-Indian war are overwhelmingly based on a perceived vulnerability to Indian territorial encroachments. Thus China sought first to deter India, and when that failed, to compel an Indian retreat. Analysts have already made clear that although China's signalling may have been faulty and its paranoia about Indian threats exaggerated, there is little dispute that Beijing was acting, as in Korea, out of defensive motives. However—and here the Korean experience continues to be instructive—it appears that in the final phase following the October offensives, China seized the opportunity provided by an advantageous military balance, to pursue wider and less defensive objectives. Unlike Korea, where China faced a far more impressive military power, Beijing could obtain its wider objectives in 1962 because Indian power was so feeble. Thus political objectives motivated the initial use of force, but military success provided the political leaders with new, and perhaps unexpected options.

To dwell excessively on the offensive phase is to miss the significance of the far more crucial defensive phase. China viewed India's forward policy as a threat for three main reasons. First, unrest in Tibet, while obviously indigenous, did have important aid from outside via India. Second, the western sector of the disputed Sino-Indian frontier was of undoubted strategic value to China. The portion of that border touching Xinjiang had become even more sensitive to Beijing in the wake of the deepening split with another state bordering on Xinjiang—the Soviet Union. Third, while China had made it plain that it was not going to insist on holding territory south of the MacMahon line in the eastern sector, it would resist any further encroachment north of the line.[5] The Dhola post set up in June was clearly north of the MacMahon line.

Chinese defensive motives seem relatively clear. It is equally clear that, as in Korea, China decided to adopt a forward defence 'at the gates' rather than be content to allow a potential enemy to be 'lured in deep'. Apparently an established state with vulnerable frontiers could not be allowed the luxury of a 'luring in deep' strategy. Forward defence was especially required not so much because the Indian threat was powerful, but more because China's hold on Tibet seemed weak.

The necessity to define China's forward defence came in response to India's forward policy, especially after April 1962. Chinese deterrence was often inconsistent in application, but the basic defensive motive was always retained. China resumed patrols in the western sector in April only after India became more bold in its patrols. In May, after the first serious shooting incidents, China's verbal deterrence changed qualitatively when it warned India privately that 'it would not sit idly by'—a key phrase from the Korean war that, as Allen Whiting points out, India should have recognized as serious.[6] But this excessive warning in the face of no new Indian moves, coupled with the wild fluctuations in the intensity of attention in Beijing given to the frontier, did not make for the clearest of communications.

Only from July, following the Taiwan Straits diversion, did China begin to engage in more coherent deterrence. But all the previous fluctuations in the Chinese line did little to encourage India to heed the warnings. Chinese ham-handedness in communication is certainly obvious when compared to the Korean war. In July 1962 the *People's Daily* warned about going to 'the brink of the precipice'[7] and the Ministry of Foreign Affairs warned that China 'can by no means sit idle',[8] but neither statement reflected any real increase in tension. Much like the Taiwan Straits hyperbole of 1954 and 1958, China was undermining its own ability to be believed when it really needed to be. This crying wolf may have moderated the Indian line on negotiations, but in the longer run it was a waste of precious verbal capital.

The August lull once again undercut Chinese deterrence as the stop–go crisis atmosphere was not conducive to credibility of communication. Chinese warnings were renewed, beginning with the secret Ministry of Foreign Affairs note of 5 September, setting the 15 October deadline for talks.[9] More importantly, China began to integrate its military actions more urgently with the verbal warnings. On 8 September Chinese pressure was applied on the Dhola post, but the fact that it came three months after the position was established, did little to reinforce India's belief in China's sincerity. On 13 September China had called the Dhola post a 'new development'.[10]

To make matters worse, after India on 19 September, seemed to accept the 15 October date, China opened fire near Dhola while issuing patently false battle reports. At least Beijing's verbal position matched its new bellicosity by warning that China could not 'look on idly while its frontier guards are being mercilessly killed'.[11] But China failed to respond to the 19 September Indian note until 3 October and even then it was an ambiguous reply.[12]

On 6 October, it was clear to China that its deterrence had all but failed when India swiftly rejected the Chinese note of 3 October that held open the door to talks. China's last attempt to deter the Indian forward policy then followed with the 10 October attack at Dhola, but Nehru still declared two days later that the PLA had to be evicted from the NEFA.[13] China's abandonment of deterrence in favour of compellence was marked by the *People's Daily* the day before the talks deadline, when it warned that a 'massive invasion' of Tibet 'seems imminent' and Chinese forbearance should not be mistaken for weakness.[14]

The coercive phase of Chinese objectives could not have been more successful. Indian forces were crushed; China seized all its objectives in the disputed territory, and more, in little more than a day. But now Chinese objectives appeared to broaden. On 22 October China had claimed it was merely trying 'to prevent the aggressive Indian troops from renewing their attack' and expanding the border clashes. China was concerned that India wanted to 'stage a come-back' and 'launch fresh attacks'.[15] But if that were truly the case, then China might have imperiously announced its unilateral ceasefire and withdrawal in the third week of October (and still demoralized India). But apparently China was not prepared for such an easy victory. Objectives were therefore changed on the run. When India was given a chance to catch its breadth and try a re-match in the NEFA, China seemed to see an opportunity not merely to defend its security (that was already accomplished) but also to teach several people a lesson. Not only was India to be taught that it was no match for Chinese power in Asia, but its claim to lead the non-aligned movement also took a knock. Lessons were also no doubt intended for other, more important, new spectators—the superpowers. Recently emerged from the glimpse of the nuclear abyss in Cuba, the superpowers could be shown that emergent China was a power to be reckoned with.

It is true that India gave China no reason to think that it had accepted Chinese terms for talks since the October fighting. But neither did India accept Chinese terms after November and then China seemed satisfied with its unilateral ceasefire. It is also notable that in the three week lull between combat China showed no signs of pursuing a new deterrent posture. Certainly there were no coherent graduated warnings of renewed combat.[16] In fact China professed pacific intentions to talk when it was essentially gearing up its logistics for a purely punitive punch.

In sum, the first Chinese objective of deterring threats to its security failed by a combination of its own incompetence and Indian insensitivity. China's second objective, compellence of India to withdraw, was a striking success. So much so that China found it convenient to pursue a third objective—the teaching of a lesson to India and other onlookers. Here too China was successful, if only because it picked on a weak and unprepared India. China could be pleased that its objectives were finally obtained, although foreign observers had reason to be concerned with the all too simple transition from defence to offence.

Operations

The operation of Chinese military strategy during the Sino-Indian war was successful primarily because of Beijing's political acumen.

To be sure there were important errors in Chinese signalling and deterrence, but when the time came for combat, there was no question of Chinese superiority. However, the causes of success are not attributable to any single strategy. Rather the reasons for success can be traced to a complex inter-weaving of strategy, fortune, and enemy errors.

The scale of combat in 1962 was obviously greater than in the Quemoy engagements, but it did not begin to approach the nature of the full-scale Korean war. The pre-war engagements were all carried out by local frontier guards who had more than sufficient local strength.[17] Even in the war itself, PLA strength rose by at most one fifth to 150,000 and it seems apparent that these numbers were by no means crucial for the actual operations.[18] The scale of losses was also relatively small. While Indian dead and missing totalled about 3000, the PLA losses are thought to have been much less. China captured 3968 Indian soldiers, but not a single PLA man was captured.[19]

Chinese success can be basically attributed to Indian folly in engaging the PLA where and when it did. There is little question that Indian military strength was far below that which could pose a serious threat to Chinese territory. This Chinese superiority was always obvious and derived from action taken to rectify previous Chinese weakness in the area. It had been the instability in Tibet and the initial military operation to seize the territory in 1950, that brought the two Chinese divisions to the area. It was continuing unrest in Tibet that kept the troops on the alert and well trained. It was also the continuing unrest that ensured superior PLA logistics, troops trained in mountain warfare, and above all a vigilant attitude attuned to local conditions.[20]

Neither did China employ any special strategy, be it Maoist or otherwise. To a certain extent the strictures of people's war were met more by China in that its forces were well integrated into local conditions. But in the final analysis it was a series of limited engagements in forbidding and barren territory. There were no people to provide the sea for the PLA to swim in. The specific strategy used was logical and practical from the PLA point of view.[21] The one aspect of strategy that was most distinctive was the evident Chinese decision to engage in forward defence. As we have already seen in previous case studies, this decision was more usual than unusual for a state sensitive to frontier encroachment. China's decision to protect

Tibet's frontiers and to develop the infrastructure and PLA power to do so, was the key strategic success.

Chinese discussions of military strategy at the time of the war also make it plain that the most crucial strategic choices were overarching political ones, and not specific military manoeuvres.[22] As was indeed vindicated by events, China had more than enough local PLA power to engage Indian forces in frontal combat. No subterfuge, or even sophisticated military camouflage was necessary—so confident was China of its military power.

The specific tactics adopted by the PLA were very impressive, but then the opposition was hardly a fair match. On only one occasion did India initiate combat (at times its patrols would encircle, but not attack PLA posts) and at no time did Indian troops even have local superiority. The Chinese had superior logistics which allowed troops and material to be brought to bear far more efficiently. The Chinese had superior training which allowed its superior equipment, especially artillery, to be used with devastating effect. The Chinese had superior intelligence which seemed to anticipate India's every move. When PLA forces struck it was with accurate and overwhelming artillery fire (as learned from the Soviet Union) and then followed by fierce assault, often by surrounding the enemy position. So-called human wave tactics were only used to take isolated and crucial positions. This combination of conventional tactics mixed with aspects of guerilla war was so overpowering that China never tried to hide its preparations for attacks (as it did in Korea).[23] The only important limits on the ability of the PLA to attack was the difficult logistical problems of the Himalayas. After the 20 October offensive, the three week lull was necessary for China to build new roads and bring up new supplies. Indian forces fled faster than the Chinese advance.[24]

The combat was entirely between ground forces. Air power was not used by India for fear of reported Chinese superiority in this service. India also feared the escalation of an air war that might bring attacks on the more vulnerable Indian cities. In fact once the combat was under way, it was suddenly, and surprisingly clear to India that it was a poor match for PLA power.

As we have already seen in other PLA operations in the 1950s, successful military operations opened up new political opportunities. In this 1962 case the vast PLA superiority opened up even more choices than before, and allowed Beijing a virtually clean sheet on which to write its objectives. It would be nice for Chinese military strategists to claim that this favourable state of affairs was due to their intelligent planning and superior strategy. Unfortunately, it seems more likely that Chinese success had more to do with Indian omissions than with Chinese commissions.

So far the analysis of Chinese military operations against India in the border war has suggested it was an entirely bilateral affair. Where were the superpowers, not to mention other Asian states, when the two major Asian powers went to war? Unlike the Korean and Quemoy incidents, in the 1962 war China was not confronting a superpower, even in an indirect fashion. The sources of China's insecurity about the Sino-Indian border may in part have involved superpower policy, but at most it was a minor consideration in Beijing.

As has already been suggested, China's concern over unrest in Tibet was aggravated by the international context. The most important change was the deterioration in relations with China's superpower ally, the Soviet Union. The significance of the Sino-Soviet split should not be underestimated.[25] But it should also be recalled that China's drift away from the Soviet orbit was in large part Beijing's own choice. China was deeply dissatisfied with various aspects of Soviet policy, too complex to be recapitulated here. But what is most important to recall is that China was not necessarily perceiving itself to be weak because of the split. China had sought an alliance with Moscow in the late 1940s when China did feel weak and vulnerable. But in the early 1960s, despite important domestic difficulties, China felt more confident in denouncing the bankruptcy of Soviet foreign policy. Thus an understanding of the Sino-Soviet split is necessary for an appreciation of Beijing's policy in 1962, but it does not necessarily indicate that China saw itself as weak.

The other superpower, the United States played a less important role in the 1962 events. There were good grounds for China to denounce American involvement in support of Tibetan rebels, but certainly by 1962 the Tibetan unrest was easily under control. The US factor was more important in the brief unrest over the 1962 Taiwan Straits crisis, but once again China had reason to feel buoyed up by its encounter with the superpower, rather than defensive and weak. The 1962 Taiwan events were in fact a pseudo-crisis, but one in which China had reason to feel confident that it had deterred Chiang Kai-shek's desires to return to the mainland.

Thus in the case of both superpowers China was of course acutely aware of their policy changes. But in both cases the superpower's actions could be seen to encourage, rather than discourage China's firm response to India. In both cases the superpowers were unable to bully China, and after recent incidents on the frontiers with Taiwan and the Soviet Union, China saw an even greater need to send a strong signal to India. Beijing's ability to send such a signal was enhanced by the fact that the superpowers were obsessed with the Cuban missile crisis. Allen Whiting has already persuasively argued that the coincidence of Himalayan and Caribbean crises was striking but not planned.[27]

It is therefore not surprising that China's build up to crisis with India made little reference to either superpower. China's grievances were stated almost exclusively in bilateral terms. To the extent that the US figured in Chinese commentaries it was in the context of the receding Taiwan crisis.[28] Beijing was far more interested in appealing to fellow third world states, as the context of the 1962 border war involved China's prestige as an Asian power far more than its relations with the superpowers.[29] Local Asian states, such as Pakistan, were particularly present in Chinese appeals of this type.

Where the superpowers did seem to play a more important role, albeit still not in a major or direct way, was after the passing of the Cuban missile crisis. It is striking that the Chinese press only began involving the US in a direct way as responsible for Indian 'aggressiveness', after the Cuban crisis had passed.[30] There was never much truth to the Chinese allegations of Western machinations, and when the US did appear to become seriously involved in support for India, it was only after the threatening Chinese attacks in November. If Chinese actions were really based on perceptions of US involvement (in fact they were not), then the Chinese military response resulted in a self-fulfilling prophecy.

The Soviet superpower did not figure directly in Chinese commentary, even after the Cuban crisis. But later Chinese comments, both about the Sino-Indian war and the Cuban crisis, make it plain that China was concerned about Soviet policy in the phase after China's first offensive.[31] Not only did the Soviet Union cease its verbal support for China in the border war, which had been given when Moscow sought support over Cuba. But more importantly China perceived the Soviet Union had given the non-communist world the wrong signal after its dismal performance in Cuba. What was needed was a more forthright, less capitulationist line in the face of imperalist threats. Thus it is possible that the important changes in Soviet policy spurred China on to teach a lesson to India. Beijing might have hoped some of the lesson would have sunk in in Moscow as well.

This analysis of the period leading up to China's offensive phase of compellence in November 1962 obviously contains a great deal of conjecture. Even if the assumptions are accepted, it still remains clear that superpower influence on the Sino-Indian border war remains marginal at most. Chinese operations were determined overwhelmingly by bilateral relations with India. Delhi's failure to respond to Chinese deterrence, and then its pathetic behaviour in the face of Chinese compellence, were the most crucial aspects in explaining the pace and scope of Chinese actions. The one remaining crucial area of analysis is the question of Chinese domestic policy and its affect on the war. It has already been suggested that China's insecurity about border provocations had a great deal to do with domestic unrest, but it seems that complex leadership politics also affected Chinese defence policy.

The Domestic Dimension

It has been suggested China might have over-reacted to the extent of the Indian threat along the frontier, but that the over-reaction was understandable in the light of China's weak internal position. It is undeniable that China did have some serious internal problems, including a revolt in Tibet and a flood of refugees across the Xinjiang border into Soviet Asia.[32] But these immense and disturbing difficulties occurred well before the 1962 crisis with India. At most these events could have served as general background for Chinese decisions in October 1962, but not anywhere near a dominating motive force. In September 1962, Mao declared that matters had indeed been bad in China, but they were now clearly improving.[33]

A similar pattern is apparent in leadership debates in China. Undoubtedly there were differences of opinion on a number of political issues in China in the wake of the Great Leap Forward's collapse. Opposition to Mao centred on Liu Shaoqi and Deng Xiaoping, and led to greater liberalization especially in the commune policy, and a toleration of dissident intellectuals such as Wu Han and Deng Tuo.[34] In 1962 there were open moves to have the verdict on Peng Dehuai reversed and in June Peng produced an 80,000 word document in his support.[35] What is more, there were clearly links to foreign policy in these opposition voices to Mao.

Some leaders urged 'three reconciliations and one reduction'; reconciliation with 'imperialists, the reactionaries, and the revisionists' and reducing support for national liberation movements.[36] Deng Tuo ridiculed Mao's 'east wind prevails over the west wind' slogan as nothing more than 'hackneyed phrases without much meaning', and urged instead an improvement of relations with both superpowers.[37] Obviously there was some dissent on foreign policy, but it is also notable that by the summer of 1962 even these leadership differences seem to be gradually resolved in Mao's favour. In August Deng Tuo's criticism was terminated and Peng Dehuai and his associates were not allowed to take part in the tenth CCP plenum in September.

Neither were there any important splits in PLA policy. In fact this aspect of Chinese politics was more stable than it had been for years, with general agreement among supporters of both the 'red' and 'expert' line in the PLA. Military training was pursued and obedience to Party control was not neglected. Obviously there were important readjustments made after the cessation of Soviet aid, but certainly by 1962 the PLA seemed to be one of the more stable Chinese institutions.[38] The PLA was also the key institution in which Mao seemed to be most influential. Neither was there any important evidence that regional/centre splits accounted for PLA reaction along the distant frontier. All analysts agree that one of the more remarkable aspects of the crisis was the firm central control maintained over combat carried on at the remotest points of Chinese control.[39]

Thus the domestic context of China's border war in 1962 was far from certain, but it certainly was not one of open and unrestrained unrest. If anything there was a trend towards greater stability and unity in Chinese policy. Following the July Taiwan Straits crisis there was in fact even more grounds for confidence, not weakness, in China. Indeed it can be argued that China's intense interest in the Sino-Indian border, which began in August, was the product of confidence, and a new determination to sort out the Indians once and for all. Previous procrastination and uncertain signals may well have had much to do with unrest in China, but the main portion of the Sino-Indian crisis occurred under conditions of growing unity and security in China.

It can be argued that the 'three reconciliations and one reduction' argument helped keep the Chinese reaction to Indian encroachments from being very vigorous. It is therefore not surprising that important differences of opinon did not recur during the course of the crisis as to just how forward the Chinese position should be. While it is not possible to identify clear factions, let alone a consistent and coherent debate on this matter, there were undoubtedly noticeable differences in some aspects of Chinese policy. Previous analysts have suggested that these differences may in part explain the less than efficient Chinese signalling process.[40]

The lengthy delay between the crucial Indian note of 19 September and the Chinese response of 3 October may well have been one of these examples of domestic politics affecting the border conflict. This was also the period of the CCP's tenth plenum where leadership unity was being re-established.[41] Also, of the first Chinese statements after the outbreak of hostilities on 20 October, some omitted a crucial conciliatory line.[42] But it could not be argued that Chinese leaders were using the crisis for domestic purposes, for the near absence of public campaigns of prominent media coverage meant no attempt at general mobilization was being made.

The absence of Chinese manipulation of external events for internal purposes did not mean that internal affairs did not affect foreign policy. The most powerful evidence for some continuation of the three reconciliations debate, came after the Chinese attack in October. At the time when decisions were being taken whether to carry on the second phase of the campaign or settle for what was already gained, important differences appeared in the Chinese press. Precisely at the time when Premier Zhou Enlai was sending pacific signals to India and even the *People's Daily* was echoing the moderate line, another, more jarring hard line was also heard. On 27 October, in the same issue of the *People's Daily* as a soft line editorial, the editorial department issued 'More and Nehru's Philosophy in the Light of the Sino-Indian Boundary Dispute'.[43] Bearing many hallmarks of Mao's punishing polemics of the Sino-Soviet dispute in the following months, this harsh article suggested a greater need for struggle and a less tolerant line towards Indian intentions.

As the decision in November to punish India more firmly

approached, this hard line slowly gained greater adherence in the Chinese press.[44] The softer line was most noticeable in statements by Zhou Enlai and Chen Yi, but it was gradually superseded by editorials in the *People's Daily* urging firmer struggle against India and its supporters in the United States. These two lines may have been merely the result of a subtle carrot and stick strategy. But they are strikingly similar to earlier disagreements in China and therefore more probably represent real differences of opinion. Whatever the case, it made for confusing signals to India.

The triumph of what was probably a Maoist harder line must not have been achieved at high cost. It is noticeable that the Cultural Revolution threw up no evidence of such a dispute even though it did offer glimpses of various other debates, including the three reconciliations one before the 1962 border war. This complex picture of undoubted but limited debate, is illuminated by other evidence of leadership politics, particularly concerning the PLA.

One of the more remarkable aspects of leadership politics during the war was the total absence of the Chinese Defence Minister Lin Biao, and his replacement in official functions by Chief of Staff Luo Ruiqing. It will be recalled that Luo was later on purged, in part for urging a more forward position in reaction to the US threat in Vietnam. Was Luo also espousing a more forward line in the 1962 war and was Lin perhaps in eclipse for having refused Mao's urgings to back this more aggressive line?

On Army Day (1 August) it was Luo not Lin who gave the ceremonial banquet and took a much harder line than many other Chinese spokesmen by specifically mentioning the Sino-Indian border. Luo warned India not to mistake Chinese forbearance for weakness.[45] Other PLA related statements at the time were not nearly as forthright about the Indian threat.[46] Lin Biao was not even mentioned in the Army Day celebrations, except in some isolated provincial examples.[47] On China's national day (1 October) Luo was present as the leading PLA official, but once again Lin Biao was not.[48] More crucially, on 6 October, after India's rejection of the 15 October talks deadline, Mao met PLA delegates to the national day celebrations. Luo was present but Lin was not.[49] Luo officiated at the PLA banquet that night, but without mentioning India in his speech. If there was a disagreement (and Lin was not simply ill), then Mao seemed to have given support to Luo and his harder line.

But such a hard line/soft line division cannot be so simply drawn.

On 25 October, after the first Chinese offensive had paused, Luo attended a banquet given by the Korean chargé d'affaires on the twelfth anniversary of the PLA entry into the Korean war. The occasion was pregnant with symbolism of Chinese determination to pursue a forward policy. But Luo's speech, in the presence of Zhou Enlai, was moderate, and certainly nothing like the sharp tone of the hard line statement that was to follow on 27 October.[50] It is possible to suggest that at this stage Luo might have felt the fighting was over, or perhaps should be over. The decision to push forward was apparently taken later, but there is reason to believe that Luo might not have been among its supporters.

It seems clear that there were important differences of opinion in the Chinese leadership as to how the war should be prosecuted. While this domestic dimension does not explain why China tried to deter and eventually compel Indian actions, it does help explain some of the less logical and less well planned aspects of Chinese policy. It is however not possible to suggest neat theories about factions and differences of opinion and how they affected policy. The apparently changing positions of Luo Ruiqing illustrate that simple factional or institutional politics do not explain the complexity of positions taken during the course of the war. Perhaps in this very complexity lies the explanation of why policy disputes were not revealed later during the Cultural Revolution. If some of the above assumptions are correct, Lin Biao and Zhou Enlai opposed action that Mao and Luo supported. This was hardly the pattern of leadership splits that emerged during the Cultural Revolution.

Conclusions

The essential flexibility in China's use of military force in foreign policy was vividly illustrated in the Sino-Indian border war. China perceived itself to be under threat from India's border encroachments and, on the basis of recent history of domestic unrest, China exaggerated the importance of that threat. These misperceptions obviously had a basis in fact, but on balance the scale of the border war, as eventually waged by China was unnecessary.

Chinese objectives, albeit irregularly pursued, were to deter Indian attacks and safeguard China's definition of the frontier. India repeatedly ignored Chinese warnings and felt that Beijing would not escalate the conflict. By October, when it was clear that negotiations had failed, the PLA struck a compelling blow. The swift collapse of Indian forces at least made plain that China never really faced an important military threat in the Himalayas. Having swiftly swept Indian forces aside, China found itself with new options, previously unplanned. Beijing then decided to punish India and teach it, and to a certain extent other onlooking states, that China was a serious power not to be trifled with. This final phase of Chinese objectives was largely aggressive, and out of keeping with the original motive for sending the PLA forward.

Chinese strategy was successful in obtaining its objectives primarily because of superior logistics and planning. No particular military strategy was employed other than the most suitable pragmatic one in Himalayan conditions. India's dismal performance, more than anything else, made Chinese military power appear impressive. Unlike the Korean and Taiwan crises, in the 1962 case Chinese aggressive phases of operations were successful largely because of the pitiful opponent.

The military success should not shroud the fact that China's diplomatic posture, in projecting deterrence messages, was pretty poor. Confusion resulted from numerous factors, including intruding external events, and above all domestic politics in China. Although it was not possible to identify coherent factions, it was clear that differences of policy did appear in China. The proponents of a harder or softer line did not fit any neat categories and some figures appeared in different groups at different times. This complex decision making process only added to a crisis based largely on mutual misperception. It was a war wanted by no one. In the end it was China that made the best of the unfortunate situation.

NOTES

1. Neville Maxwell, *India's China War* (London: Penguin, 1972), p. 374.
2. On the Indian side see *ibid*. On China see especially Allen Whiting, *The Chinese Calculus of Deterrence* (Ann Arbor: The University of Michigan Press, 1975). Also Melvin Gurtov and Byoong-Moo Hwang, *China Under Threat* (Baltimore: Johns Hopkins University Press, 1980). For the great power context see Gerald Segal, *The Great Power Triangle* (London: Macmillan, 1982) Ch. 3. For some modification of Whiting's approach see Edward Freedman, 'Comment' in *The China Quarterly*, No. 63, 1975, pp. 528–38 and a reply in No. 65.
3. Details for this section based on *ibid*.
4. For details see Whiting, and Gurtov and Hwang, *ibid*.

5. On the Chinese border position see Alastair Lamb, *The China–India Border* (London: Oxford University Press, 1964).
6. Whiting, *Chinese Calculus*, pp. 58–9.
7. *People's Daily*, 9 July 1962 in *SCMP* No. 2778 pp. 24–5. See also *Observer*, 21 July 1962 in No. 2786, pp. 25–8.
8. *SCMP* No. 2787, p. 27.
9. Whiting, *Chinese Calculus*, pp. 95–6.
10. NCNA 13 September in *SCMP*, No. 2821, p. 33.
11. *People's Daily* Editorial, 22 September 1962 in *SCMP*, No. 2827, p. 25.
12. Released 6 October 1962, *SCMP*, No. 2837, p. 23.
13. Whiting, *Chinese Calculus*, pp. 112–14.
14. *People's Daily* Editorial, 14 October 1962 in *SCMP* No. 2842, pp. 25–6.
15. Ministry of Defence, 22 October 1962 in *SCMP* No. 2846, pp. 23–4.
16. Zhou Enlai, 4 November 1962 in *SCMP* No. 2856, p. 37; Chen I on 7 November in No. 2858, p. 27; *People's Daily* Editorial, 8 November in No. 2860, pp. 36–8; *People's Daily Observer*, 11 November in No. 2861, pp. 25–8.
17. For example NCNA, 23 September 1962 in *SCMP* No. 2828, p. 21, and NCNA, 24 September p. 22.
18. Whiting, *Chinese Calculus*, p. 93.
19. *Ibid*, p. 149.
20. Two revealing glimpses of Indian weakness and Chinese strength came from two Indian military men's memoirs. J. P. Dalvi, *Himalayan Blunder* (Bombay: Thacker and Co., 1969); B. M. Kaul, *The Untold Story* (Bombay: Allied Publishers, 1967).
21. See a report on PLA training in *Nang-fang Jih-pao* 26 July 1962, in *SCMP* No. 2834, pp. 7–8.
22. For example Hsiao Hua in Red Flag No. 15–16, 1 August 1962. *SCMM* No. 328, pp. 7–8. T'ang Ping-chu in *People's Daily* 15 May 1962 in *SCMP* No. 2753, pp. 2–5. Huang Sen in *Kung-jen Jih-pao*, 27 July 1962 in No. 2799, pp. 2–3.
23. See note 20 and Maxwell, *India's War*, pp. 363, 367, 374, 387.
24. Whiting, *Chinese Calculus*, p. 137.
25. Segal, *The Triangle*, Ch. 3.
26. *Ibid*, and Whiting, *Chinese Calculus*.
27. Whiting, *Chinese Calculus*, pp. 15–18.
28. *People's Daily Observer*, 21 July 1962 in *SCMP* No. 2786, pp. 25–8; Lo Jui-ch'ing on Army Day in *Liberation Army Daily*, 1 August 1962 in No. 2801, pp. 4–7; *People's Daily* Editorial, 22 September 1962 in No. 2827, pp. 24–5.
29. Segal, *The Triangle*, Ch. 3.
30. *People's Daily*, 27 October 1962, 'More on Nehru's Philosophy in the Light of the Sino-Indian Boundary Dispute', *BBC*/SWB/FE/1055/A3/5–9. Chen I, 7 November 1962 in *SCMP* No. 2858, pp. 27–8; *People's Daily* Editorial, 8 November 1962 in No. 2860, pp. 36–8.
31. Segal, *The Triangle*, Ch. 3.
32. Gurtov and Hwang, *China Under Threat*, pp. 98–103.
33. Mao at 10th Plenum on 24 September 1962, translated in Stuart Schram, *Mao Tse-tung Unrehearsed* (London: Penguin, 1974), p. 190.
34. Gurtov and Hwang, *China Under Threat*, pp. 106–7. Ellis Joffe, *Between Two Plenums: China Intraleadership Conflict, 1959–1962* (Michigan Papers in Chinese Studies No. 22, 1975); Richard Baum and Frederick Teiwes, *Ssu-Ch'ing: The Socialist Education Movement of 1962–1966* (University of California: China Research Monograph No. 2, 1968).
35. Joffe, *Between Two Plenums*.
36. *Chinese Law and Government*. Spring 1968, pp. 78–9.

37. Merle Goldman, 'The Unique Blooming and Contending of 1961–1962', *The China Quarterly* No. 37, January 1969, pp. 76–82.
38. Gurtov and Hwang, *China Under Threat*, pp. 110–14; Ellis Joffe, *Party and Army* (Cambridge: Harvard University Press, 1971).
39. This was despite earlier control problems noted in the PLA Bulletin of Activities. J. Chester Cheng ed., *The Politics of the Chinese Red Army* (Stanford: Hoover Institution, 1966).
40. Developed in both Whiting, *Chinese Calculus*, and Gurtov and Hwang, *China Under Threat*.
41. Whiting, *Chinese Calculus*, pp. 108–9.
42. *Ibid*, p. 122.
43. *People's Daily* Editorial, 27 October 1962 in *SCMP* No. 2850, pp. 22–5; Editorial Department in *BBC*/SWB/FE/1085/A3/5–9.
44. Zhou Enlai, 4 November 1962 in *SCMP* No. 2856, p. 37; Chen I on 7 November in No. 2858, p. 27, and 9 November in No. 2860, p. 31; *People's Daily* Editorial, 8 November in No. 2860, pp. 36–8; *People's Daily Observer*, 11 November in No. 2861, pp. 25–8; *Red Flag* Editorial in NCNA, 17 November in No. 2864, pp. 25–8; on the same day Zhou's moderate letter, pp. 28–30.
45. *SCMP* No. 2794, pp. 1–2, and 2801 for full text.
46. *People's Daily* 1 August 1962 in *SCMP* No. 2794, p. 3; Huang Seb in *Kung-jen Jih-pao*, 27 July 1962 in No. 2799, pp. 2–3; *Liberation Army Daily*, 1 August reprinted in *People's Daily*, 2 August No. 2801, pp. 4–7; Hsiao Hua in Red Flag No. 15–16, 1 August 1962 in *SCMM* No. 328.
47. Canton, *Nan-fang Jih-pao*, 1 August 1962 in *SCMP* No. 2814, pp. 4–6.
48. *BBC*/SWB/FE/1063.
49. *SCMP* No. 2842, pp. 1–2.
50. *SCMP* No. 2850, pp. 25–6.

9

Vietnam, 1964–1965

China's role in the Vietnam war is a special example of the use of armed force in Chinese foreign policy. Its importance is derived in part from the fact that for long portions of the war, the US saw its involvement as the necessary attempt to block the spread of China's extremist brand of communism. It is one of many ironies in this war that by the time the US pulled out of Vietnam, it had come to see the war as more an anti-Soviet struggle, with China as a tacit ally against Moscow's influence.

The distinctiveness of this war for Chinese foreign policy is also based on at least four other aspects. First, more than any other post-war conflict, the Vietnam war dominated China's perception of a hostile outside world for the longest period. Second, the most intense period of the war, from 1965–8, was also the peak of the greatest period of Chinese domestic unrest, the Great Proletarian Cultural Revolution. Third, the war was a complex affair for China, particularly in that in many senses China perceived two discrete sub-wars—the air and the ground threats. Finally, unlike any of the previous case studies, the war had no clear end to hostilities until 1975 and thus for close to ten years China never fully lowered its guard. Neat theories of crisis management do not suit this messy war.

Thus this chapter only deals with part of the Vietnam war. However, it is the part in which China's basic approach was established and most of what followed amounted to variations on the same theme. Certainly to the extent that China ever perceived the war to be a crisis, this was confined to the 1964–5 period.[1]

The Course of Events

Three important phases of this part of the Vietnam war can be identified. The first began slowly in early 1964, as the Johnson administration gradually increased its air attacks on the Democratic Republic of Vietnam (DRV).[2] China moved to deter the attack with strong words of support for Hanoi including the statements that China 'could not sit idly by' and expressions of unity 'as lips and teeth'. This exaggerated response to a relatively minor American threat was seen to have failed to deter US threats to North Vietnam when, following the 2 August Gulf of Tonkin incident, the US replied with direct attacks on the DRV.

China responded by even more prominent public statements of support, but more importantly it also began to act in military terms. New airfields and joint operations with the DRV into 1965 lent a more concrete meaning to Chinese words. However although the air war did not cease, once the initial crisis passed China did come to feel more secure. Coupled with political reassessments following the removal of Khrushchev in October 1964, in China the Vietnam war came to be seen as less serious than it had been in mid–1964.

The second phase of the war began in March 1965, when US ground troops began to be introduced into Vietnam. It was the threat of war on the ground that potentially posed the most serious threat to the DRV and ultimately to China. Beijing began to offer troops to Hanoi and, especially by June, the Chinese expression of concern reached new levels. However the military response was complicated by evident disagreements in China on various issues, including domestic policy, relations with the Soviet Union, and the strategic response to the US threat. By September China reinforced its words with action by the despatch of support troops to the DRV.

It is difficult to pinpoint the date when China felt fairly confident that it could contain even the US ground threat. Debates, and above all the uncertain US response made any calculation in Beijing inevitably short term. The opening shots of the Cultural Revolution and the purge of PLA Chief of Staff Luo Ruiqing in November indicates that by then at least a certain amount of confidence was felt by those in charge. As in the first phase of the air war, no clear end to tensions is identifiable. So long as US air and ground forces remained in strength, it would have been foolish to lower the guard entirely.

Thus the third phase began in uncertainty and continued largely unchanged until the DRV victory in 1975. Certainly from 1966 onward, Beijing seemed fairly confident that the threat of war would be contained. Fluctuation in this confidence did occur, notably in March, May, and July 1966 when domestic and foreign policy debates flared up. The embers of conflict and uncertainty were not to be extinguished until 1975.[3] Those seeking precise ends to crises or neat patterns to Beijing's use of force are hampered by the expedient conduct of conflict and the uncertainty over how wars end.

Objectives

Chinese objectives in the Vietnam war were not very similar to previous conflicts already analysed. The special characteristics are derived mostly from the fact that Beijing's objectives remained fairly consistent, low key and defensive. While policy debates obviously raged, China tended to hold to limited, safe policies.

In the first phase, from March 1964 to March 1965, Chinese objectives seemed primarily to deter air threats to the DRV. This was neither an objective to be pursued at all costs, nor one that obtained complete success. By its very vagueness, the objective left room for expedient policies and judgement of relative success. Certainly from March to June 1964 China did not appear unduly alarmed at US threats to the DRV. In February 1964 Mao had even said, 'If the Americans quit Formosa (Taiwan) there is no reason why they should not be our friends too.'[4]

In June, China suddenly stepped up its warnings, as if it only then came to see the growing escalation of the US air war. High value deterrence phrases such as 'not sit idly by' and 'lips and teeth' were used by Chinese leaders and in the media without any coherent pattern or build up of warnings.[5] Chinese signalling of its concern was inconsistent and it is not surprising that the US ignored the Chinese words. Beijing's attempt at deterrence of US action failed in early August when the US retaliated against the DRV for the Gulf of Tonkin incident.

As serious as these challenges were to China, Beijing still seemed less concerned that the air war posed a serious threat to Hanoi. Zhou Enlai told a Vienna paper on 1 August that China would only intervene if US forces crossed into North Vietnam.[6] To be sure, China did react firmly to the Tonkin incident, but what was most crucial was the new military rather than the verbal response. The promise to 'not sit idly by' reappeared in August,[7] but as has already been pointed out, the importance of this warning was already devalued by China's earlier misuse of the communication code.

During the next five months China tried to reinforce its deterrence posture by moving MIG aircraft to the DRV, extending its air defence system, concentrating its own MIGs in new airfields, and by January 1965 was engaged in joint air defence operations with Hanoi.[8] These actions, amounted to more than China did at the similar phase of the Korean war, and they were undertaken with a sense of potential risk of escalation of the conflict to Chinese territory. China still saw the threat as limited, and so far mainly to the DRV.[9]

By early 1965 China seemed to express some confidence that the air threat was under control. The by now vacuous pledges to not sit idly by remained in some comments,[10] but did not appear to reflect real high levels of Chinese concern. In January, Mao told Edgar Snow that:

Only if the US attacked China would the Chinese fight. Wasn't that clear? The Chinese are very busy with their internal affairs. Fighting beyond one's own borders was criminal. Why should the Chinese do that? The Vietnamese could cope with their own situation.[11]

Mao may have been merely reflecting the reduced tension since August 1964, but he flatly contradicted Zhou's remarks about the defensive line being drawn at the DRV frontier and indeed contradicted China's own behaviour in the Korean war. If Mao is to be believed, then it seems that by January 1965 China still saw a threat, but only to the DRV and a limited one at that.

In February 1965 the return of the Soviet Union to concern with Vietnamese affairs gave a new twist to Chinese objectives. Following Khrushchev's ousting in 1964, but most especially after Kosygin's visit to Hanoi in February 1965, China became concerned that its influence with the North Vietnamese would wane as Moscow's waxed. But at least in the initial stages of this new phase, China was content to let the Soviet Union bear the brunt of deterring US air attacks. For its part China apparently felt it had done all that was necessary to meet its limited objectives.[12] Beijing's complacency was abandoned when the nature of the war changed yet again.

When the US announced the arrival of its first ground combat troops, in March 1965, Chinese objectives had to be altered somewhat to concentrate on deterring escalation of the ground war. This type of threat brought with it special fears for China. In February a *People's Daily* editorial had taunted:

U.S. imperialism is doing its utmost to intimidate us. It endlessly rattles its sabres thus: We have naval and air superiority, aren't you afraid? But what is that naval and air superiority after all....what can they do since the outcome of the war has to be decided on Terra Firma?[13]

The arrival of US troops on Terra Firma led China to draw the deterrence line not at China's borders as Mao did, but at the DRV border. A *People's Daily* editorial in March said 'every inch of land north of this boundary (DRV border) is sacred and inviolate. A single step over this boundary by the US constitutes an aggression against the DRV and against the Socialist camp.'[14]

Chinese verbal deterrence was not merely confined to the 'lips and teeth' declaration, for in late March China made clear that it was prepared to send its troops 'to fight shoulder to shoulder' with Vietnam.[15] However, the most forceful Chinese reaction to the US threat did not come until July when it became clear that the United States was bent on fighting a ground war.

The reasons for the delay and the low key Chinese reaction to the American escalation of the war may have been due to the creeping nature of that escalation and the fact that American troops did not cross the DRV frontier. It may also have been affected by various debates raging in Beijing. Whatever the case, by early August China took concrete action to support its new open pledge to provide soldiers for Hanoi.[16] From September to December China openly moved 35,000 air defence troops into the DRV. They engaged in combat and suffered losses although their activities were deliberately not reported,[17] so as to reduce the threat of escalation. China also constructed a huge base at Yen Bai in the northern part of the DRV, apparently in case Hanoi had to be evacuated. China openly sought blood plasma on the world market.

Few could be under any illusions, especially in the light of misread Korean war signals that China meant what it said. Chinese policy up to this point was more forward than it had been in Korea, but it was hoped that Washington was being deterred, not antagonized. It is impossible to say with certainty just when Beijing became confident that the ground war threat would not expand and its deterrence conditions were understood in Washington. It is more clear that by November 1965 the Cultural Revolution was under way and China seemed fairly confident that the DRV could cope with the present level of threat.[18] It is possible that some participants in the Chinese debates were less confident of the limited nature of the threat (see below), but by November their voices fell silent.

In the third and final phase, Chinese objectives were merely to uphold its deterrence. Various events originating either from internal politics, the Soviet Union, or the war itself led to some uncertainty about the deterrence lines. Yet China's objectives did not change: to deter major air threats to the DRV and especially to prevent the movement of ground troops into the DRV.[19] Fifteen thousand more PLA troops were added to the Chinese contingent in the North in early 1966 but China remained confident that the DRV would win.[20] The PLA men were not withdrawn until March 1968, when it was clear that the US itself was pulling out of the ground war.[21]

Therefore most Chinese objectives were met. Not all US attacks on the DRV by air or within South Vietnam by ground forces could be prevented. But Beijing was notably successful in deterring any threat to China, in preventing unrestricted air raids on the DRV, and above all in keeping US ground troops south of the DRV frontier.

Operations

The most important aspect of China's military operations during the Vietnam war had less to do with combat, and more with the politically determined doctrines that helped keep the military option in low key in the first place. More than any other single factor, China's careful deterrence set the stage for the minimum of military moves. Although this posture resulted in part from policy debates in Beijing, (see below) it was in part an even more forward deterrence than in previous conflicts. Certainly, in comparison to the Korean War, it is striking that, in Vietnam, China committed its own troops to defence of the North before any American troops crossed into the northern communist state.

The over-arching doctrine that allowed China to draw its deterrence line at threats to the DRV and left the US to carry on massive air attacks right up to the Chinese frontier, was of course the Maoist belief in people's war. The doctrine, especially as espoused by Lin Biao[22] incorporated the crucial aspect of trusting the DRV to attain victory, albeit slowly. If the US threat had been extended to China itself, the doctrine suggested that nothing short of total invasion would have a chance of success—and that was unlikely. In such circumstances the quality of US arms meant less than the collective wrath of an aroused Chinese people. To be sure, the people's war doctrine was not one of total passivity, for in keeping with Mao's strategy of expedience, Lin repeated the exhortation to 'despise the enemy strategically, but take him seriously tactically'.

Thus the Chinese tactical response was a degree of military involvement in the war, while staying calm in strategic terms. Yet this was only possible so long as the US played by the same limited rules of conflict. No test of the effectiveness of people's war for China was really made, but China could have a high degree of confidence that the threat to wage a people's war served its basic deterrence in dissuading an all-out US attack.

One should however be wary of suggesting any tight and coherent Chinese deterrence policy just because the US did not challenge China's basic deterrence. As has already been suggested, Chinese verbal signals were far from consistent or credible.[23] Rather it was the idiom of military action that made China's seriousness evident and, coupled with the limited nature of the US war effort, Chinese crisis management appeared more efficient than it actually was.

The success of Chinese deterrence, however, meant that little actual combat involving Chinese forces took place, thereby offering scant ground for comment on China's military operations. PLA anti-aircraft and logistics troops engaged and shot down American aircraft and suffered casualties during American air raids. Nevertheless, several points can be noted. First, it is obvious that tight political control was maintained over all military operations. There were no known cases of local military action uncontrolled by Beijing. For example, when a US aircraft was shot down over China, Beijing attributed the kill to a stray US missile, not to Chinese troops. Neither China nor the United States desired to commit their prestige to a direct clash that might well escalate. China also made it clear that it knew that US forces were tracking PLA operations closely and so it was not always necessary to publicize every incident. At least on one occasion China attributed its own successful attack on US aircraft to DRV action.[24] This tight control merely strengthens the view that PLA action was intended more for its political signals than for military utility.

Second, to the extent that Chinese troops were used, it was only for logistics and air defence. We know little about what kinds of tactics the PLA used in these operations, but there were few indications of special tactics. Chinese troops were in part effective in these defensive operations, but not startlingly so. After all, they were there more for political rather than military purposes.

Third, China clearly differentiated between different types of potential military threats. Although most combat was seen by air-defence related services, the primary Chinese concern was the ground war. As has already been suggested, Chinese deterrence lines were drawn most distinctly to prevent the US crossing into the DRV. The 50,000 PLA troops were a clear symbol of this policy, despite their air-defence role.

Therefore it is not surprising that the potential American nuclear threat did not appear to disturb the Chinese. For Chinese commentators it was clear that nuclear weapons did not change the nature and laws of war. Men, not weapons, decide wars and thus atom bombs could be seen as paper tigers.[25] However, it was by now clear that this paper tiger thesis was never meant to suggest that nuclear weapons could not be devastating only that they had limited utility in dealing with a guerrilla war.

China accepted that 'the outbreak of a nuclear war would indeed bring a tremendous loss to mankind'[26] but the weapons remained 'tools in the hands of certain classes' and by themselves do not decide the outcome of war. In June 1964 Mao declared,

If they want to drop an atom bomb then there's nothing more to say, they want to drop it. If they drop an atom bomb, we'll run. If they go into the cities, we'll go into the cities too, and then the enemy won't dare to drop an atomb bomb; we'll do battle in the streets, in short we'll fight them.[27]

But Mao was not so simple-minded as to ignore at least the limited use of nuclear forces to threaten China. Perhaps Mao, like Stalin in 1945, was blasé in public about nuclear weapons, while privately developing China's own stockpile.

From October 1964 China's own nuclear programme came to fruition, moving rapidly through to a hydrogen bomb test in 1967 and then greater sophistication of delivery vehicles. At a time of great domestic unrest and a low-key deterrence posture in Vietnam, the nuclear commitment is all the more striking. Mao himself set the rationale for this programme—to deter threats by denying the enemy the possibility of victory. Even if nuclear weapons could not defeat China, they could be used as threats against which China needed to show it could defend itself and offer a credible threat to fight. In discussing nuclear threats, Mao said,

You have to manufacture some weapons in peacetime, because if you wait until the war has started, it'll be too late...when war starts we must depend on China to stand firm; to depend on revisionism just won't do...In short, we are prepared to fight...and even if they drop an atomic bomb we still mustn't get flustered...If they kill half (of us) there's still half (of us) left. The more one's fear, the less one's strength. If you're prepared and you're not afraid, then you'll have strength.[28]

Mao was at least consistent, for his theory of despising the enemy strategically but taking it seriously tactically, applies as well to nuclear as it does to conventional weapons.

The attitude towards nuclear weapons is of course strongly linked to China's view that the Soviet Union no longer provided an adequate security umbrella. Thus it is not surprising that China's relations with the Soviet Union during the Vietnam war, and just after the 1963 public split, were crucial to the conduct of Chinese operations during the war. The core question was whether China should engage in united action with Moscow against the US in Vietnam, or whether because of other differences the Soviet Union was an unsuitable partner.

The issue received wide attention both within China, in part in the form of a strategic debate, and also outside China as foreigners looked for signs of how domestic unrest affected Beijing's foreign policy (see below). Suffice it to say that at this stage, the Soviet question was important for Chinese policy, especially until March 1966 when Sino-Soviet Party ties were severed.[29] In the period until October 1964, the Soviet factor in China's calculus was not crucial.

In his last months in office, Khrushchev seemed resigned to opening the Sino-Soviet split wider and minimizing the conflict in East Asia. His removal in October 1964, and especially the Kosygin visit to Hanoi in February 1965, reopened the issue of Soviet involvement in Vietnam. At first, China seemed prepared to listen to the new Soviet leadership. Perhaps new policies might emerge.[30] But in early 1965, and especially after the Kosygin visit, many Chinese leaders began to see that at least in the Sino-Soviet realm, little had changed.

The Soviet Union was now returning to an active policy in East

Asia seeking new friends, but not at any cost. Moscow bought Hanoi's friendship with increased military aid, and as Beijing's perception of the military struggle in Vietnam became more radical, Hanoi found even greater reason for Soviet friendship. China saw scant reason to engage in united action as the Soviet Union stood to gain most in Hanoi, and perhaps even in Soviet–American relations, by 'delivering' a Vietnam deal. By mid-1965 the option of united action was not entirely closed, but there was certainly little more than a crack left in the doorway.

By September, and certainly November, the united action proposal was all but rejected in China. But much like other aspects of the strategic debate, it never completely disappeared. The most prominent revival of the issue came in response to the February 1966 Soviet invitation to the CCP to attend the 23rd CPSU Congress.[31] Mao's eventual rejection of the invitation, despite domestic opposition, marked a crucial watershed in Sino-Soviet ties, but even then the issue was never entirely laid to rest.[32]

The Soviet factor, important as it was in theory, never actually affected Chinese operations during the war. Obviously, the potential import—for example if Moscow had provided China with aid for intervention as in Korea—was enormous. But a great deal had changed, especially since 1963, in Chinese foreign policy. While China continued to be deeply affected by superpower policy, it no longer sought alliance with one against the other. Chinese operations were therefore not free from outside influence, but China certainly appeared more independent. It is hard to judge just how much more independent China was in reality, for it (as well as the US) opted to fight limited campaigns in Vietnam. Hence the outer limits of Chinese policy were not really tested. However, it was clear that the era of potential Sino-Soviet alliance in Chinese military policy had passed.

The Domestic Dimension

Earlier chapters had to bend over backwards to find even scanty evidence of domestic division affecting China's use of military force. The Vietnam chapter in this respect is a stark contrast, for few would argue that domestic politics during the Cultural Revolution were not crucial. Leadership cleavages, especially from November 1965 were clear for all to see, culminating in the following years in high level purges and open factional strife. The central question for this chapter is not whether leadership divisions existed, but rather whether they had a foreign or defence policy dimension and whether foreign or defence policy was changed as a result.

Two possible cleavages stand out in importance, and at times they overlap. First, to what extent was there a pro-Soviet group in China—or at least a group favouring less hostility towards the Soviet Union? This question has been chewed over, in an occasionally vicious personal manner, by several Western academics.[33] The conclusions are far from unanimous or clear cut, but the following lines of argument seem most apparent.

From February 1965, the Chinese began to take seriously the extent to which the Soviet Union was returning to an active East Asian policy and not all Chinese leaders supported a hard line against united action. This is not to say that anyone was purged for their beliefs. But at a minimum, an important difference of emphasis was noted. Some, perhaps including such leading officials as Deng Xiaoping, were apparently less willing to be hostile towards Moscow and saw more cause for co-operation.

By September 1965, few people were prepared to support, in public at least, united action with the Soviet Union. The option on united action however still lingered on until November, when other aspects of the strategic debate seemed to come to a resolution.[34] No one was purged exclusively for their line on the Soviet Union, but in some cases it could have been a contributing factor in their demise. While it is not clear what influence a mildly pro-Soviet leader might have had, it is not possible to point to any change in Chinese policy as being due to the victory of Mao and Lin Biao's view against any deal with Moscow.

In March 1966 the united action issue arose again in response to the CPSU invitation, but once again Mao's line was dominant. This time the opposition group seemed even more broadly based, and included the Premier Zhou Enlai.[35] However, in the heightened tension of the Cultural Revolution, the Soviet invitation, and united action in general were probably not fundamental policy questions. Indeed, of the entire range of issues possibly at the heart of the leadership debate, the most crucial one was less strictly concerned with foreign policy, and more with defence strategy.

The second major, and most important cleavage was on the question of how China should meet the perceived US threat in Vietnam. Once again it seems clear that divisions of opinion in China existed, but their effect on foreign and defence policy is harder to pinpoint. The main line of conflict pitted the Chief of Staff, Luo Ruiqing, against Lin Biao on the question of how to defend against the US threat. Both agreed that US action in Vietnam was serious, but Luo appeared to urge greater preparation and more 'active defence'. In early to mid-1965 Luo's line might well have also included a call for greater co-operation with the Soviet Union, but the main cleavage was on the best policy response to the US threat. If Luo's line had been adopted, then Mao would have been distracted from his main task of the Cultural Revolution, and above all resources could have been devoted to military preparedness.

This general context of the dispute—conflicting national priorities—requires further elaboration. Although Luo was accused of many sins during the Cultural Revolution, his disputes with Mao and Lin Biao seemed to centre on two dimensions and were aggravated by apparent personality clashes with Lin.[36] First, Luo's belief that more should be done to meet the US threat, would have meant an increase in professionalism in the PLA.[37] Luo was not particularly well known as a believer in 'expert' over 'red', but he did appear to lay greater emphasis on professionalism than did many of his colleagues.[38] Differences in emphasis can be crucial, and in this case it did seem to contribute to Luo's split with Mao and Lin. Luo apparently wanted more time spent on professional pursuits and less involvement with the unprofessional militia. In addition, Luo seemed to concentrate more on central PLA organs and paid less attention to the regional, and less professional parts, of the PLA.

Luo also seemed to be out of step in his military strategy. He apparently saw China as less prepared to meet a sudden US attack, and his policy seemed to call for greater defence expenditure. In May 1965, Luo was unusual in arguing for worst-case planning and praising the World War II Soviet leadership for making more active plans to defend the state. Luo's strategy seemed to involve more formal planning so as to halt the enemy 'before high mountains and outside fortified cities'. It might even require 'strategic pursuit to destroy the enemy at his starting point, to destroy him in his nest'.[39] Later Chinese commentaries accused Luo of wanting to keep the enemy from entering China by 'blocking the water' and 'engaging the enemy outside the gates'.[40] This was labelled a passive defence as it would rely on fixed positions. China was urged to follow Mao's more flexible and active strategy that would 'lure the enemy in deep'. Mao was said not to fear 'the breaking of jars' that might result from fighting on Chinese soil.

Obviously there is some falsification of the historical record in the later criticisms of Luo's position. What is more, the simplistic notion of 'two military lines' is patently absurd when one considers that the Maoist strategy of the Korean war sounded enormously like Luo's supposedly bankrupt Vietnam strategy. It is important not to lose sight of the fact that Luo was perfectly well within the flexible definition of Mao's strategy, for Mao was not always opposed to fighting outside the gates. Unfortunately for Luo, in 1965 he was out of step with a Mao then emphasizing a different aspect of his theories. It is also crucial to keep in mind that, although Luo may have been purged in November/December 1965, his ideas were not entirely rejected. China's policy in Vietnam was more forward than the equivalent phases of the Korean War and China did make certain preparations, albeit not on the basis of Luo's worst-case scenarios. Even during the height of the Cultural Revolution, Maoist military doctrine never lost its sense of balance. Its 'walking on two legs' involved both red and expert, both man and weapons, and above all it urged 'people's war under modern conditions.'[41]

Luo Ruiqing fell as a result of a complex factional struggle rather than one that simply pitted Party against Army or red versus expert. The cleavages cut across each other and further intersected with far more complex cleavages on foreign policy and above all on the Cultural Revolution itself. Hence no simple picture can be constructed of one faction supporting one policy or another, although it is clear that differences existed. As for the effect on China's foreign and defence policy in the Vietnam war, the verdict must remain uncertain. It seems likely that the extent of the external threat influenced how the Cultural Revolution was launched in only a minor way. The timing of the Cultural Revolution was no doubt delayed until the foreign policy threat was properly assessed and controlled. Mao's determination to launch the upheaval contributed heavily to his low key approach to the war and the desire to implement a limited defence. To that extent, the Cultural Revolution was a brake rather than a boost to foreign policy adventure.

Second, Chinese debates on the Soviet Union and united action also had some impact on Chinese foreign policy. Not that Beijing adopted a new policy as a result of the debate, but a simmering dispute might have meant a delay in rejection of united action, and China's careful attention to further possibilities for change in Moscow's policy. Once again the impact of the debate was more in terms of timing of Chinese rejection of united action, than the adoption of a new strategy.

Third, the defence debate in China seemed to result in compromise. Thus the balance between red and expert, and especially between forward and passive defence, was adjusted in a way apparently not at first sought by Mao. Certainly, his 1965 promise not to fight beyond China's borders was violated by September of that year. This is not to suggest that foreign and defence policy formed a fundamental part of the Cultural Revolution. Far from it. But foreign and defence policy in the Vietnam war were affected by part of a Chinese struggle that was concerned with broader aspects of Chinese society and Maoist vision.

Conclusions

In comparison to many of the previous cases, China's use of military force in the Vietnam war seemed remarkably successful. However, the success was due neither to brilliant Chinese crisis management nor to the efficiency of the PLA. Most Chinese objectives were obtained because of two main factors. First, China itself set relatively limited objectives. Second, the US, it seems, never realistically planned to put ground troops into the DRV, thereby drawing a Chinese response.

These mutually limited objectives made the crisis management appear more successful than it really was. Indeed it is obvious that Chinese declaratory signals were confusing and certainly followed no clear pattern. Neither was the use of the Chinese military instrument particularly impressive. The limited forward defence beyond China's gates was pre-eminently a political signal that China would not tolerate a Korea-like crossing into the communist state bordering on China. Although Chinese troops did suffer casualties, there is little to be learned about Chinese military strategy from this limited operation.

The most revealing aspects of military strategy were made evident in the strategic debates. Competing aspects of so-called Maoist strategy were apparent as both sides could plausibly argue that their positions were in keeping with previous policy. The resulting compromise strategy of some forward defence, but essential reliance on defence behind the gates, reflected the compromise nature of the debate, and above all the complex high policy debate in Beijing. The Vietnam debate again made plain that it is not possible to identify any single unchanging Chinese military strategy.

These policy compromises are crucial to understanding why China set its limited objectives in Vietnam. Not only did compromise and debate lead to a low key policy while the differences were sorted out. But, more crucially, the domestic dimension finally supported the Cultural Revolution, which required a non-threatening international environment and a limited foreign policy. Thus debates in China led to greater caution, not greater adventurism.

Similarly, this was the first, albeit limited, use of the Chinese military instrument after China had walked out from under the Soviet nuclear umbrella. China acted more cautiously as an independent power, fully appreciating the dangers of nuclear war. However this greater caution was not a result of a changed view of nuclear weapons, but rather because the domestic priority of the Cultural Revolution meant China did not seek foreign conflict. It does not take any wild imagination to speculate on how much more forward and adventurist Chinese foreign policy might have been, if the Cultural Revolution had not been Mao's current obsession.

NOTES

1. Gerald Segal, *The Great Power Triangle* (London: Macmillan, 1982), Ch. 4.
2. Details for this chronology are drawn from Gerald Segal, 'From Bipolarity to the Great Power Triangle', Ph.D. dissertation, the London School of Economics, 1979. Allen Whiting, *The Chinese Calculus of Deterrence* (Ann Arbor: University of Michigan Press, 1975).
3. Thomas Gottlieb, *Chinese foreign policy factionalism and the Origins of the Strategic Triangle* (Santa Monica: Rand Corp. R-1902 NA, Nov. 1977).
4. *New York Times*, 21 February 1964. See also in this period Chen Yi to Xuan Thuy, 2 March 1964 in *SCMP*, No. 3173, p. 23; and *People's Daily* 4 March in No. 3174, pp. 26–7. Michael Yahuda, 'Chinese Foreign Policy After 1965: The Maoist Phases', *The China Quarterly*, Oct–Dec. 1968. Harold Hinton, *Communist China in World Politics* (Boston: Houghton Mifflin, 1966) p. 36.
5. Chen Yi, 24 June 1964 and *People's Daily* Editorial, 1 July in *Peking Review*, Vol. 7, No. 27, pp. 8–13; Chen Yi to Xuan Thuy in *SCMP* No. 3255, p. 38; Chen Yi, 19 July and *People's Daily* Editorial, 20 July in No. 3265 pp. 29–42.
6. Text in U.S. Department of State Research Memo, RFE-55, 5 August 1964, to Dean Rusk from Thomas Hughes. Papers of James Thomson, Far East, Communist China, 7/67–10/64. Box No. 16, *John F. Kennedy Library*.
7. *SCMP*, No. 3276, p. 26. The term 'not sit idly by' was a crucial signal of Chinese determination to intervene in the Korean war. US decision-makers appreciated the importance of the term. See Whiting, *Chinese Calculus*.
8. *New York Times*, 12 August 1964; Whiting, *Chinese Calculus*, pp. 176–7.
9. Hanoi radio interview with General Giap noted the US threat to the DRV at China but the NCNA version dropped the reference to China, *BBC*/SWB/FE/ 1629/A3/3–5.
10. Zhou Enlai, 24 November 1964 in *SCMP*, No. 3346, p. 34. *People's Daily* Commentator, 29 November in No. 3349, p. 39 and *People's Daily* Observer, 12 December in No. 3358, p. 345.
11. *The New Republic*, Vol. 152, No. 9, 27 February 1965, p. 22.
12. *SCMP*, No. 3395, pp. 35–9, No. 3396, pp. 28–31, No. 3397, pp. 24–8.
13. 19 February 1965 in *SCMP*, No. 3403, pp. 42–3.
14. 4 March 1965 in *SCMP*, No. 3411, p. 36.
15. Chen Yi, 28 March 1965 in *SCMP*, No. 3429, p. 44, but Zhou Enlai's similar comments the same day were dropped by NCNA. Jay Taylor, *China and Southeast Asia* (New York: Praeger, 1976), p. 46.
16. PRC Government statement, 7 August 1965 in *SCMP*, No. 3515, p. 36.
17. Whiting, *Chinese Calculus*, pp. 185–9.
18. People's Daily Commentator, 15 and 21 September 1965 in *SCMP*, No. 3541, pp. 41–2, and No. 3544, pp. 33–4. Chen Yi on 29 September in No. 3555, pp. 21–9. *People's Daily* Editorial, 8 and 9 November in No. 3577, p. 37 and No. 3584, pp. 37–9.
19. Segal, *The Great Power Triangle*.
20. *People's Daily* 27 February 1966; 28 February in *SCMP*, No. 3679, pp. 33–4. 4 March in No. 3653, p. 37; 1 May in No. 3691, pp. 41–2.
21. Whiting, *Chinese Calculus*, p. 186.
22. Lin Piao, 'Long Live the Victory of People's War' *Peking Review*, No. 36, 3

September 1965. D. P. Mozengo and Thomas Robinson, *Lin Piao on 'People's War'* (Santa Monica: Rand Corp. RM 48-M, No. 1965).

23. Whiting, *Chinese Calculus* and Segal, *The Great Power Triangle*.
24. NCNA, Peking, 9 April 1965 in *SCMP*, No. 3438, p. 42; *People's Daily* Editorial 12 April in No. 3439, pp. 42–3; Whiting, *Chinese Calculus*, p. 180.
25. Jonathan Pollack, 'Chinese Attitudes Towards Nuclear Weapons' *The China Quarterly*, No. 50, 1972, Gerald Segal, 'China's Nuclear Posture in the 1980s', *Survival*, Jan–Feb. 1981.
26. Kuang-ming Jih-pao, 27 August 1965 in *SCMP*, No. 3539, pp. 2–8.
27. Mao, 16 June 1967, text in *Chinese Law and Government*, Vol. 10, No. 2, Summer 1977, p. 78.
28. *Ibid*, pp. 79–80.
29. Gottlieb, *Chinese Policy*.
30. Segal, *The Great Power Triangle*.
31. *Ibid*.
32. Gottlieb, *Chinese Policy*.
33. See especially *Ibid*, and Segal, *Great Power Triangle*. Other key sources for this section include, Harry Harding and Melvin Gurtov, *The Purge of Lo Jui-Ch'ing* (Santa Monica: Rand Corp. R-548-PR) Feb. 1971. Uri Ra'anan, 'Peking's Foreign Policy "Debate", 1965–1966' in Tang Tsou ed., *China in Crisis*, Vol. 2 (Chicago: Pegasus, 1967); Michael Yahuda, 'Kremlinology and the Chinese Strategic Debate, 1965–1966', *The China Quarterly*, Jan.–March 1972. Gerald Segal, 'Chinese Politics and the Soviet Connection', *Jerusalem Journal of International Relations*, Vol. 2, No. 1, Fall 1976.
34. *People's Daily* and *Red Flag* editorial, 11 November 1965, in *Peking Review* Vol. 18, No. 46, 12 November 1965.
35. Kikuzo Ito and Minoru Shibato, 'The Dilemma of Mao Tse-tung', *The China Quarterly*, No. 35, July 1965. *Chinese Law and Government*, Vol. 10, No. 2, Summer 1977, p. 107.
36. Red Guards, 'Report on the Problem of Lo Jui-Ch'ing's Mistakes' 30 April 1966, *Chinese Law and Government*, Vol. 4, No. 3–4, Fall–Winter 1971.
37. Based on *Ibid*, Harding and Gurtov, *Purge of Lo*; The Red Guards, 'The Fundamental Difference Between the Proletarian Military Line and the Bourgeois Military Line', 7 September 1977; *Chinese Law and Government*, Vol. 4, No. 3–4, Fall–Winter 1971. 'Basic Differences Between the Proletarian and Bourgeois Military Lines', *Peking Review*, No. 48, 24 November 1967. Lo Jui-Ch'ing, 'Commemorate the Victory Over German Fascism!' and *People's Daily* Editorial Department, 'The Historical Experience of the War Against Fascism', *Peking Review*, No. 20, 14 May 1965. Ho Lung, 'Democratic Tradition of the Chinese PLA', *Peking Review* No. 32, 6 August 1965. Red Guards, 'Lo Jui-Ch'ing's Towering Crimes Against the Party, Socialism and Mao Tse-tung's Thought', *SCMM*, No. 641, 20 January 1964.
38. Morton Halperin and John Wilson Lewis, 'New Tensions in Army–Party Relations in China, 1965–1966', *The China Quarterly*, No. 26, April–June 1966; Ellis Joffe, 'The Chinese Army Under Lin Piao' in John Lindbeck ed., *China's Management of a Revolutionary Society* (Seattle: University of Washington Press, 1971).
39. Lo, 'Commemorate the Victory' and Lo Jui-Ch'ing, 'The People Defeated Japanese Fascism and They Can Certainly Defeat US Imperialism Too', *Peking Review*, No. 36, 3 September 1965.

40. Red Guards, 'The Fundamental Differences', 'Basic Differences', and 'Report on Problems'. According to Chen Yi on 29 September 1965, 'some people' believed the PRC could stand on its own and some people did not. Luo was no doubt one who did not. *SCMP*, 3555, p. 21.
41. *Ibid*, especially 'Basic Differences', p. 13.

10

Soviet Union, 1969

The 1969 Sino-Soviet border clash and its ensuing threats of nuclear war, are special for three major reasons. First, the events of 1969 were the first and only crisis that involved at least a somewhat plausible threat to use nuclear weapons against China. Thus an evaluation of China's use of military force in its foreign policy in 1969, requires special emphasis on China's nuclear weapons doctrine.

Second, this is the first crisis involving the use of Chinese military force against the Soviet rather than American superpower. The character of the military threat is therefore radically changed. Serious potential land threats had to be confronted, rather than the less pressing threat from an offshore and distant sea power. What is more, since the Soviet Union was an ideological rival in the communist world, a Sino-Soviet crisis was more complex ideologically for China than the previous relatively straightforward confrontation with the United States. Third, this crisis is special in that there seemed to be virtually no attainable military objectives for either side. The crisis was pre-eminently political, in that one side was either trying to teach the other a lesson, or to avoid being 'educated'.

In part because of these special characteristics, the 1969 crisis has already been well analysed in several studies.[1] Many analysts have paid special attention to the domestic dimension of the crisis and have painstakingly assessed the factional politics.[2] Obviously these excellent analyses make subsequent research easier. But such studies have concentrated mostly on the Sino-Soviet border clashes themselves, and less on the following seven months of tension when the Soviet Union forced China to the negotiating table. Thus there are two crucial phases to the 1969 crisis.

The Course of Events

The March 1969 Sino-Soviet border clashes have some of their origins in ancient territorial rivalry, but more immediate causes date from 1963, when China first raised the issue of 'unequal treaties' imposed on China's weak Qing dynasty. Talks about the border were terminated in 1964 because of Soviet sensitivity to China's hard line and the fall of Khrushchev in October of that year.[3] In the mid-1960s the Soviet Union began the process of reinforcing its military presence along the Sino-Soviet border, and especially in 1966 when it signed a pact with Mongolia allowing the stationing of Soviet troops in strength in Mongolia. By 1967 China began to match some of this Soviet build up.

The immediate pre-crisis build up commences with the Soviet invasion of Czechoslovakia and the proclamation of the Brezhnev doctrine in September 1968. China, then undergoing the Cultural Revolution, perceived itself to be vulnerable to Soviet attack and on 16 September publicized Soviet border violations. The cool Soviet response in October minimizing the border tension, followed by a flurry of hopes for an improvement in Sino-American relations towards the end of 1968, provided a lull in the tense atmosphere.[4]

At this stage China seemed determined to convince the Soviet Union that it would not be another Czechoslovakia. On 27 December China tested a hydrogen weapon and, after a serious Sino-Soviet border clash along the Ussuri river at Zhenbao Island, on 23 January, China stepped up its aggressive patrols and changed its tactics to provide a covering patrol for the vulnerable lead patrol.[5] Tension was further heightened by Soviet warnings after another clash on 16 February.

On 2 March the first of two major clashes at Zhenbao occurred when, apparently, a Soviet attempt to halt the leading Chinese patrol was ambushed by the Chinese covering patrol. Casualties were high and the Soviet seemed to get the worse of the exchange.[6] Both sides exchanged propaganda barrages with China taking the lead. On 15 March the Soviet Union apparently 'taught the Chinese a lesson' by orchestrating a second incident at Zhenbao, where superior Soviet manpower and firepower decimated Chinese troops.

On 21 March Soviet Premier Kosygin tried to contact the Chinese by phone with the aim of reducing tensions, but was rebuffed. On 29 March the Soviet government called for talks but China still deferred a reply until after the 9th Chinese Communist Party Congress had taken place in April. On 26 April the Soviet Union offered to resume river navigation talks as an interim measure and on 11 May the Chinese agreed to meet in June. On 24 May the Chinese finally responded to the call by the Soviet government on 29 March for general talks and agreed in principle to meet, but without setting a date or place.[7]

The Soviet Union responded on 13 June, calling for talks in the next two to three months. In the meantime the Moscow conference of communist parties opened on 5 June and in his speech of 7 June, Brezhnev kicked off the Soviet campaign for an Asian collective security scheme, aimed obviously against China. However, Soviet impatience with China grew, despite the conclusion on 8 August of the river navigation talks.

On 13 August two months after the 13 June Soviet note, major Sino-Soviet clashes took place in Xinjiang, apparently at Soviet instigation.[8] In the next two weeks the Soviet Union dropped broad hints about the possibility of escalation to nuclear war, including perhaps a Soviet surgical strike against China.[9] On 28 August Pravda warned in unusually harsh terms of the dangerous situation. Soviet pressure to talk was obviously being stepped up in the 2–3 month period after 13 June.

On 3 September the leader of North Vietnam, Ho Chi Minh, died and Communist leaders flocked to Hanoi. Zhou Enlai arrived on 4 September but did not meet Kosygin, who arrived later. Ho's testament called for Sino-Soviet reconciliation and, on 11 September, Kosygin met Zhou at Beijing airport. Kosygin was returning from Ho's funeral and had already reached Soviet central Asia on his return journey before turning back to Beijing.[10] Apparently the decision to talk was not taken easily in China.

Indeed the Zhou–Kosygin talks delayed, but did not end, Soviet pressure for formal talks. Soviet warnings about the dangers of nuclear war continued into September,[11] and on 18 September Zhou's letter to Kosygin proposed talks, but talks laced with added conditions. On 4 October, while the crisis was contained but not eliminated, China announced two nuclear tests carried out on 23 and 29 September. On 6 October China responded to a 26 September Soviet note on arranging talks. Following a swift Soviet response, on 7 October China agreed to meet the Soviet Union on 20 October. While Moscow made minor concessions, such as calling the talks negotiations rather than consultations and agreeing to meet in Beijing rather than Moscow, the Chinese had capitulated on the basic demand of agreeing to talks. From 7 October Chinese reports of Soviet threats dropped off and talks opened on 20 October.

Objectives

In one sense Chinese objectives in this crisis can be seen as the most straightforward of any crisis so far: to deter a Soviet threat. However, analytical complications set in when it becomes apparent that the Chinese perception of the nature of the threat varied and, what is more, Beijing adopted more or less forthright deterrence postures in response. Taking these variations into account, it becomes apparent that Chinese objectives in the Sino-Soviet crisis underwent important alterations.

China's sense of threat became focused following the August 1968 Soviet invasion of Czechoslovakia. Threats were seen as being posed in Europe, but also more directly to China. After labelling the Soviet Union 'social imperialists' China seemed very concerned about Soviet threats to Europe and the fact that some Asians, such as the North Vietnamese and North Koreans, 'cherished illusions' about the nature of Soviet power.[12] Following the official Albanian withdrawal from the Warsaw Pact in 1968 China tried to link its security with that of Albania and offered protection in the wake of the Czech invasion. But as the Chinese proverb has it, 'distant waters cannot quench fires', and there was a limit to how far Chinese deterrence could be extended.

After the Soviet invasion of Czechoslovakia, China became most concerned with its own security for, by the autumn of 1968, China saw itself as under threat from the Soviet Union.[13] The Chinese acknowledgement on 16 September of Soviet air intrusions made it plain that China was vulnerable to Soviet attack. But there was little sense of an immediate Soviet threat to Chinese territory. China tested its nuclear device in late December, and during January continued to see a mixture of both Soviet strengths and weaknesses.[14] This was apparently an uncertain time in Chinese politics in general, as domestic debates seemed to affect foreign policy, especially concerning policy towards the superpowers (see below).

Chinese deterrence of the Soviet threat took a more forward turn on 23 January when patrolling tactics in the Zhenbao area were made more aggressive. When the Soviet Union refused to back down from confrontation at Zhenbao, the forward Chinese policy was likely to be tested soon. The crunch came in the dead of winter when frozen conditions permitted larger scale military confrontation. On March 2 the Chinese escalated the quality of their deterrence strategy from shoving to shooting, and thereby astonished the Soviet

Union. China was probably not trying to 'punish' the Soviet Union, but was trying to teach them that China was not Czechoslovakia.

The Chinese having raised the ante, forced the Soviet Union either to challenge Chinese deterrence, or suffer at least psychological defeat. Moscow then chose to 'lean forward' in its own defence and prevent China from 'bleeding the Soviet Union to death' with many small-scale confrontations.[15] The 15 March Soviet counter-punch was merely part of a series of responses intended to 'teach the Chinese a lesson'. Moscow also advertised its border reinforcements, reminded China of the Soviet Union's past use of military force in the Far East,[16] and spread initial hints of willingness to use nuclear weapons if China persisted in its forward posture.[17]

The immediate result of the two clashes was a Soviet victory. China apparently decided not to raise the military stakes and made no significant troop reinforcement.[18] China of course raised a large propaganda campaign denouncing the Soviet threat, but professed not to be scared.[19] Even supposed superpower collusion in nuclear threats to China were dismissed in Beijing as being deterred by China's own nuclear forces.[20] But in reality, China did seem to change its policy to one that challenged the Soviet Union less forcefully. On 28 April Mao said that China would fight small scale attacks on the border, but the reality of Chinese policy seemed to be an even more defensive strategy.[21] This is not to say that China yielded territory, but rather it recognized that it did not have to meet each Soviet patrol as if it were a crucial test. By flexibly changing the definition of the threat, China was able to adjust its deterrence policy in the face of inferiority under certain conditions.

However, from the Soviet point of view, this flexible Chinese deterrence did not solve the problem of how to avoid bleeding to death by small incidents. A new Soviet strategy was needed. Somehow the Chinese had to be compelled to reduce the threat to the Soviet frontier and come to the negotiating table. China's new objective now became to deter such Soviet compellence. If China failed to do so, then its overall foreign policy of deterring the Soviet threat would be seen to fail. If China could be pushed around on the Sino-Soviet frontier, then serious doubt would be cast on the overall credibility of Chinese foreign policy. So, while the type of Chinese deterrence had changed somewhat, it was still part of an over-arching objective of deterring Soviet threats to China.

From 21 March to 20 October, China managed to avoid succumbing to Soviet demands for talks. The reasons for China's ability to withstand Soviet pressure for seven months are complex and often overlapping. First, Soviet signals of serious intent to force Chinese compliance with Moscow's demands for a reduction of tension were less than coherent and consistent.[22] The Soviet Union was at times playing to the galleries, either of the Communist Parties or the new US administration. Soviet nuclear threats faded away after March, only to return again in August and September. China then felt free consistently to disparage Soviet nuclear sabre-rattling as the antics of a paper tiger. In large part because the Chinese did not take Soviet threats seriously, China might well have thought that there was no immediate danger of war.[23] The Chinese remained in control of Zhenbao Island and some patrols did continue after the March incidents, so Beijing could properly feel that the Soviet military was still being restrained.[24] Thus from China's point of view there seemed to be no pattern of escalating Soviet military pressure necessitating a Chinese response.

Second, China did not reject the option of talks entirely. Not only did it agree to river navigation talks in early May, but on 24 May the Chinese government accepted the principle of talks with the Soviet Union on broader issues. Beijing was careful to suggest that this agreement was not 'a sign of weakness' or a sign that China was cowed by 'nuclear blackmail'. Therefore partial concessions and belated replies dragged out the sequence of events, turning it into a slow-motion crisis.

The Soviet Union's patience did eventually run out and China was compelled to talk. Chinese deterrence of Soviet pressure to come to the negotiating table failed for several reasons. First, because from 13 August the Soviet Union was far more consistent in its series of warnings. Hints of a possible surgical strike against China came in the Soviet press and via third parties in August and September.[25] On 13 August the Soviet Union launched a major raid in Xinjiang, inflicting large casualties and reminding China of Soviet military superiority. Coupled with the 28 August sharply worded and urgent *Pravda* statement, Beijing could be under no illusion that the Soviet Union was serious. It is notable that in this phase of the crisis China issued far fewer and less categorical statements of confidence about withstanding nuclear threats.[26] China soon was to begin a major campaign of war-preparedness, including the building of civil defence shelters, something it had never done in the face of previous supposed US and Soviet nuclear threats.[27]

Second, the death of Ho Chi Minh and the publication of his political testament gave China a face-saving reason to accept the idea of talks. China's basic problem was not whether to talk to the Soviet Union (they had already agreed to that), but rather how to do so without appearing to be coerced. By having Ho's dying plea as an excuse, China could claim to be acting for the good of the socialist community, and not under the Soviet gun. After all, the views of the international communist gallery were an important part of why China tried to avoid submitting to Soviet pressure.

Third, China could claim to have obtained some concessions from the Soviet Union. The talks were called negotiations and not consultations, thereby indicating that there were real issues of dispute along the border. The talks were to be held in Beijing and not Moscow as originally stated by the Soviet Union. Finally, Premier Kosygin was met by Premier Zhou at Beijing airport after being forced to fly most of the way home and then backtrack to Beijing. If saving face was an important element for China, certainly Kosygin had lost some himself. Not only was his 21 March phone call refused by Chinese leaders, but his 11 September meeting with Zhou was seen to wait on Chinese whims.

Fourth, China found it easier to capitulate to Soviet pressure because it did so in stages. The Zhou–Kosygin meeting on 11 September did not end the crisis, although it did severely minimize the dangers. Thus China was allowed more time to save face by prevarication and symbolic gestures like the twin nuclear tests in late September. The delayed announcement of the tests[28] was most unusual for China and probably indicated recognition of the sensitivity of nuclear sabre-rattling in this crisis. Nevertheless, China did not wait until after 7 October, and the real end of the crisis, as it probably felt that it could not be seen to give in to Soviet blackmail.

In sum, China had only partial success in its basic objective of deterring Soviet threats. When China tried to teach lessons to its powerful northern neighbour, the Soviet Union eventually delivered a firm rebuff. When China adopted a more defensive definition of deterrence it had more success. Although in the end China was forced to the negotiating table, it was not at the cost of a huge loss of prestige. Thus, on balance, two conclusions emerge most starkly. First, Chinese objectives in this crisis, as well as the previous ones already outlined, changed over time in response to changes in the internal and external environment. Second, China did succeed in its most basic desire of making plain to the Soviet Union that it was not subject to the Brezhnev doctrine and could not be treated as a vassal state. However, Chinese leaders did learn that China was weaker than they thought to start with, and would have to tailor its deterrence posture and use of military force accordingly.

Operations

The nature of Chinese military operations in the 1969 crisis is difficult to evaluate. The conventional phase—including various border clashes—seemed simple and pragmatic. The nuclear phase—including Soviet threats and Chinese bravado—did seem to introduce some new twists to Chinese doctrine.

In the build-up to the March border incidents, both sides engaged in some predictable escalation, with the Soviet Union consistently taking the lead in building up its forces.[29] In 1968 China shifted 4–5 divisions to the Soviet frontier, including some artillery from Fujian. However this hardly constituted even the beginning of an offensive potential. The border clashes were clearly a frontier incident, albeit of a larger scale.

The 2 March clash apparently only involved frontier troops and no replacements. China had altered its patrol pattern to include back-up forces (seen by the Soviet Union as ambush forces), but no large set-piece conventional war was planned by either side.[30] The resulting 'fire-fight' had more political than military significance and revealed no distinctive Chinese style of military operations. Chinese casualties, although including twenty dead, were apparently less than those suffered by the Soviet Union and reflected China's apparently better planned frontier patrols.[31]

On the other hand, the 15 March clash showed greater Soviet cunning and planning, as a Chinese patrol was lured into a trap and was badly mauled by superior Soviet fire-power.[32] The nine-hour battle resulted in higher casualties on both sides, and Chinese deaths numbered in the hundreds. This time the Soviet Union also sent its aircraft into action, but they took no offensive role. This second incident was to set a pattern for later clashes, where superior Soviet equipment punished Chinese forces. But in no case did the incidents expand in military terms beyond frontier fire-fights.

Apparently, the Chinese saw the Soviet border threat as more political than military. In April 1969 Mao outlined a version of

Chinese deterrence by denial. In a reversal of the Korean and Vietnam examples, where China saw fit to engage the enemy beyond China's gates, in the 1969 clash Mao felt that, at most, small scale clashes should be met at the gates, and all other threats could be defeated by people's war.

Others may come and attack us but we shall not fight outside our borders. We do not fight outside our borders. I say we will not be provoked. Even if you invite us to come out we will not come out, but if you should come and attack us we will deal with you. It depends on whether you attack on a small scale or a large scale. If it is on a small scale we will fight on the border. If it is on a larger scale then I am in favour of yielding some ground. China is no small country. If there is nothing in it for them I don't think they will come. We must make it clear to the whole world that we have both right and advantage on our side. If they invade our territory then I think it would be to our advantage, and we would then have both right and advantage. They would be easy to fight since they would fall into the people's encirclement. As for things like aeroplanes, tanks and armoured cars, everywhere experience proves that they can be dealt with.[33]

The denigration of military equipment of course suited the essentially politically determined view of a limited threat. By minimizing the threat, there could be less argument in favour of military professionalism. Not surprisingly, the general tone of Chinese comment in early 1969 on military affairs, made much of the superiority of man over weapons.[34]

However, one should not be misled by verbal bravado. There were clear signs, especially after the August 1969 Xinjiang border clash, that China did make military preparations against a Soviet attack.[35] Certainly Chinese troops were soon to be increased along the frontier and new patrolling emphasized China's need to defend its fixed frontiers and thereby undertake at least a somewhat more positional defence.[36] Most importantly, China did eventually give in to Soviet pressure and resume bilateral negotiations. China was impressed by the Soviet military threat, although this seemed to result from a complex combination of conventional and nuclear power in support of a determined political campaign. Perhaps the most intriguing question is the extent to which China was coerced by the Soviet Union's threat to use nuclear weapons and how China's own nascent nuclear doctrine was affected.

On the surface it seems clear that Soviet nuclear weapons threats were dismissed as vain attempts at blackmail, threatening China with a paper tiger's nuclear claws. But few would suggest that, simply because the Soviet Union in 1962 dismissed US threats in the Cuban Missile Crisis as insufficient to force Soviet compliance, Moscow was not acutely sensitive to the potential for nuclear pressure. Similarly, it seems that in 1969 China may well have doubted that Soviet nuclear threats were close to being realized, but Chinese leaders eventually seemed to calculate that discretion was perhaps the better part of valour when all the Soviet Union wanted was an agreement to talk.

China certainly became acutely sensitive to Soviet nuclear threats. Prior to August, when Soviet threats were vague and unco-ordinated, Chinese dismissal of the problem seemed more confident and continuous.[37] After the August escalation of the Soviet campaign, China became relatively quiet about the threats and later in 1969 began its own massive programme of civil defence. No such campaign was undertaken in the face of supposed United States nuclear threats in the previous decades.[38]

Chinese sensitivity to nuclear threats in 1969 should be neither surprising, nor taken to be a reversal of the people's war doctrine which Mao asserted to be China's ultimate defence. It is obvious that for well over a decade China had appreciated the importance of nuclear weapons, even if they were not seen as decisive. China's own nuclear weapons programme made it plain that it saw some use for these weapons in deterring an aggressive opponent.[39] While deterrence of a general invasion of China could be achieved by the threat of people's war, China had come to understand that more limited threats required a more credible counter-threat of nuclear weapons.[40] China's view of nuclear weapons as paper tigers meant only that their power was exaggerated, not that they had no important impact.[41]

Unfortunately for China, in 1969 there developed several reasons why China was forced to take the Soviet nuclear threat more seriously than it had in the past. First, unlike the case of threats from the United States, China faced a genuinely angry and worried Soviet Union who shared a long and vulnerable frontier with China. Thus Moscow might be more motivated to wield a nuclear stick than was the United States. Second, although China had tested nuclear devices for five years, it was far from having an invulnerable second strike capability.[42] Chinese aircraft could deliver a limited number of weapons, but Beijing's missile force was not yet operational.

Chinese weapon tests in December 1968 and September 1969 indicated that Beijing recognized the deterrence value of its weapons, but also accepted its state of relative weakness. China was in that notoriously sensitive position where it had some nuclear power, but not a secure second strike. It was thus notionally highly vulnerable to a pre-emptive strike from the Soviet Union. China could therefore dismiss nuclear weapons in the strategic sense of a possible general war with the Soviet Union as being paper tigers. But China accepted that, in the short term, and in more limited crises it was vulnerable.[43]

It is difficult to suggest that the 1969 Soviet threats forced China to change its nuclear doctrine, but it did seem to give impetus to a programme already under way. Not only did China move to secure its second strike capability, it also embarked on passive defence measures to enhance China's credibility of survival in case war broke out. None of these changes contradicted the principles of people's war or the concept of nuclear weapons as a paper tiger, but they did indicate the flexibility of these principles. By despising nuclear weapons strategically, China could still take them seriously tactically. Hence China's bending to Soviet nuclear pressure in the short run did not necessarily mean a policy of long-term obedience.

The striking aspect of the use of the Chinese military instrument in the 1969 crisis, was the bilateral nature of the conflict. Few outside influences seem to have intruded, as China tried to cope with the changing Soviet threat. However, several, less immediate types of third party influence can be outlined.

Chinese policy was in part designed to appeal to other parties in the Communist world. The Asian communists, especially in Vietnam and to a lesser extent in Korea, were crucial targets for a China trying to warn about the danger of the Soviet threat. It can be plausibly argued that China's forward defence in the face of the Soviet threat had much to do with China's insistence to Vietnam that an uncompromising attitude should be taken toward the US threat in Southeast Asia.[44] The parallel growth of Soviet power and the decline of US involvement in Asia was undoubtedly an important part of China's strategic overview. Vietnam was equally relevant for the course of Chinese policy in September, when Beijing seized on the Ho Chi Minh testament as an excuse to capitulate to Soviet demands. If Hanoi had been an important forum for China's early hard line, then it also made sense to serve as a forum for China's revised policy.

The other state which figured in a passive way in Sino-Soviet crisis management was the United States. The role of the great power triangle at this time has already been comprehensively analysed elsewhere.[45] Suffice it to say that two possible areas for a United States role have been outlined. First, there is the suggestion that China bent to Soviet wishes because the option of a Sino-American detente was fore-closed. Had China been able to develop the early signs of detente in November 1968, then it would not have felt the need either to take on the Soviet threat, or, on the other hand, it would have felt more able to withstand Soviet pressure.

Where both of these hypotheses fall down is on the view that China was challenging the Soviet Union out of a perception of weakness. The most striking aspect of the early phase of the Sino-Soviet clashes was that China seemed to feel that Moscow could be taught a lesson not to apply the Brezhnev doctrine to China. What is more, for China to seek United States assistance in times of weakness, would not have been characteristic for Beijing. In fact, at no time did China seem willing to deal with the United States out of weakness. The cancellation of the February Warsaw talks on the excuse that a Chinese chargé d'affaires had defected in Holland no doubt indicated part of such Chinese sensitivity to appearing weak. Factional politics in Beijing may have also played its part (see below). But there seems little evidence that China undertook a specific policy towards the Soviet Union that was dependent on Sino-American relations.

Similarly, it is notable that the eventual Sino-American detente followed rather than preceded the reduction in Sino-Soviet tension. Not only did China respond to American initiatives (that were only seriously put forward in 1970, after the US recognized the depth of Sino-Soviet problems) but China did not scurry to the US, not even when faced with Soviet sabre-rattling.[46] The Chinese decision to reduce tension with the Soviet Union resulted from an assessment of the specific Sino-Soviet balance. The decision may well have had a spin-off effect in making it easier to take up US detente initiatives, but it is crucial that Sino-American rapprochement followed the Sino-Soviet clash and therefore was possibly a result of and certainly not a causal factor in Sino-Soviet crisis management.

The United States factor was more important in the passive role as a transmitter of Soviet seriousness in threatening China. The August nuclear weapons threats, made public by American government officials after discussions with Soviet officials in Washington, were high quality and plausible signals to China that Moscow was genuinely worried. Their credibility was no doubt enhanced by the already well established Chinese view of super-power collusion on nuclear matters.[47] The announcement on 14 March, just prior to the second Sino-Soviet border incident, of the American anti-China, Anti-Ballistic Missile system (ABM) no doubt enhanced this Chinese image of superpower collusion. Thus while one may rightly cast doubt on just how seriously the Soviet Union was sounding out US intentions on the idea of a surgical strike against China,[48] one cannot dismiss the importance of such action as a high quality signal to Beijing. Therefore the United States, like Vietnam, served as a forum for Sino-Soviet signalling. But beyond such passive involvement, it is difficult to suggest that outside powers had an important impact on the conduct and outcome of the 1969 Sino-Soviet crisis.

The Domestic Dimension

It should come as no surprise that China's turbulent domestic politics had an impact on foreign policy, but it is far from easy to identify the precise nature of that impact. China, in 1969, was moving from the final stages of the Cultural Revolution to the first phases of Defence Minister Lin Biao's challenge to Mao's rule. While both issues were overwhelmingly concerned with domestic politics, it has already been suggested that foreign policy was not untouched. Three domestic aspects of the 1969 Sino-Soviet border crisis are most often cited as most important.

First, it has been suggested that following the Soviet invasion of Czechoslovakia, Zhou Enlai and Mao Zedong, saw the need for greater vigilance against Moscow.[49] Others, including parts of the PLA and Mao's wife Qiang Qing and her radicals, were less con-cerned about the problem and saw less need to alter policy. It is argued that in November, Zhou was able to take initial steps to improve relations with the United States and therefore improve China's defence against the Soviet Union. The radical counter-attack by December reversed the opening to the United States.

While it is undeniable that the Chinese leadership was debating domestic policy and had begun the process of stepping back from the Cultural Revolution in October 1968, it is less clear that foreign policy divergences were either so evident or relevant to Sino-Soviet relations. Furthermore, it is unclear where such important actors as the PLA Chief of Staff Huang Yongsheng fit in.[50] He seemed to assume different positions depending on where and when he spoke. What is more, the option of developing relations with the United States was not then seriously available to appeal to some elements in the Chinese leadership. China's opening to the United States was not only a less sudden change than some suggest, but it also was dependent on a positive United States response, which was not apparent at the time. No doubt the defection of the Chinese chargé d'affaires was crucial in killing any idea of dealing with the United States for the time being.

It is also important to note that there was no necessary link between Sino-American and Sino-Soviet relations in early 1969. While there may have been a dispute in Beijing over whether to talk to the United States, this did not necessarily mean that there was a debate on how to respond to Soviet policy. It seems likely that there were some foreign policy issues where the Chinese leadership was divided, but the link to Sino-Soviet crisis politics is more asserted than established.

The second important aspect, where domestic politics were said to affect the course of the Sino-Soviet crisis, is the question of why China triggered the 2 March clash. Various conspiracy theorists adopt one or other variation on the line that Zhou and Mao went behind the back of Lin Biao and engineered the incident, so as to trigger a policy giving special attention to the Soviet threat and thereby sanctioning Sino-American detente.[51] Such a convoluted theory has its problems.

First, there exists a more plausible and simple explanation for the outbreak of fighting—that mutual escalation boiled over into open hostilities when patrol policy was altered by China so as to teach the Soviet Union a lesson. Second, it is unlikely that Lin's command of the PLA could have been circumvented for so long and so flagrantly.[52] Third, it is difficult to imagine that Zhou and Mao could have envisaged that a major clash with the Soviet Union would weaken Lin as the defence minister. Indeed, his position reached new heights after the incident, as he was appointed Mao's heir apparent.[53] Fourth, such a conspiracy theory goes against the grain of previous exercises of PLA power in foreign policy and also assumes a higher risk Chinese foreign policy.

A more likely explanation is that various groups in the Chinese leadership, divided primarily on internal policy issues, had differing perspectives on foreign policy, but not necessarily those that need erupt into open conflict. Zhou may well have seen the Soviet Union as more threatening than Lin, and therefore thought a controlled border conflict might serve usefully to raise the issue to the fore. Lin may well have gone along with the policy, assuming that the Soviet response would be low key and his own stature as defence minister would be enhanced by new tension. Consensus in complex policy-making situations is often arrived at by stranger means than these.

Whatever the specific alignment of forces, it seems probable that both Lin and Zhou misread Soviet intentions. Zhou found that the Soviet Union would not so easily succumb to being taught lessons, and Lin discovered that the risks were higher than he thought. Throughout the summer, and especially after August, a new decision was being forced on the Chinese by the Kremlin. China's response in September/October is the third possible area where factional politics played a crucial role.

It is strange that those who make much of possible factional debates over the decision to engage the Soviet Union along the border often ignore the termination of the crisis. Surely the factional politics do not stop in March. In fact, it seems more likely that the extent of debate in the autumn was little different than in the spring. In September/October it seems that China gradually gave way to Soviet pressure—and in a way where different leaders could find their own rationalization. All groups were no doubt satisfied that the Soviet Union had made some concessions. Zhou was probably most concerned with the seriousness of Soviet threats and the need to lower China's conflict with both superpowers. Lin was probably most impressed by the Ho Chi Minh testament as an excuse to back down and the new campaign for war-preparedness which would strengthen his position.[54] It is striking that, at the highest level, there was no debate or recrimination over the decision to talk to the Soviet Union. Not even after Lin's purge, or the attacks on Zhou later in the 1970s, was there any mention of possible 'capitulationism' to Soviet pressure.

There are of course important grounds for speculation on possible factional politics.[55] The Chinese invitation to Kosygin on 11 September obviously came very late and may have resulted from some last minute Beijing debates. On the other hand the delay might have merely been to embarrass Kosygin. What is more, there were some lower level reports of disunity at the time when talks were resumed with the Soviet Union. Apparently, 'some people' did not think the Soviet threat very serious and did not see the need for war prepara- tion. In reply, the Chinese press recalled that Mao said 'without preparedness, superiority is not real superiority' and therefore urged preparation against the Soviet Union.[56]

It seems possible that such passive views were perhaps held by radicals wishing to pursue the Cultural Revolution. But the main power centres—Lin, Zhou and Mao—probably agreed that the Soviet threat was real, and something had to be done. Lin may have stressed preparedness and Zhou may have emphasized diplomatic concession, as befitting their respective bureaucratic positions. But, whatever the case, the conclusion was a relatively united policy leading to a reduction of Sino-Soviet tension. On 1 October Lin and Zhou's speeches represented nearly identical foreign policy lines,[57] and on 15 October wide coverage was given to Mao and Lin's appearance in front of PLA men.[58] The new line favouring negotiation may have caused some problems, as some saw China's line as backtracking from previous firmness.[59] However, such a policy is always easier to sustain if there is relative unanimity among the major decision makers. This seemed to be the case in 1969.

In sum, there were clearly debates in China running on from the Cultural Revolution.[60] But while these debates may have had some foreign policy implications, they were primarily unconcerned with the Sino-Soviet crisis. Undoubtedly Chinese management of the crisis was made more complex by these domestic dissensions, but clear-cut factional lines on the crisis are not evident. It is important to appreciate this complexity of policy-making, but it is impossible to even outline a persuasive theory on how it *determined* Chinese policy in the crisis. In fact, the most important implication of the Cultural Revolution's domestic dimension was the over-arching sense of domestic unrest. This general policy-making environment apparently led Chinese leaders first to feel overly threatened by the Soviet Union, and then to over react to these misperceptions by trying to teach the Soviet Union a lesson after the invasion of Czechoslovakia. That such a policy failed is not unusual, for the Cultural Revolution with its overblown hopes and rhetoric also failed. New realism came to Chinese foreign policy before it came to domestic policy, in large part because of Soviet pressure. In the end, it was China that learned lessons in both domestic and foreign policy.

Conclusions

China's basic objective in the 1969 crisis—to deter perceived Soviet threats—was largely achieved. However, the immediacy of the Soviet threat and the level of the crisis was largely brought about by China's own misperceptions and offensive policy. China's paranoia led it to believe there was a Soviet threat to China in the form of the Brezhnev doctrine and that a forward policy of deterrence would disabuse the Soviet Union of the illusion that China could be treated like the East Europeans. When Chinese forward deterrence failed and the Soviet Union's paranoia about China was activated, China struggled to deter Soviet attempts to compel China to negotiate over the dispute. The eventual compromise offered only minor comfort to Beijing and in the end illustrated Soviet military superiority. To be sure, China was seen to be a harder nut to crack than Czechoslovakia, but then it is unlikely that anyone seriously thought the two to be similar, except in the Chinese paranoia about Soviet strategy.

The Chinese put themselves through this unnecessary test in part due to the deep fears generated by the hostile mood of the Cultural Revolution. In the end, China was revealed to be more of a paper tiger than the Soviet Union and China was taught more of a lesson than the Soviet Union. China's weakness in conventional military power was consistently demonstrated along the frontier, so long as the Soviet Union was not caught unaware. A forward Chinese deterrence of the perceived Soviet threat would have involved defence beyond the gates (as in Korea or Vietnam) but was ruled out by superior Soviet power. When China recognized this weakness, it chose to stand and fight on the border. Even here, China was consistently mauled by superior Soviet fire-power. So long as the Soviet Union held its troops at the frontier, it would do the punishing and not the Chinese. Mao's people's war might well have deterred a large-scale Soviet operation, but then none was apparently planned. When the Soviet Union chose only to apply limited power, China found it not only needed more flexible responses, but also more fire-power. This was a lesson only learned by China in the course of combat.

On the nuclear level, China showed similar adaptability in responding to the enemy's power. While at first denigrating, and then later taking seriously the Soviet threat, China applied Mao's dictum of taking Soviet nuclear power seriously tactically, while despising it strategically. Chinese nuclear doctrine did not so much evolve as illustrate just how flexible it always had been. In the context of limited crises, as in 1969 where Chinese power was weak, Beijing was forced to take nuclear weapons and strategy most seriously and retreat in the face of Soviet pressure.

These aspects of defence policy were of course carried out in the context of domestic politics riven by factional debates. In one respect the outbreak of the crisis can be blamed on excessive defensiveness, growing out of domestic unrest. Thus, without the domestic dimension of crisis, there might well have been no Sino-Soviet crisis. But it is far more difficult to establish precise links between domestic factions and foreign policy crisis management. Domestic factions certainly complicate any full analysis, but it also seems clear that foreign policy resulted largely from changing consensus and not the victory of one faction over another. The fact that China got itself into an unnecessary crisis, from which it then struggled to extricate itself, must be blamed on the leadership as a whole. But as we have already seen from previous case studies, less than perfectly rational and consistent formulation and execution of Chinese defence policy was not unknown in the past. China, like other great powers, can make mistakes.

NOTES

1. Richard Wich, *Sino-Soviet Crisis Politics* (Cambridge: Harvard University Press, 1980); Melvin Gurtov and Byoong-Moo Hwang, *China Under Threat* (London: Johns Hopkins University Press, 1980); Thomas Robinson, 'The Sino-Soviet Border Conflict' in Stephen Kaplan, *Diplomacy of Power* (Washington: Brookings, 1981); Thomas Robinson, *The Sino-Soviet Border Dispute* (Santa Monica, California: The Rand Corp. RM-617-PR, August 1970); Harold Hinton, 'Conflict on the Ussuri', *Problems of Communism*, Jan–April 1971.
2. Kenneth Lieberthal, *Sino-Soviet Conflict in the 1970s* (Santa Monica, California: The Rand Corp. R-2342-NA, July 1978); Thomas Gottlieb, *Chinese Foreign Policy Factionalism and the Origins of the Strategic Triangle* (Santa Monica, California: The Rand Corp. R-1902-NA, Nov. 1977); Roger Braun, 'Chinese Politics and American Policy', *Foreign Policy*, No. 23, Summer 1976.
3. For background detail see O. Edmund Clubb, *China and Russia* (New York: Columbia University Press, 1971).
4. This section draws heavily on Wich, *Sino-Soviet Crisis*.

194   *Defending China*

5. *Strategic Survey, 1969*, (London: IISS, 1970); *Military Balance, 1967–68* (London: IISS, 1967); and *Military Balance, 1968–69* (London: IISS, 1968). Also Harry Gelman, *The Soviet Far East Buildup and Soviet Risk-Taking Against China* (Santa Monica, California: The Rand Corp. R-2943-AF, August 1982); Neville Maxwell, 'The Chinese Account of the 1969 Fighting at Chenpao', *The China Quarterly*, No. 56, 1973.
6. The question of responsibility for the 2 March clash has obsessed many analysts. What seems least important is who fired first, for the clash was made virtually inevitable by the Chinese decision to patrol actively the disputed territory. Although the Chinese reported the clash several hours after the Soviet Union, Beijing clearly had a swifter and better orchestrated propaganda campaign. Early Soviet reaction was remarkably low key and responsive to Chinese charges. Also, Soviet satellite launches in this period occurred after the First clash, but were not recovered until after the 2 March incident. However, new ones launched soon after were recovered before the 15 March clash. *Soviet Space Program: 1976–80*, US Senate, Committee on Commerce, Science and Transportation, 97th Congress, 2nd Session (Washington: USGPO, December 1982), pp. 411–13. Thus in many respects the outbreak of combat was less a premediated choice by one party, but rather a case of a heavily boiling pot, boiling over. However, it does seem clear that the Chinese hand was the last one to turn up the heat.
7. Wich, *Sino-Soviet Crisis*.
8. *Ibid*, Gelman, *Soviet Far East*, and similar pattern of Kosmos launching in *Soviet Space Program*.
9. *New York Times*, 29 August 1969; Henry Kissinger, *The White House Years* (London: Weidenfeld and Nicolson and Michael Joseph, 1979) reports, pp. 183–4, that on 18 August a middle level State Department specialist on Soviet affairs at lunch with a Soviet embassy official was asked what the US reaction would be to a Soviet attack on Chinese nuclear facilities. In late August, US intelligence detected a stand-down of Soviet airforces in the Far East which permitted all aircraft to be brought to a high state of readiness. He also noted new Soviet statements on war in the Pacific in World War II. See also the very idiosyncratic reports by H. R. Haldeman (with Joseph Dimona), *The Ends of Power* (London: Sedgwick and Jackson, 1978), Ch. 2.
10. Wich, *Sino-Soviet Crisis*.
11. On 16 September, Victor Louis wrote in the *London Evening Standard* that 'well informed sources in Moscow said there were Soviet nuclear weapons aimed at Chinese nuclear facilities' and the Soviet Union preferred the use of rockets to manpower in dealing with China. He noted Soviet plans to attack Chinese facilities at Lop Nor.
12. Wich, *Sino-Soviet Crisis*, pp. 56–72.
13. Gelman, *Soviet Far East*, pp. 26–8; Gurtov and Hwang *China Under Threat*, pp. 216–221.
14. NCNA 28 December 1968 in *SCMP* No. 4330, pp. 10–11; NCNA 31 January 1969, in No. 4354, pp. 31–3; and *People's Daily*, 2 February in No. 4355, pp. 25–6.
15. Gelman, *Soviet Far East*, pp. 31–4.
16. John Despres, Lilita Dzirkals, Barton Whaley, *Timely Lessons of History* (Santa Monica, California: The Rand Corp. R-1825-NA July 1976); Lilita Dzirkals, *'Lightning War' in Manchuria* (Santa Monica, California: The Rand Corp. P-5589, January 1976).
17. 8 March article in *Red Star* and 15 March, *Radio Peace and Progress*, both cited in Gelman, *Soviet Far East*, p. 37.
18. Gurtov and Hwang, *China Under Threat*, pp. 230–4.

19. Various reports from 2–15 March in *SCMP*, Nos. 4372–82.
20. NCNA 9 March 1969 in *SCMP* No. 4376, p. 24 and NCNA 17 March in No. 4382 p. 16–7. This latter article noted the US decision to deploy an anti-China ABM as part of US–Soviet collusion against China.
21. Cited in Stuart Schram, *Mao Tse-Tung Unrehearsed* (London: Penguin, 1974), pp. 285–6. Mao also said China would not fight beyond its borders although it had done so several times since 1949.
22. Gelman, *Soviet Far East*.
23. For example Chinese government statement, 24 May 1969 in *SCMP*, No. 4426, pp. 24–32. Also NCNA, 3 June in No. 4433, pp. 23–5.
24. Maxwell, 'Chinese Account', NCNA 13 April 1969, in *SCMP*, No. 4398, p. 9; NCNA 17 May in No. 4419, pp. 14–16.
25. See note 9 and Gelman, *Soviet Far East*. Also Seymour Hersh, *The Price of Power* (New York: Summit Books, 1983), pp. 357–8.
26. For the few exceptions see *Peking Home Service*, 19 September 1969 in *BBC*/SWB/FE/3186/A2/5.
27. Lin Biao on 1 October in *BBC*/SWB/FE/3192/C/1–2; 10 and 16 October in No. 3207/B/2–5.
28. NCNA 4 October 1964 in *BBC*/SWB/FE/3195/C/1.
29. Robinson, 'Sino-Soviet Conflict', pp. 269–273; Gurtov and Hwang, *China Under Threat*, p. 226.
30. Robinson, 'Sino-Soviet Conflict', pp. 273–276; Maxwell, 'Chinese Account', pp. 735–6. Gurtov and Hwang, *China Under Threat*, p. 236.
31. Maxwell, *Ibid*, notes China's claim of 20 dead and 34 wounded on its side, with up to 70 dead and wounded on the Soviet side. Wich, *Sino-Soviet Crisis*, notes 31 Soviet dead.
32. Robinson, 'Sino-Soviet Conflict', p. 277, Maxwell, 'Chinese Account', pp. 736–8, Wich, *Sino-Soviet Crisis*, pp. 109–10.
33. See note 21.
34. *People's Daily*, 31 January 1968, in *SCMP*, No. 4111, p. 52; *People's Daily*, 1 February 1969, in No. 4359, pp. 1–5; NCNA 13 April 1979, in No. 4398, p. 9; NCNA 24 May 1969, in No. 4427, pp. 29–32.
35. Hinton, 'Conflict on the Ussuri', pp. 50–2. Lieberthal, *Sino-Soviet Conflict*, p. 50. Also, *Strategic Survey*, pp. 71–2.
36. NCNA 13 April 1969 in *SCMP*, No. 4398, p. 9; NCNA 14 May in No. 4419, pp. 14–16.
37. NCNA 17 March 1969 in *SCMP*, No. 4382, pp. 16–20; PRC Government statement 24 May in No. 4426, pp. 31–2. NCNA 25 May in No. 4428, pp. 14–16; NCNA 3 June in No. 4433, pp. 23–5; *People's Daily, Red Flag, Liberation Army Daily*, 1 August in No. 4470, pp. 14–15.
38. For low key PRC responses in August see NCNA 14, August 1969, in *SCMP* No. 4480 p. 29. *Peking Home Service*, 19 September, in *BBC*/SWB/FE/3186/A2/5. Lin Biao on 1 October, in No. 3192/C/1–2. On civil defence see Donald McMillen, 'Civil Defence in the People's Republic of China', *The Australian Journal of Chinese Affairs*, No. 8, 1982.
39. Jonathan, Pollack, 'Chinese Attitudes Towards Nuclear Weapons, 1964–69'. *The China Quarterly*, No. 50, April 1972.
40. Gerald Segal, 'China's Nuclear Posture for the 1980s', *Survival* Vol. 23 No. 1, Jan/Feb. 1981; Gerald Segal, 'Nuclear Forces' in Gerald Segal and William Tow eds., *Chinese Defence Policy* (London: Macmillan, 1984); Gerald Segal, 'Strategy and Ethnic-chic', *International Affairs*, Vol. 60 No. 1, January 1984.
41. Morton Halperin, *China and the Bomb*. (London: Pall Mall, 1965.)

42. Alice Langley Hsieh, 'China's Nuclear Missile Programme', *The China Quarterly*, No. 45, June 1971; Michael Minor, 'The Chinese Nuclear Development Program', *Asian Survey*, June 1976; *Strategic Survey 1968* (London: IISS, 1969), p. 41. China seemed to be having trouble reducing its warhead size to fit its missile force.

43. Pollack, 'Chinese Attitude'.

44. Wich, *Sino-Soviet Crisis*, pp. 81–3.

45. The points that follow draw on Lieberthal, *Sino-Soviet Conflict* and Gelman, *Soviet Far East*. An otherwise idiosyncratic analysis by Greg O'Leary, *The Shaping of Chinese Foreign Policy* (London: Croom Helm, 1980) does make the valid point that China did not initiate the change in Sino-American relations, but rather it was the US that changed its policy. See also Robert Sutter, *China-Watch* (Baltimore: Johns Hopkins, 1978).

46. The July 1969 lifting of US–China trade restrictions had no immediate impact on Sino-American relations. However, the November 1969 ending of Taiwan Straits patrols by the United States was a more important signal of intent that was taken seriously in China. Kissinger, *The White House Years*. It should also be noted that there is no evidence that Soviet policy towards China during the crisis was in any way affected by the course of United States policy, despite Kissinger's hints to the contrary. Gerald Segal, 'An Assessment of the Great Power Triangle' in Gerald Segal ed., *The China Factor* (London: Croom Helm, 1982).

47. NCNA 17 March 1969 in *SCMP* No. 4382 pp. 16–17; NCNA 3 June in No. 4433 pp. 23–5.

48. See notes 9 and 11. Also Gelman, *Soviet Far East* pp. 38–40.

49. Thomas Gottlieb, *Chinese Foreign Policy Factionalism and the Origins of the Strategic Triangle* (Santa Monica, California: Rand Corp. R-1902-NA, November 1977) pp. 84–112.

50. On Huang see Wich, *Sino-Soviet Crisis*, p. 70.

51. Gottlieb, *Chinese Factionalism* pp. 116–120; Roger Brown, 'Chinese Politics and American Policy', *Foreign Policy* No. 23, Summer 1976.

52. Gurtov and Hwang, *China Under Threat*, pp. 238–9.

53. Lieberthal, *Sino-Soviet Conflict*, pp. 6–7.

54. For background see Gurtov and Hwang, *China Under Threat* pp. 229–232; Wich, *Sino-Soviet Crisis* pp. 194–9.

55. Some have suggested that Chinese defence spending was affected by the Sino-Soviet crisis. Recent western analysis of Chinese spending finds no grounds for such suppositions. Central Intelligence Agency, *Chinese Defence Spending, 1965–79* (July 1980).

56. Chekiang Provincial Service, 1 September 1969 in *BBC*/SWB/FE/3174/B11/1; NCNA reports of 10 and 16 September in No. 3207/B/2–5. Also, Robinson, *Sino-Soviet Border*, p. 47.

57. *BBC*/SWB/FE/3192/C/1–2.

58. *BBC*/SWB/FE/3205/B/2.

59. PLA Nanking united cited in *BBC*/SWB/FE/3208/i.

60. Generally see Gurtov and Hwang, *China Under Threat*, pp. 187–208.

11

Xisha, 1974

China's seizure of the Xisha (Paracel) Islands in January 1974 was ostensibly merely a natural reassertion of control over Chinese territory. Like the take-over of Tibet it's outcome was largely determined by the availability to China of sufficient offensive power and the relative unconcern of outside powers. In the Tibet case the losers were obscure Tibetan nationalists, and in 1974 in the Xisha Islands the loser was the rapidly disappearing regime in Saigon. Unlike the Taiwan Straits incidents, this resolution of Beijing's irridentist claims met no superpower opposition and therefore was swiftly successful.

Also like the Tibet operation, and unlike other cases of China's use of military force in support of its foreign policy, the Xisha case has been virtually ignored in previous Western studies.[1] This oversight is surely not due to the scale of casualties, for they were comparable to the Taiwan and Zhenbao cases. Rather the neglect seems due to a complex series of reasons, including the fact that the superpowers took no part because they were unable to decide whom to support, and because it was a swift operation that involved merely Asian killing Asian for coral reefs in the South China Seas.[2] But in a study of how China uses force in its foreign policy, the Xisha case should not be so easily ignored.

Course of Events

China had long claimed sovereignty over South China Sea islands and at regular intervals, but lacked the power to support its cause. For example, in February 1959 when forces from South Vietnam expelled Chinese residents and fishermen from Shenhang (Duncan) Island in the Yongle (Crescent) group of the Xisha Islands, China meekly suffered the humiliation and in the meantime reinforced its hold on the Xuande (Amphitrite) group of the Xisha.[3] However, fifteen years later, another South Vietnamese provocation received a devastating Chinese riposte.

On 20 July 1973 Saigon awarded oil concessions to Western companies that in part encompassed the Nansha Archipelago. On 6 September the Vietnamese authorities tried to clarify the legal position for the companies by incorporating several islands in the archipelago under the control of South Vietnam's Phuoc Tuy province. However, various states who had competing claims protested at the action. China's response came four months later, after initial surveying and drilling had revealed exploitable oil deposits.[4] On 11 January 1974 a Chinese Ministry of Foreign Affairs statement denounced the South Vietnamese action and 'reiterated' China's claim to the islands, as well as to the Northern Xisha Archipelago and surrounding resources.[5]

Despite that fact that attention had so far focused on the Nansha Islands, military moves took place in the Xisha Archipelago. Since both sides held different islands in the Xisha area and China could deploy sufficient military force only in these northern islands, the new venue was logical. According to Beijing's version, on 15 January Saigon troops intruded in the Yongle Group, especially around Ganquan (Robert) Island and attacked Chinese fishermen and naval vessels on patrol. China had not previously held the Yongle Group. China reported further incidents on 17 January at Ganquan and Jinqing (Drummond) Islands, in the group where South Vietnamese forces landed and removed the Chinese flag, apparently planted on the 16th. Chinese naval forces were reinforced on the 17th but on the following day further incidents took place in the area. While South Vietnamese forces apparently opened fire first, Chinese troops had provoked them by contesting islands previously held by Saigon troops.[6]

After having failed to dislodge Vietnamese troops by a show of force, China then removed the mailed fist from its protective glove. On 19 January, China expressed 'strong indignation' at South Vietnamese action and warned Saigon that if it persisted, the South Vietnamese were 'bound to eat their own bitter fruit'.[7] But this was less an exercise in judicious crisis management, and more a declaration of intent, for on the same day China brought to bear superior air and naval power and defeated the South Vietnamese forces. After losing one patrol boat with 50–60 of their own people on board, the PLA sank two South Vietnamese boats of similar size and, with a force of 600 men, launched an amphibious operation on Shenhang Island, where Saigon troops had landed in the previous few days.[8] On 20 January China wrapped up its gunboat diplomacy by occupying Jinyin (Money) and Shanhu (Pattle) Islands as Vietnamese troops withdrew.

On 29 January China announced it would begin returning the 48 South Vietnamese and 1 American captured,[9] and began reinforcing its newly acquired coral reefs. Attention now turned south to the Nansha Islands where Saigon immediately began reinforcing its garrison. On 4 February, the Chinese Ministry of Foreign Affairs protested at these new moves[10] and many feared this was a prelude to yet another Chinese strike. However, while Taiwan, Indonesia, and the Philippines all made their positions clear, China made no military moves.[11] Having lost the element of surprise, and lacking sufficient naval punch at this long reach, Beijing escalated no further and international concern about a second phase of military operations swiftly faded away.

Objectives

In the 1959 Xisha engagement, China's objective of imposing its definition of territorial sovereignty was thwarted due to lack of military power. Fifteen years later, China's revenge was sweet, but its basic objective had not changed. The Xisha action, like the take-over of Tibet twenty-five years earlier was essentially a result of Beijing's desire to compel others to accept its definition of Chinese territory. China's success in 1974 was largely due to the weakness of its opponent, and the propitiousness of the moment chosen.

China's 11 January statement makes plain the central desire to safeguard China's sovereignty.[12] Saigon's 'wanton infringement of China's territorial integrity and sovereignty' was not new, but now China thought it could act to restore its own control. The specific moment was apparently chosen for a number of reasons. First, Saigon's provocation in the previous September and the encouraging signs of reasonable oil deposits made it relatively urgent that China pre-empt any further international involvement in Chinese-claimed territory. Second, the imminent collapse of South Vietnam meant that if China wanted to avoid a clash with its own ally in North Vietnam over whether the islands were Vietnamese or Chinese,

Beijing had to act before Saigon's forces were defeated by the north. Third, the United States, now embroiled in the Watergate affair, had only recently discovered the 'China card' and was dropping its commitment to South Vietnam. Thus Washington was less likely actively to oppose Chinese action as it repeatedly did in the Taiwan Straits crises.

Therefore it was not Chinese objectives that changed in 1974, but rather the international circumstances had altered so that Beijing could now achieve its objectives. Three phases in this process are evident. First, the 11 January statement emphasized concern over the Nansha rather than Xisha Islands, but this was less a case of Chinese deception, and more a general announcement of China's intent to safeguard its sovereignty. It provided the excuse for action triggered by Saigon's move in September to change the status quo.

In the second phase China shifted the scene to the Xisha Islands themselves, where from 15–19 January Beijing tried 'showing the flag' on its gunboats and fishing vessels in the hope that Saigon would back down without a fight.[13] When the South Vietnamese decided to fight, perhaps in the hope that North Vietnam might restrain China,[14] Beijing moved into the third of its three offensive phases and seized the Yongle Group. When Saigon then shifted its attention to the protection of the Nansha Islands, China did not move into phase four, despite ominous statements indicating as much concern with Nansha as for Xisha. Chinese restraint had more to do with an absence of capability than with a surfeit of respect for Vietnamese claims.[15]

A striking feature of China's pursuit of its primary objective—securing its sovereignty when faced with minimal opposition—was the speed of its execution. Little time was left for anything but a military solution and certainly there seemed to be little attempt to manage the crisis peacefully. The military operations began four days after China's first statement and ended on 19 January, at the same time as China issued what could be seen as its first warning. The suddenness of the operation led to military success, but cast serious doubt on the view that China's use of force always follows a carefully orchestrated campaign.

Two other Chinese objectives were relevant to Beijing's 1974 calculation, although neither was particularly important in the 1959 Xisha events. First, there was China's concern to safeguard possible oil resources in the islands. It is obvious that the trigger for Chinese action was Saigon's move on oil prospecting, and above all the new evidence that there were in fact real exploitable resources at stake. This is not to say that China urgently required Xisha or Nansha oil, for it already had more readily accessible resources in less disputed territory.[16] But especially after the October 1973 Arab–Israeli war and the OPEC oil embargo, the oil issue had assumed much greater international importance than before. The near panic and evident uncertainty in the West following the embargo may well have helped make China jumpy about protecting its own valuable resources. China's 11 January statement made it plain that Beijing was reiterating its claim to the islands and 'natural resources'.[17] Thus the safeguarding of oil prospects may well have been a contributory, rather than a determining reason, for Chinese intervention.

China's final objective is harder to pin down, but also seems to have contributed to the decision to act. It is apparent that China had emerged from the Cultural Revolution and the Lin Biao affair with a new interest in a more active foreign policy. While most of this policy was concerned with wider aspects of international affairs, and some of it was under debate in Beijing (see below), the new policies did have some impact on the Xisha events. First, China's new firm line against Soviet hegemonism had, since the early 1970s, became concerned with the growth of Soviet naval power, especially in the Indian Ocean.[18] It is important to note that the seas between the Xisha and Nansha Islands provided the only access for shipping from north east Asia to the Indian Ocean. The coral reefs in the area had served as mid-sea anchorages for both superpowers, but access through the area was especially crucial for the Soviet navy operating out of Vladivostok.[19]

Second, since the early 1970s there had been a growing maritimist trend in the Chinese navy, which marked a move away from the previous strictly coastal role.[20] Along with expansion in the Chinese merchant navy and development of new port facilities, China seemed far more involved in extended naval policy. Finally, with its entry into the United Nations in 1971, and China's prominent role in the UN Law of the Sea conference, Beijing was generally paying more attention to the strategic significance of naval power.[21] In this atmosphere, it is not surprising that the Xisha issue received such forceful attention from China. Official Chinese statements rarely made much of the islands' strategic value,[22] but certainly the concern with the expansion of Soviet naval power in general[23] was becoming a major string in China's anti-Soviet propaganda bow.

In sum, China's three-fold objectives were all swiftly met in what appeared to be a neatly scripted model of coercive diplomacy. Chinese objectives did not change in the course of the combat, although China had to adjust its timing when Saigon failed to capitulate immediately. Such pragmatism was in fact in keeping with the spirit of the operation, for China had waited fifteen years until the circumstances were right before having the courage of its objectives and taking the islands. That China has not fulfilled its stated objectives of controlling the Nansha as well as Xisha Islands, must be blamed primarily on the lack of military power at that distance. Similar limits constrained China in 1959 but not 1974 regarding Xisha, and by 1990 China may be ready for the complete attainment of its objectives.

Operations

On the one hand China's conduct of military operations in 1974 entailed low risk. Proper conditions were judiciously chosen so that great power intervention would be least likely and the risks of war contained. On the other hand, the Xisha campaign can be seen as one of higher risk when it is considered that China pursued the military option with ruthless determination. Confusing and inaccurate signals were sent to Saigon and no opportunity was given for a peaceful solution. Perhaps more than any other example of the use of force in Chinese foreign policy, the Xisha case illustrates Beijing's confidence, bordering on arrogance, in the use of military power.

China did not deploy a massive show of military power, but considering the paltry South Vietnamese fleet and garrison, China's 7–11 ships, including several of the Komar class carrying modern styx missiles, were enough to overwhelm the enemy. The 19–20 January operation was in fact a combined-arms operation, including some 600 men involved in an amphibious landing supported by MIG aircraft based on island of Hainan. While most Chinese troops were drawn from those already based in the Xuande Group of islands, including local militia, clearly a certain degree of central planning was required to co-ordinate the three service arms. Furthermore, the intervention of the modern Komar class ships provided the decisive punch that forced Saigon to back down.[24]

Despite some Vietnamese claims that China used human wave

tactics to overcome the garrison, there is no evidence to support or deny this allegation.[25] Despite China's claim that this was example of a 'people's navy' at work, which did not fear using old equipment,[26] in reality the victory was achieved with very modern equipment, using modern tactics against a hopelessly out-classed opponent. It is possible that the militia's role was emphasized for reasons of domestic factional politics (see below) but the operation was a brief, modern example of gunboat diplomacy where superior steel and electronics triumphed.

Chinese casualties are not known, but if the reports of the loss of one patrol ship are accurate, then at least 50 Chinese died. Saigon also reported that it inflicted heavy shelling on Shenhang Island where more Chinese soldiers were said to have died.[27] Vietnamese casualties were acknowledged to be more than 130 dead, mostly inflicted when ships were sunk. Whatever the precise total of casualties, China clearly got the better of the clash and could be satisfied that this was a small price to pay for the swift military and political gains. The success of the operation hinged in fact on attaining surprise, and such swift results.

A longer campaign might well have thwarted Chinese objectives because other states might then have become involved. As it was, the military operation involved only the two protagonists. China's greatest skill in the Xisha operation was in choosing the moment when the superpowers and the Democratic Republic of Vietnam (DRV) were unlikely to oppose Chinese action. As best illustrated by the pathetic antics in the United Nations Security Council, none of the major powers wanted to call the Council into session for fear of illuminating their ambiguous positions.[28] China, as a recently seated member of the Council, would in any case have been likely to veto any resolution.

The most crucial superpower was obviously the United States. Not only did it have overwhelming military superiority in the area, with Seventh Fleet forces still involved in the nearby Vietnam war but, more importantly, it was the US forces which had blocked previous Chinese irridentist claims in the area in support of Taiwan. But the Xisha incident marked the first time China used military force after the United States had improved its relations with China, and the Nixon administration was loath to lose the leverage it thought the opening to China provided. Thus Washington was caught at a time of waxing support for China and waning support for

Saigon, and therefore maintained a strictly hands off policy.[29] The ironies for the United States, that only recently had lost more than 50,000 dead in Vietnam in opposition to the spread of communism, were keenly felt in Washington.

United States forces were expressly ordered to avoid any involvement in the Xisha clash and Washington even refused Saigon's appeal for aid when the battle was lost.[30] United States officials called for a peaceful solution, but refused to take sides. Secretary of State Kissinger, recently returned from yet another Middle East shuttle, was unwilling to be distracted, especially as the Watergate trauma was already sapping the strength of US foreign policy.[31] The fact that one American was among the 49 captured by the PLA was a cause for embarrassment in Washington rather than an excuse for its own gunboat diplomacy. It is also possible that the US helped the Chinese cause by convincing Saigon to withdraw after the first defeat. But even if this advice was not made explicit, certainly Washington's implicit policy encouraged such retreat. China had deftly played the Washington card.

The Soviet Union was less crucial as a potential actor. It was anyway neutralized, as was the DRV, by the timing of the Chinese operation. By choosing the time when the islands were still held by the common South Vietnamese enemy, little could be said in public opposition to Chinese strategy. The sounds of anguished silence from both Moscow and Hanoi were clearly audible. The Soviet Union, like the DRV, both had maps showing the Xisha Islands as Chinese territory, but the Soviet Union especially had reason to denounce Chinese policy on disputed territorial claims. Moscow resolved the problem by quoting hostile references to Chinese action in its press, along with perfunctory citation of the Chinese line.[32] By February some Soviet reports took a more openly hostile attitude towards Chinese action, decrying the deliberate worsening of tension in the area.[33] However, despite the Chinese expulsion of five Soviet citizens on alleged espionage charges in late January, Moscow still refused openly to make an issue of China's Xisha action. In 1975 more open Soviet criticism was made, but by then the crisis was long over.[34] By exploiting ambiguities in the communist world, in part created by the Sino-Soviet split, Beijing was able to ensure superpower silence in January 1974.

Hanoi was similarly gagged by China's timing. Tight-lipped spokesmen grumbled 'no comment', when questioned about ownership of the disputed islands. Vietcong representatives in Beijing and Hanoi replied tersely that the problem was 'complex' and should be resolved peacefully.[35] China's disagreement with the DRV in fact only became public after Hanoi's victory over the South in 1975 and its immediate replacement of Saigon's forces on the Nansha Islands. The dispute over offshore islands would later become a sideshow of the much more violent and complex Sino-Vietnamese conflict in the late 1970s[36] (see next chapter). Thus the DRV, like the two super-powers, was silenced by the swift and surgical execution of Chinese policy.

Despite the complexity of the legal claims over the disputed islands, no other states had a major role to play. China undoubtedly antagonized some South East Asian states by its sudden use of military force, raising fears of Chinese southward expansion.[37] But Beijing's limited operation against an unpopular regional dictator-ship on its last legs, meant that opposition to China was muted. Taiwan, while occupying some of the Nansha Islands, at least agreed with Beijing that the Xisha Islands were Chinese. Even Indonesia supported the Chinese claim to the Xisha Islands.[38]

In sum, the conduct of Chinese operations in 1974 could hardly have been more efficient. In military terms it was a textbook amphibious landing by combined arms forces. While Chinese troops were undoubtedly skilful, their victory can be attributed to superior technology, and above all a superior political position. Indeed, it was in political terms that China was most adept—choosing the perfect moment to enforce its claim when no one was willing to support the pariah regime in Saigon.

The Domestic Dimension

The international politics of China's Xisha operation were smooth and consistent, but what of the domestic dimension of this policy? Were there disagreements about the use of force? While it is clear that major questions of domestic and foreign policy were under debate in Beijing at this time, there is far less evidence to substantiate any link to the conduct of the Xisha operation.

At least two issues of domestic policy were in debate during 1974, but neither has an evident link to the Xisha question. The most important debate over the anti-Confucius campaign had begun in the autumn of 1973, just when Saigon awarded oil contracts for the

Nansha area, but there is no evidence that offshore islands figured at all in the campaign.[39] The course of the campaign shifted at least twice as radicals and moderates battled for its control, but none of the shifts correspond with changes in policy over the islands. Undoubtedly there were debates in Beijing, but they were very complex, and apparently not related to the Xisha question.

Similarly, defence spending and strategy also came under debate later in 1974, with an even more complex array of radicals, moderates, and centrists slugging it out for advantage.[40] However, despite the obvious differences of opinion on how much should be spent on defence and what kind of forces were most appropriate, the Xisha question was not raised in support of any of the protagonists. In fact, the defence spending question was so Byzantine that radicals, who at first supported the idea of higher spending so as to appeal to elements of the PLA, ended up having the campaign stolen from them by Deng Xiaoping and other moderates.

Debates on foreign policy issues were perhaps more clear cut than those on domestic policy, but even here there is no evidence of a link to the Xisha campaign. Apparently, the radicals opposed the new Chinese foreign policy that brought increased trade with the West and urged co-operation with the second and third worlds against Soviet power. The radicals called for greater self-reliance and an even harder line against the Soviet Union.[41] It is surmised that the expulsion in February, 1974 of five Soviet citizens was engineered by radical groups, but there is no evidence for a similar link to the Xisha venture. What is more, the divisions of opinion on foreign policy issues were often most complex, with figures like Zhou Enlai and Mao Zedong often shifting ground and the PLA largely sitting on the sidelines. If the Xisha question had been important, even as an example of one or other group's approach to broader foreign policy questions, one would have expected to see at least allegorical reference to the islands in the otherwise fairly obvious allegorical debates of the time. However, there is no evidence that the Xisha issue was used in such a way, nor did it feature as did other issues in retrospect after the fall of the radical Gang of Four. At the time of the crisis in 1974, the Xisha issue received very little national press coverage and, unlike the 1969 Sino-Soviet clash, was apparently not used for domestic purposes. The virtual black-out on the Xisha question in the domestic media was especially striking when compared to previous cases of the use of force in China's foreign policy.

While it is evident that domestic politics in China continued to be turbulent in early 1974, there is no evident link to the course of the Xisha events. The most obvious, albeit speculative, explanation for this is that different groups in China had different, but complementary reasons for supporting the Xisha operation. The most influential voice was apparently that of Deng Xiaoping. He returned to prominence at the 10th Party Congress in August, 1973, and in December was made a Politburo member and a Vice-Chairman of the Military Affairs Committee.[42] In late December a massive shift of China's powerful regional military commanders went off smoothly and Deng is credited with engineering this feat. His close relations with these regional bosses and his acceptability as a moderate leader no doubt smoothed his way. Deng also had close contacts with the head of the navy, Su Zhenhua, and was said to be a leading voice supporting a more maritime approach for the PLA navy. Thus Deng Xiaoping appeared to be closely linked with Xisha events, as the operation no doubt enhanced the general role of the PLA (and pleased the shifted commanders) and more specifically furthered the cause of those favouring a more maritimist role for the navy in Chinese foreign policy.[43]

The radicals no doubt also supported the operation for a mix of reasons. Not only would their support enhance their appeal to the PLA, but, if interpreted in the proper manner, could enhance the role of one of their pet institutions, the militia.[44] It is notable that official PLA comment on the campaign did play up the role of the militia and local military units. In 1976 the radicals were to bolster their campaign against military modernization by suggesting that the Xisha (and Zhenbao) cases proved that modern equipment was not necessary.[45] Clearly the nature of the arguments shifted with the movements of the quicksand of Chinese domestic debates, but to the extent that the Xisha question figured at all, it was often it contradictory and changing ways. What is most important however is that radicals, like moderates, had good reason to support the Xisha campaign.

Similarly those groups in the centre ground also had reason to support the campaign. Obviously large segments of the PLA, especially those urging a return to greater professionalism, would have been pleased by an efficient show of military prowess.[46] This was no doubt especially appealing to those PLA groups, especially in the navy and other services, utilizing modern arms.

The nature of the opponent in this operation and the very swiftness and success of the Xisha campaign no doubt made it much easier to reach such a consensus. Had the campaign dragged on, or met setbacks, then recrimination and debate might well have surfaced. But as it was, the Xisha campaign was a smashing success, thereby encouraging domestic groups to jump on the Xisha bandwagon. These factions may well have been fiercely debating other, perhaps even related, topics, but on the Xisha question the domestic dimension seemed to play no important role.

Conclusions

The Xisha operation seems to show how China would like to act if its movements in international relations were less fettered by realities of power. Beijing seemed to move without any neat patterns of escalation or consistent and precise signals to the opponent. Instead China simply issued declarations and then launched a powerful strike to overwhelm the opposition. While it is true that the first military manœuvres were less than immediately successful, the mistake of underestimating the enemy's will to fight was swiftly corrected by increasing the power of China's military punch.

The real success in the Xisha operation must be attributed to superior political planning. Coupled with efficient military execution, this meant that the campaign was over before either domestic or foreign opposition could be mustered. Few events in international relations unfold in as favourable a set of conditions as those prevailing for the Xisha operation. Under normal circumstances the opposition is stronger and the international environment more complex, so that China is unable to launch coercive operations at times and places of its own choosing. But, if such similarly low risk conditions do return, for example regarding the Nansha Islands or Taiwan, then there is ample evidence to suggest that Beijing will strike when it feels the iron to be hot.

NOTES

1. The only exception is Marwyn Samuels, *Contest for the South China Sea* (London: Methuen, 1982). See more generally Lee Laai-to, 'The PRC and the South China Sea', *Current Scene* Vol. 15 No. 2, February 1977.
2. Note the excessive attention paid to the fate of one American captured by the Chinese.

3. Geographic names in this bewildering maze of coral reefs will be the Chinese ones. The Xisha archipelago lies some 750 km north of the Nansha (Spratly) Archipelago. The Yongle Group of the Xisha is to the south and west of the Xuande Group. The Xisha Archipelago lie 1334 km from Taiwan, 278 km from Hainan and 445 km from Da Nang, Vietnam. The Nansha Archipelago lies 650 km from Vietnam, 1,000 km from Hainan, 160 km from Malaysia, and 100 km from the Philippines. For details see Samuels, *Contest*.

4. *Ibid*, pp. 98–9.

5. *BBC*/SWB/FE/4499/A3/1–2.

6. *International Herald Tribune*, 22 January 1974. *The Guardian*, 24 January 1974. *The Financial Times*, 24 January 1974.

7. NCNA at 2306 GMT in *BBC*/SWB/FE/4505/A3/1–4. A further warning was issued in the more official form of a Ministry of Foreign Affairs Statement on 20 January but by then the military operation was all but over. No. 4506/A3/1–2.

8. *Japan Times*, 18, 20 January 1974. *New York Times*, 19, 20 January 1974. Also Saigon version of 17 January in *BBC*/SWB/FE/4504/A3/4, and 19 January in No. 4505/A3/1–4.

9. NCNA 29 January 1974 in *BBC*/SWB/FE/4513/A3/1.

10. *BBC*/SWB/FE/4519/A3/1–3.

11. *The Times* (London), 6 February 1974.

12. *BBC*/SWB/FE/4499/A3/1–2.

13. NCNA 19 January 1974 in *BBC*/SWB/FE/4505/A3/1–4.

14. See Saigon's appeals in *Ibid*, 19 January 1974 and 30 January in No. 4514/A3/4.

15. Selig Harrison, *China, Oil and Asia* (New York: Columbia University Press, 1977), p. 198.

16. *Ibid*, pp. 189–203. Samuels, *Contest* generally on the oil factor in the area, and *Far Eastern Economic Review*, 28 January 1974, p. 32.

17. See note 12.

18. Bruce Swanson, *Eighth Voyage of the Dragon* (Annapolis: Naval Institute Press, 1982), pp. 262–3.

19. Harrison, *China, Oil*, pp. 191–2.

20. Swanson, *Eighth Voyage*, pp. 262–70.

21. *Ibid*, and Samuels, *Contest* Ch. 7.

22. *Guangming Daily*, November 1974 in Samuels, *ibid*, p. 139.

23. For example *Guangming Daily*, 2 January 1974 in *SPRCP* No. 5540–5544, p. 84.

24. Based on reports in *Japan Times*, 20 January 1 1974. *Sunday Times* (London), 20 January 1974. *The Times*, 21 January 1974. *BBC*/SWB/FE/4504/A3/4; No. 4505/A3/1–4; No. 4507/A3/1; No. 4514/A3/4; Harrison, *China, Oil*, p. 192; Samuels, *Contest*, pp. 100–101.

25. Saigon on 19 January 1974 in *BBC*/SWB/FE/4505/A3/1–4.

26. For example *People's Daily*, 17 April 1974 in *SPRCP* No. 5615 pp. 166–9 carried an article under radical inspiration that seemed deeply confused. On one hand it said, 'in the short period of 30 minutes the heroic armymen and civilians defeated the Saigon army with modern equipment in a neat and clean manner' but later on said no Komar class boat or guided missiles were used.

27. Saigon on 21 January in *BBC*/SWB/FE/4507/A3/1.

28. According to the *Japan Times*, 15 February 1974 the US and UK gave lukewarm support to Saigon's appeal, along with Austria, Costa Rica and Australia. The Soviet Union, Byelorussia, Iraq, and Indonesia were against a meeting, while Kenya, Cameroon, Mauritania, Peru, and France sat on the fence.

29. *Japan Times*, 18, 20 January 1974.

30. *New York Times*, 22 January 1974.

31. *New York Times*, 23, 25 January 1974. *Japan Times*, 11 February 1974.

32. *International Herald Tribune*, 29 January 1974.
33. *New York Times*, 10 February 1974, citing *New Times*. Also *Soviet News*, 12 February 1974, citing *Pravda* of 10 February.
34. Harrison, *China, Oil*, p. 203. Also, *FEER*, 12 December 1975, pp. 28–9.
35. *New York Times*, 20 January 1974. *BBC*/SWB/FE/4516/i.
36. *Beijing Review* No. 34, 24 August 1979, and *China's Indisputable Sovereignty Over the Xisha and Nansha Islands* (Beijing: Foreign Languages Press, 1980).
37. *FEER* 31 December 1973, pp. 39–40, and 28 January 1974, p. 32.
38. Taibei in *BBC*/SWB/FE/4520/A3/1, and Indonesia in No. 4519/A3/3.
39. On the campaign see Merle Goldman, *China's Intellectuals* (Cambridge: Harvard University Press, 1981) pp. 166–179; Kenneth Lieberthal, *Sino-Soviet Conflict in the 1970s* (Santa Monica, California: The Rand Corporation R-2342-NA, July 1978).
40. See for example two *Red Flag* articles in No. 12, December 1974, in *SPRCP* No 5758 pp. 192–6, and *SPRCM* No. 834 pp. 13–27. See also Harry Harding, 'The Domestic Politics of China's Global Posture' in Thomas Fingar ed., *China's Quest for Independence* (Boulder, Colorado: Westview Press, 1980).
41. Harding, *ibid*, pp. 96–121.
42. *Ibid*, and Goldman, *China's Intellectuals*, p. 179.
43. Swanson, *Eighth Voyage*, pp. 269–70; *FEER* 7 January 1974.
44. Lieberthal, *Sino-Soviet Relations*, p. 112.
45. Three articles in April 1974 praised the militia and 'man over weapons' in the Xisha campaign. But it is notable that these articles and the poem 'Battle of the Xisha' were primarily tools in a wider political debate on the relevance of the 'new born things' of the Cultural Revolution. The aspects of military strategy were at most examples used in passing, but certainly not the centre of the debate. *SPRCP* No. 5615, pp. 166–9; No. 5616, pp. 217–8; No. 5617, pp. 15–17. See also Harding, 'Domestic Politics', p. 121; and Swanson, *Eighth Voyage*, p. 269.
46. Ellis Joffe and Gerald Segal, 'The Chinese Army and Professionalism', *Problems of Communism*, Vol. 27, No. 6, Nov–Dec. 1978.

12

Vietnam, 1979

We would not mind military achievements. Our objective is a limited one—that is to teach them they could not run about as much as they desired.
Deng Xiaoping, February 1979.[1]
You can't know the reaction of the tiger if you don't touch his arse.
Deng, March 1979, quoting Mao.[2]

Trying to teach political lessons by military means to a superior military power is always a dangerous game. It is therefore not surprising that China's attempt to do just that to Vietnam failed. Arguably the 1979 Sino-Vietnamese war was China's most important foreign policy failure since 1949, and the main reason for this failure was the poor performance of the PLA. In essence, the failure of policy can be attributed to China's incorrect assessment of the link between the political and military dimensions of war. The 1979 war was intended to achieve difficult political objectives with insufficient military means.

Of course, the notion of China teaching a lesson to its neighbours is not unprecedented. But unlike the 1962 crisis with India, in 1979 Chinese military power was weaker and the political circumstances were less favourable. The 1979 war, like the 1974 Xisha operation, was arrogantly conceived. Unlike the situation in 1974, the political and military balance favoured China's opponent.

The importance of the 1979 war lies not merely in its striking failure or in the high number of casualties. It was also China's first military engagement after the death of Mao and Zhou, and thus provided a comparison to assess the relative importance of these two great helmsmen of past Chinese foreign policy. In its first try, post-Mao China did not excel. This was not because Mao and Zhou never chose to fight beyond the gates, for they surely did, but rather the poverty of the political judgement in 1979 indicated a rashness and arrogance unlikely to have been pursued by their predecessors.

Course of Events

The roots of the Sino-Vietnamese war, as with the Sino-Soviet split, are to be found deep in history and ideology. The more immediate sources of conflict can be traced to 1977–8, when the recently unified Socialist Republic of Vietnam (SRV) and Kampuchea, both recently victorious in war against US supported governments, began to establish their control. Kampuchean–Vietnamese conflict soon emerged over various issues, with China taking Phnompenh's side. Also, the SRV began a collectivization scheme in March that led to the exodus of ethnic Chinese. Thus in May 1978 China cancelled aid projects to the SRV and in July border clashes became more common. Sino-Vietnamese talks were held from 8 August to 26 September but no solutions were found to their developing problems.

This increasing polarization was also connected to divisions in the broader foreign policies of both states. China's tilt towards greater co-operation with the West was enhanced in August with the Sino-Japanese Friendship Treaty, which included a clause opposing Soviet hegemonism. On 11 October the Carter administration took concrete steps that were to lead towards normalization of Sino-American relations. On 3 November Vietnam consolidated its tilt towards the Soviet Union by signing a Friendship Treaty of its own with Moscow. In June Hanoi had joined the Soviet-dominated CMEA.

China's perception that the struggle against Soviet power in general and Vietnamese influence in particular was not going well, was heightened on 3 December when Vietnam sponsored the establishment of a united front of Kampuchean forces, led by Heng Samrin and opposed to the Chinese supported Pol Pot regime in Kampuchea. The deterioration of the Shah's position in Iran and the failure of the US to respond forcefully to protect its interests there, was also a cause of concern to China.

China therefore tilted more clearly to the West when, on 12 December, Deng accepted the 4 December US proposals for normalization of relations.[3] The third plenum of the CCP Central Committee apparently ratified this action in its meeting on 18–22 December, and also agreed to respond to increasing signs that the Vietnamese would invade Kampuchea and install the Heng Samrin regime. On 25 December Vietnam's military drive began and by 7 January Phnompenh fell.

China responded to the deteriorating situation by priming its military cannon along the frontier with Vietnam and by sending Deng Xiaoping to the United States and Japan to sound out reaction to a punitive Chinese strike against Vietnam. While in Washington, at the end of January 1979, it seemed clear that Deng's mind was already made up to launch a didactic war.[4] By the time of his return to China, on 8 February, Deng apparently felt that he had heard nothing to dissuade him from his purpose.

There was no consistent pattern of escalating Chinese warnings to Vietnam that China would strike, for even the final warning from the Ministry of Foreign Affairs, on 16 February, was no different from earlier statements. The following day Chinese troops crossed the Sino-Vietnamese border in five major spearheads. After initially running out of steam, China renewed its offensive on 23 February and found that advances were slow and costly. While regularly issuing statements to deter Soviet intervention, China claimed it would only stay in Vietnam for a short while, without saying when the operation would end.

On 27 February the PLA began a major assault on Lang Son, a provincial capital on the final hills before the plains open up to the Red River Delta and Hanoi. China finally captured the town on 5 March and immediately announced its intention to withdraw. By 16 March all Chinese troops were pulled out. On 4 April Vietnam finally responded favourably to Chinese proposals for further talks and on 6 April China agreed to send a delegation to Hanoi on 14 April. Border clashes have continued intermittently since then, with periodic war scares about a 'second lesson'. In the meantime Vietnam's hold on Kampuchea remains firm.

Objectives

As with many previous cases of China's use of its military instrument, the stated reasons were several, and not always in their real order of priority. According to Beijing, China was merely responding to a prior Vietnamese attack across the frontier,[5] but few analysts see this as anything but at best an excuse. To be sure, China's calculus was complex and various factors laid the groundwork for Beijing's operation.[6] But, in general, three clusters of objectives can be outlined.

First and foremost, China sought to punish Vietnam. This objective was listed in various ways in official and private Chinese statements, but rarely as the prime motive.[7] China had much to be angered with, as Hanoi had rejected Chinese guidance, expelled its ethnic Chinese citizens, and above all toppled China's Kampuchean ally Pol Pot. However, the main evidence for the primacy of this punishment motive, or its variant of teaching a lesson, is to be found in the timing of the Chinese attack. What seemed to trigger Beijing's invasion was less a real border threat, and more the sense that Vietnam was rampaging unchecked and engineering Heng Samrin's victory. Certainly when China decided to halt its invasion of Vietnam in March, it tried to link its pull-back with that of a hoped-for Vietnamese withdrawal from Kampuchea.[8]

In November and December 1978, China issued various protests about Vietnam's alleged border violations,[9] and issued vague warnings about 'consequences' if the actions continued. But only after the Vietnamese invasion of Kampuchea did Deng Xiaoping and other Chinese leaders begin to speak about teaching Vietnam a lesson. Chinese troop movements only began after Vietnam's true intentions became clear in December/January.[10] Beijing's official warnings continued to be issued in response to border incidents,[11] but it was clear that the real changes had taken place along the Kampuchea–Vietnam border.

The timing of China's attack was also constrained by other factors. First, the climate. An attack could not be launched in the rainy season, beginning in April, but to attack too early would mean the ice along the Sino-Soviet border would still be frozen and would favour possible Soviet counter-pressure on China. Beijing's window was not wide.[12]

Second, China seemed concerned about possible international reaction. Thus Deng's trips to the United States and Japan were essentially designed to test the waters.[13] His open talk of teaching lessons on both visits left his hosts in little doubt that Deng had decided to attack, and primarily because of the situation in Kampuchea, rather than incidents along the Sino-Vietnamese frontier itself.[14] Therefore Chinese signals to Vietnam were on the one hand very clear that some kind of response would be forthcoming, but the reasons were less than clear. Due to this confusion in objectives, and the distinction between official and private statements, there was no consistent and graduated Chinese escalation of warnings. Vietnam was clearly warned that China would respond, but there was no tidy escalation of statements to indicate that a breaking point had been reached.[15] After the six weeks of talk about punishment following the demise of the Pol Pot regime, China probably had to ensure some kind of strategic surprise in order to enhance the chances of victory for an operation already facing numerous objective problems. Vietnam had obviously been warned of Chinese intentions, but it could not be sure when China would strike. The absence of much of Hanoi's top leadership from the capital on 17 February, the day Chinese troops crossed the border into Vietnam, indicates at least initial Chinese success in creating surprise. But it also indicates China's failure to communicate its intent clearly in crisis.

The second major cluster of Chinese objectives concerns Beijing's stated motive—defence of its territory. If the first objective of punishing Vietnam was derived from China's more aggressive and arrogant definition of its right to determine the nature of political alignments in its backyard, then this second objective is more concerned with defensive definitions of threats to its actual frontiers. Whereas the first objective was to compel Vietnamese withdrawal from its new positions, in Kampuchea, the second objective was to deter Hanoi's extension of its power across the Chinese border itself.

It is of course arguable whether there was any real Vietnamese threat to China along the frontier. Certainly the logic for such aggressive intentions on Hanoi's part would have to be very strained. Nevertheless, of greatest concern to this analysis, is that China perceived (or misperceived) such a threat. Every important Chinese statement on the conflict made this perception clear.[16] China repeatedly spoke of Vietnamese incursions, causing loss of life, destruction of property, and unnecessary costs when China was trying to pursue the four modernizations.

However, extreme caution must be exercised in accepting these Chinese claims. Undoubtedly border incidents did take place, but as with other Chinese frontier problems, the rate of clashes seems too closely linked to rising tensions derived from other causes.[17] In 1969 what really bothered China was a perceived general Soviet threat and in 1979 it was a perceived rise in Vietnamese power in the area. What is more, the Chinese attack on Vietnam did not have an appreciable effect on continuance of border incidents, for clashes continued during the Chinese invasion.[18] By and large, the perceived threat to the border seems exaggerated. Prior to the late 1970s there were no reported disagreements on the frontier, although the two parties did contest offshore islands.

If there was a real threat to Chinese national security it stemmed less from border issues, and more from the general Chinese sense that, in order to establish its importance as a great power even in regional terms, it could not let politics in the area go their own way without Chinese guidance. After the war was over, China claimed to have destroyed the image of Vietnam as the third largest military power,[19] a position unofficially claimed by Beijing for itself. If China was perceived to be a paper tiger even in its own backyard, then Chinese national security would suffer elsewhere. To the extent that security is guaranteed by enhancing credibility of deterrence threats, China could not allow itself to be seen as a paper tiger.

In fact, the notion of paper tigers brings us to the third cluster of Chinese objectives—demonstration of Soviet weakness. By attacking Moscow's key Asian ally, Beijing could hope to prove its own mettle, and cast doubt on the meaning of Soviet power. In many respects China could not but challenge Vietnam, and through it the Soviet Union, for the 1970s had been a decade of vociferous Chinese claims that Soviet power had to be forcefully met by deeds not words. China had loudly denounced those who seek accomodation with the Soviet Union when all that was required was more backbone.[20]

Thus China sought to teach lessons to both Vietnam and the Soviet Union. The importance of such tutorials was increased in late 1978 with the fall of the Shah of Iran and the Carter administration's impotence to prevent the loss of an ally.[21] China, by attempting to raise the cost of Vietnam's Kampuchean venture and perhaps save Pol Pot, might be able to show that great powers can act in a more forthright manner. As Deng Xiaoping said in February 1979,

If we really want to be able to place curbs on the polar bear, the only realistic thing for us is to unite....(with the US). We are an insignificant poor country, but if we unite, well it will carry weight.[22]

This Chinese willingness to take on the Soviet bear of course did not necessarily mean that China had no respect for Soviet power (see next section). But Beijing did feel that something had to be done to stem the tide of Soviet influence in East Asia and that a swift sharp shock delivered to Hanoi would avoid a Soviet threat to China, while at the same time dealing a blow to Soviet prestige.[23] However, a razor-sharp military instrument was needed to ensure success. Unfortunately for China, its blunt sword failed to deliver its blow and so China's objective went unrealized.

In sum, none of China's three main objectives was met. The only real lessons taught in this educational war, were delivered to Beijing by Hanoi and Moscow. China failed to punish Vietnam for, while it inflicted heavy casualties on the Vietnamese in seventeen days of hostilities, China also suffered heavily. First-line Vietnamese troops were only used in the final battle for Lang Son. China's troops were held by mere border guards. Nor was Hanoi forced to pull back troops from Kampuchea or in any way loosen its grip on its new conquest. Because Hanoi was never in serious danger, the Soviet commitment to its ally was not seriously called into question either. Thus the Soviet Union was also not taught a lesson. Finally, if China was merely trying to protect its own frontiers, it failed in that task as well. Border incidents continued. As for dispelling the image of China as a paper tiger, it is true that Beijing showed it would act to uphold its interests, but the poor military performance showed the Chinese tiger to be virtually toothless.

Overall, China's basic problem in the war was that, in order to achieve its main objective of teaching a lesson, it had to strike hard and fast. However, to strike too firmly and swiftly would draw in the Soviet Union in support of Hanoi. Thus China had little room for error in a strategy highly dependent on the surgical use of the military instrument. When the PLA failed to strike an impressive blow, Chinese strategy collapsed. Because of the poor political calculation that set such difficult, and at times contradictory tasks, China never stood much chance of success in the first place. This failure to achieve basic objectives, coupled with poor communication in crisis, must make the 1979 war one of China's most striking defence policy failures. As the PLA paper said in March 1979, '...war is a practical question...whether we'll have to fight is not decided by our subjective wishes'.[24] The 1979 war was just such a case, but still China persisted in waging it. Not surprisingly then, China paid the price for ignoring the link between disposable military force and politics.

Operations

The PLA operations in the Sino-Vietnamese war were the most extensive, and costly, since the Korean war. But in the almost thirty years between the two wars, little seemed to have improved in Chinese equipment and combat performance. To stand so still in military affairs, is to fall fatally behind. In the same thirty years the Vietnamese had been fighting almost continually against modern Western equipment and were as well trained as anyone to take on an invader. Thus China's decision to wield its military instrument was taken in the face of distinctly unfavourable military conditions. The war was in its conception and execution a political act, for professional military men would most likely have counselled caution.

That there were important political motives for the war has already been outlined. It is equally clear that the decision to fight beyond China's gates was not unprecedented for Beijing. Although such leftist and adventurist strategy had been condemned (and continues to be condemned) in China, it was practiced by Deng's predecessors.[25] Equally, that China chose to engage in compellence by trying to force Vietnam to quit Kampuchea is also not unprecedented. There was no doubt an element of deterrence involved in China's attempt to prevent a further growth of Vietnamese and Soviet power, but in essence China was trying to regain by force its prestige and position in Asia. In its most positive construction, the 1979 war was didactic, and thus hardly defensive.

It is clear that in the 1979 war the most crucial aspects of Chinese military strategy were set by political authorities. Thus the PLA was operating under massive initial handicaps, at a time when it was debating military doctrine (see below). In many senses, then, the specific tactics adopted by the PLA during the war were predetermined by the political strategy and the well-known limitations of out-dated armed forces. Nevertheless, certain important characteristics of China's conduct of the war require elaboration.

First, as with previous large-scale wars, China set up an *ad hoc* military front to conduct the war, replacing the pattern of peacetime military regions. The southern front encompassing the Kunming and Guangzhou regions was established in January, when large-scale troop movements were under way. Xu Shiyou, a Deng supporter and Guangzhou commander, was put in charge, with Wang Bicheng, the Kunming commander who lacked mountain warfare experience, being passed over in favour of Yang Dezhi as

Deputy Commander. Yang had Korean war experience and reportedly had direct operational control in 1979. Zang Tingfa, a Politburo member, air force commander, and expert on militia affairs, was brought in as chief of staff of the front.[26]

Along the Sino-Soviet border a northern front was established under the Li Desheng, incorporating the Xinjiang, Lanzhou, Beijing, and Shenyang military regions, and civilians were reportedly evacuated from border areas in case of Soviet frontier pressure. Although China claimed that the war with Vietnam was waged by frontier guards and militia, this was patently absurd.[27] In fact troops were drawn from 10 military regions, with the militia and frontier guards providing rear security and logistical support. Up to 20 main force divisions were used, bringing to bear 300,000 soldiers, 700–1000 aircraft, 1000 tanks, and 1500 pieces of heavy artillery. While most of the tanks, infantry, and all aircraft were held in reserve, the initial strike was made by 6–7 divisions, later joined by 4 more. At the climax of combat, China had around 80,000 soldiers in Vietnam, mostly in the Lang Son struggle. They faced 75,000–100,000 Vietnamese border and militia troops.

Second, PLA tactics showed no special flair or individuality as they engaged in largely set-piece frontal assaults on well dug-in positions. The war was indeed a pragmatic affair, with China's forces coping with political constraints, geographic difficulties, and the antiquity of PLA weaponry. These conditions of course also allowed for a certain amount of stealth and surprise and both sides tried to outflank each other as PLA columns headed down main roads towards provincial capitals.[28] However, the constraints also meant that in the end the fierce battles were fought for fixed positions.

Despite initial tactical surprise[29] and a five pronged advance,[30] the PLA quickly ground to a snail's pace. The main set-piece battles certainly did not work out well for China, although the main targets were eventually seized.[31] The battle for Lang Son was the most dramatic. PLA forces had to fight a fierce house-to-house, and rock-to-rock battle. Inevitably, under such circumstances, Chinese casualities were high as the PLA advanced 'wave after wave'.[32] Chinese Deputy Chief of Staff Wu Xiuquan admitted to 20,000 casualties of which roughly half were killed. Hanoi claimed the figure for Chinese losses was more than twice that total. Vietnamese casualties, according to China, were in the 40–50,000 range. Confidential Chinese reports admitted to roughly equal casualties.[33]

In comparison with other wars of the 1970s, the Sino-Vietnamese one could have taken place thirty years earlier for all that modern equipment or tactics were used. The PLA infantry performed well under the difficult conditions, but by and large this was a one-dimensional war with a smattering of tank and artillery support. Both sides kept back their air force and navy in an attempt to limit the combat. China certainly could have little confidence that the air force would perform well against Vietnamese forces, who had only recently taken on United States airpower.

Some of the most glaring problems in operations involved anti-quated logistics and poor reconaissance. One report says Qing dynasty maps were used in some areas.[34] But despite these problems, matters might have been worse had the PLA moved beyond Lang Son to the open Red River delta. If Chinese forces had moved into such territory, where modern war could have been more easily waged, the weakness of PLA logistics, equipment, and air defence (to name but a few problems) would have become crushing. To the extent that the PLA had an opportunity to wage a modern war after 5 March, they wisely declined to do so.[35] At least in this instance China's limited political objectives made the PLA's task easier.

In conducting PLA operations on such a vast scale China, of course, had to consider the reactions of other interested parties. As in the Taiwan crises, where United States power supporting Taiwan could not be ignored in Beijing, so in 1979 China had seriously to consider Soviet power behind Vietnam. That China was highly sensitive to Soviet reactions seems beyond doubt. Deng Xiaoping, for one, made it plain that China had seriously calculated Soviet reactions before embarking on the war.[36] Chinese evacuations and troop adjustments along the Sino-Soviet border indicate the serious-ness with which Beijing took the potential threat of Soviet action.[37] And above all, the pains to which China went to indicate that its operations was limited, seems to have been primarily related to a fear of Soviet reaction, perhaps as had taken place in the 1971 India–Pakistan war.[38] Finally, as has already been outlined, one of the prime objectives of the Chinese attack was to show up the Soviet Union as a 'paper ally' and more generally to cast doubt on the importance of Soviet power.

Certainly, the conduct of Chinese operations seemed to show acute sensitivity to Soviet reactions. The timing of the operation seemed in part designed to reduce the chance of large-scale Soviet aid for Vietnam.[39] The scale of PLA operations was also intended to minimize risks of Soviet counter-action. Even China's public statements about the Soviet Union during the war were kept relatively low key.[40] What is more, Sino-Soviet river navigation talks continued as usual during the war, even though China was at the time holding territory of a close Soviet ally.[41]

It has been suggested that such Soviet passivity proved China's point, that the Soviet Union was an unreliable ally. However, it seems more likely that it was the very limited nature of the Chinese operation, and its poor performance, that allowed the Soviet Union to sit back so calmly. To be sure, there were clear signs that Moscow was surprised by the outbreak of war and temporized in its intial reactions.[42] But as the great power backing the winning side, the Soviet Union was not called upon to take decisive action. To the extent that evidence of support was required by Hanoi, Moscow did send some military aid by air and moved some of its ships closer to the combat zone as a sign of support.[43] Vietnam had little need for anything more dramatic, and therefore the recently concluded Soviet–Vietnamese Friendship Pact was not put to the ultimate test. It is however reasonable to assume that if necessary Moscow would have offered Hanoi as much support in 1979 as it did to Delhi in the 1971 war. Because of the PLA's failure, even this level was not called for.[44]

Thus China not only failed to teach the Soviet Union and the world a lesson about Soviet power, more importantly China itself seemed forced to learn from its mistakes. While it is difficult to establish a causal link between Chinese performance during the war, and the September 1979 resumption of Sino-Soviet negotiations, it does seem plausible that China had been encouraged to re-evaluate its strategic posture in the wake of the Vietnam episode.[45] Obviously the Chinese decision to resume talks with the Russians was complicated, and wrapped up in continuing debates on the Soviet Union. The actual course of the 1979 war no doubt encouraged those who sought some sort of reduction in tension with Moscow. However, the December 1979 Soviet invasion of Afghanistan soon torpedoed this nascent detente process, which was only gingerly resumed some three years later.[46]

As with previous shifts in China's strategic perception, changes seem to take place in Beijing's view of both superpowers. In 1979 the United States played a far less crucial role in Chinese calculations, but the nature of United States action did seem to have an important impact on some aspects of Chinese policy. In the first place, it seems clear that the timing of Sino-American normalization had something to do with Beijing's desire to consolidate support before the war. While it is plain that the United States initiated the normalization process,[47] it is equally obvious that Deng's decision to accept US terms in mid-December was related to the imminent Vietnamese invasion of Kampuchea and the recent Soviet–Vietnamese Friendship Pact.[48] What is more, the failure of United States power in the simultaneous Iran crisis no doubt encouraged the Chinese to dwell on the need for more backbone in foreign policy.

Deng Xiaoping's visit to the United States before finally embarking on the attack on Vietnam seems to suggest a link between the two elements of Chinese policy. It would certainly have been prudent for China to at least appear to garner United States support for its punitive operation. While Deng no doubt had all but made up his mind to strike, it is likely that a bright red light from Washington would have made him pause.[49] As it turned out, the light was neither red nor green, but amber. Intense factional politics in the United States no doubt added to the vagueness of the signal. In any case it seemed rather in keeping with the generally dithering character of the Carter administration.[50]

During the course of the war the United States continued to send confusing signals to China. Secretary of the Treasury Blumenthal's scheduled visit to China was not cancelled, but while in China he did deliver harsh messages about US disapproval of the war.[51] After the war, the anti-China lobby in Washington did gain strength and Soviet–American détente (despised by Beijing) did go ahead, at least until the Afghan invasion. For those in China who counted on firmness from the United States in the face of Soviet power, the fainthearted United States reaction no doubt caused concern. Just as the war probably encouraged alterations in China's view of Soviet power, so it probably encouraged a minimization of China's expectations of United States power.

Apart from the superpowers, a few other states did figure in the conduct of Chinese operations against Vietnam in 1979. As it had with the United States, China also seemed to seek support, or at a minimum an amber light, from the Asian states and others such as Japan and India. Deng's visit to selected south East Asian states in November 1978, and his brief stay in Japan in February 1979, were all no doubt part of this process. All parties apparently sent vague signals similar to those from Washington.[52] Equally, these states, and especially India, were displeased with the war itself. The Indians found their foreign minister caught in China when hostilities broke out. Whether this was part of a canny Chinese attempt to surprise the Vietnamese, or was simply shoddy Chinese foreign policy, India was most angered at being embarrassed.[53] The Asian states and Japan had every reason to fear resurgent Chinese military power, designed to dictate the East Asian political order, but the poor PLA performance no doubt reassured them that China was less powerful than it claimed. Paradoxically, China's military failure was an advantage in at least some aspects of its foreign policy.

The Domestic Dimension

Like many of the previous crises already reviewed, the 1979 war took place against the background of a certain amount of domestic unrest, but the conduct of the war did not seem to be appreciably affected. Neither were there any major changes in domestic politics after the war that could be attributed to the course of the combat. Several potential areas of dispute did emerge but, as with previous cases, it is enormously difficult to establish a link between the war and domestic politics.

First, although there were alterations in military commands just prior to the war, none seemed to be anything more than sensible *ad hoc* arrangements to put the most capable people in charge of a military operation that required certain types of skills.[54] It is notable that no PLA purges took place before or after the war, despite the army's poor performance. Apparently it was recognized that, under the very difficult conditions set by the political leadership, such unfair dismissals would cause too much unrest within the PLA.[55]

Second, while it is true that the PLA was debating its basic military strategy and the meaning of people's war under 'modern conditions', the discussions were going on before the war started.[56] The discussions were given added impetus by China's poor performance in combat. As the *Liberation Army Daily* noted, the war had 'lent a big impetus to the modernization of our army'.[57] But earlier comments had gone to great length to point out that China must adopt a new pragmatic approach to strategy. The PLA paper noted on 18 December that,

since war is a developing situation, then war theory must develop accordingly...military theory has been developing and has never stopped at any
fixed level. Mao Tse-tung's military thinking itself has also developed
according to military developments....[58]

Su Yu told the PLA military academy on 19 January that 'Comrade
Mao Zedong's basic principles for directing wars are still applicable
under today's objective conditions, but they must be applied flexibly
in the light of actual conditions.' He cited Clausewitz in noting that
'theories should be a kind of observation, not rigid rules'.[59] It is true
that some people held 'some erroneous ideas on the question of
war', and the 1979 war helped clear them away,[60] but by and large
the shift to a more open debate of the pragmatic military options
was well under way before the war. The removal of the radical
influence some three years earlier had opened those floodgates.
The war itself only justified the professional critics.[61]

   Third, there were continuing debates among the Chinese leadership in general on the extent to which the radical influences should
be eradicated. The end of 1978 was marked by wall posters urging
the reversal of verdicts on victims of the Tienanmen incident and
calls for the removal of Wang Dongxing and Wu De. But it is
notable that despite these aspects of house-cleaning after the purge
of the Gang of Four, the Sino-Vietnamese war did not figure in
leadership politics. In fact, the war itself was not the focus of any
mass campaigns, nor did it receive saturation coverage in the Chinese
media.[62] Certainly there were no obvious differences of opinion on
the war evident in speeches of the leadership. One *People's Daily*
editorial on 5 March noted that 'many leading comrades' did not
understand the new anti-leftist trend, but did not explicitly link this
problem to the war. The paper did, however, note that the war with
Vietnam 'remains a protracted and serious task' and therefore may
have been implicitly linking leftist remnants to those who thought
the war would be easier.[63] It is notable that Wang Dongxing had led
a delegation to Kampuchea just before the Vietnamese invasion
and may have been especially involved in support for Pol Pot. But
even if this was the case, Deng Xiaoping clearly stood out as the
most vocal spokesman on the war, and certainly United States
negotiators seem clear that Deng was firmly in charge of foreign
policy.[64] Once again, while there may have been differences of
opinion on domestic policy, the groups did seem to agree generally
on the need to punish Vietnam in 1979.

Fourth, there were obviously more specific discussions in China at the time about the need for readjustments in economic plans. But as in the case of the decision to alter defence strategy, there had been a discussion of economic matters before the war that was simply encouraged by the outcome of the battle.[65] It is notable that the high costs of the war further aggravated the problems caused by initial exuberance in economic planning after the fall of the Gang of Four. The 1979 war required special financing, further straining the budget. In the years following the war, the military budget was cut back to pre-war levels.[66] The extent to which military modernization should take precedence over other aspects of the four modernizations obviously was wrapped up in these shifts. However, this discussion over the relative position of military modernization had begun well before the war[67] and after 1979 it was still decided to keep the PLA as the fourth of the four modernizations. After 1979 there were more clear cut emphases within the PLA on those aspects of modernization that did not cost a great deal of money, for example in training and professional skills.[68]

The economic plans as a whole were scaled down and, to the extent that Deng Xiaoping was seen as responsible for the initial euphoria, and for added military costs in particular, his position after the war suffered to a certain small extent.[69] However, as has already been suggested, many of these changes were already well under way before the war. What is more, Deng was not alone in favouring the 1979 war. Thus Deng alone was unlikely to de demoted. In any case this was in a relatively rare period of consensus decisions in Chinese politics. Following the trauma of the Gang of Four, consensus politics tended to make for changes of policy that did not result in massive purges. To be sure leadership changes did take place in the early 1980s, but none seemed dramatic, and none were apparently related to the 1979 Sino-Vietnamese war.

Fifth, as has already been pointed out, China's views of both superpowers changed for a time after the war. It is unclear just how much this resulted from the war, or was merely yet another shift in a constantly changing Chinese assessment of the relative positions of the superpowers. There is some evidence that Hua Guofeng was less bothered about Soviet power than was Deng,[70] and therefore would have seen less need to take on Vietnam in 1979. One *Liberation Army Daily* commentary after the war made it plain that 'certain people's superstitions over hegemonism' were shattered by the war as it showed that there was no need to have 'a morbid fear of the Soviet Union'.[71] It is difficult to know to whom this applies, for it can be argued that those who feared the Soviet Union would have been less likely to support the war. It seems most likely that there were voices who opposed the war for fear of Soviet reactions, but there was a sufficient coalition of voices who thought the war could be controlled. While the specific breakdown of who sat in which group is impossible to make, the importance of this aspect, as well as the four previous policy disagreements, points to the fact that leadership politics were complex and cut across the various issues at stake. But as with previous crises and debates, despite the disagreements, the course of the military operations was not affected. There may well have been a greater impact on ensuing policy, but by and large the war only lent greater impetus for a process of change already well under way before the war.

Conclusions

Four months after China's punitive war against Vietnam, Li Xiannian admitted that Hanoi had not been taught a sufficient lesson.[72] In fact, the failure of the Chinese operation was evident almost as soon as the combat ceased. China failed to force a Vietnamese withdrawal from Kampuchea, failed to end border clashes, failed to cast doubt on the strength of Soviet power, failed to dispel the image of China as a paper tiger, and failed to draw the United States into an anti-Soviet coalition.

This Chinese defeat, perhaps the most serious in its thirty years of foreign policy, was swiftly seen as a bad dream in Beijing. As US President Kennedy noted after a less costly foreign policy fiasco, 'Victory has a thousand parents, defeat is but orphan'. Thus important changes in Chinese domestic and foreign policy were given added impetus as China tried to forget the fiasco in Vietnam. Foreign policy changes included an abortive détente with the Soviet Union that, but for the invasion of Afghanistan in December 1979, might have got properly under way in 1979 rather than 1982. Chinese defence policy planners also became more pragmatic, ensuring modernization of PLA training and that at least certain services obtained new weapons.

The fact that China, and not Vietnam or the Soviet Union, were taught a lesson in 1979 has many causes. That China embarked on a strategy of compellence rather than deterrence was not unprecedented, but it was a foolhardy policy when based on weak political and military grounds. That China embarked on a strategy of fighting beyond its gates was similarly not new, except for the flimsy basis on which it too was founded. That China undertook no coherent pattern of escalation leading to war was also not unusual in the thirty years of the People's Republic.

The Chinese defeat was, however, limited by the very limited nature of the war that helped ensure its failure. By insisting on a limited war, China kept the risks of its action well under control. Similarly, the limits on the war no doubt helped maintain domestic leadership unity and ensured that none suffered for fathering the orphan.

In sum, China lost a great deal in the 1979 war, whether the balance sheet is measured in lives or political cost. But perhaps the greatest loss was in a more intangible product—China's reputation. If anyone had any illusion prior to 1979 that somehow there was something especially pacific or low risk in China's approach to defence policy, they were surely disabused. China seemed to act like any other power, whether in the way it wielded its military instrument, or the objectives of establishing influence beyond its frontiers. Coupled with the passing of Mao and his revolutionary generation, China's pragmatic conduct of the 1979 war ensured that China would be seen for the ordinary great power that it is, and always has been.

NOTES

1. 26 February 1979, in *BBC*/SWB/FE/6054/A3/2.
2. 11 March 1979, in *BBC*/SWB/FE/6065/A3/7.
3. Announced on 15 December. For details of this process see Zbigniew Brzezinski, *Power and Principle* (New York: Farrar, Straus, Giroux, 1983).
4. *Ibid*, p. 410. The German Ambassador in Beijing suggests the final decision was taken only days before the attack. Erwin Wickert, *The Middle Kingdom* (London: Harvill Press, 1983), p. 224.
5. PRC Government Statement, 17 February 1979, in *BBC*/SWB/FE/6046/A3/4; *Liberation Army Daily* Editorial 8 March in No. 6062/A3/1–2. Also on 26 March in No. 6078/A3/11–12.
6. On background to the war see Herbert Yee, 'The Sino-Vietnamese Border War'. *China Report*, Vol. 16, No. 1, Jan–Feb., 1980; Sheldon Simon, 'China, Vietnam and Asia', *Asian Survey*, Vol. 19, No. 12, December 1979; Bruce Burton, 'Contending Explanations of the 1979 Sino-Vietnamese War'. *International Journal*, Vol. 34, No. 4, Autumn 1979; Melvin Gurtov, 'China Invades

Vietnam', *Contemporary China*, Vol. 3, No. 4. Winter 1979; Michael Leifer, 'Post-Mortem on the Third Indo-China War', *The World Today*, June 1979; Nguyen Manh-Hung, 'The Sino-Vietnamese Conflict', *Asian Survey*, Vol. 19, No. 11, November 1979; Douglas Pike, 'Communist vs. Communist in Southeast Asia', *International Security*, Vol. 4, No. 1, Summer 1979; Jonathan Mirsky, 'China's 1979 Invasion of Vietnam', *RUSI Journal*, June 1981. Edgar O'Ballance, *The Wars in Vietnam, 1954–1980* (N.Y. Hippocrene Books, 1981), Ch. 16.

7. See note 5 and also PRC Government Statement, 7 January 1979, in *BBC*/SWB/FE/6010/A3/3. PRC Government Statement, 14 January, in No. 6017/A3/1.

8. For example PRC Government Statement, 5 March 1979, in *BBC*/SWB/FE/6059/A3/2.

9. *Peking Home Service*, 6 October 1979, in *BBC*/SWB/FE/5937/A3/3–5. *People's Daily* Editorial, 10 November, in No. 5966/A3/1–2.

10. AFP in *BBC*/SWB/FE/6023/A3/7. See also Harlan Jencks, 'China's "Punitive" War on Vietnam', *Asian Survey*, Vol. 19, No. 8, August 1979; King Chen, 'China's War Against Vietnam, 1979', *The Journal of East Asian Affairs*, Vol. 3, No. 1, Spring/Summer 1983.

11. Ministry of Foreign Affairs, 24 December 1978, in *BBC*/SWB/FE/A3/1–2. See note 7.

12. Jencks, 'China's War' pp. 804–5; Yee, 'The Border War', p. 22.

13. Daniel Tretiak, 'China's Vietnam War and its Consequences', *The China Quarterly*, No. 80, December 1979, p. 742. Also reports on Deng in *BBC*/SWB/FE/6032/A1/3. While in Thailand in November Deng said China's response to Vietnamese action would depend on what happened in Kampuchea. Yee, 'The Border-War' p. 16. By not placing the Kampuchean issue in the forefront, China may have hoped to make a Vietnamese withdrawal easier. If so, Chinese signals were confused as a result.

14. Brzezinski, *Power and Policy*, pp. 406–13. Jimmy Carter, *Keeping Faith* (London: Collins, 1982) pp. 202–6. Cyrus Vance, *Hard Choices* (New York: Simon and Schuster, 1983), pp. 113–22.

15. Statements in notes 5, 7, 11. Also Ministry of Foreign Affairs, 18 January 1979, in *BBC*/SWB/FE/6020/A3/1–2. Also on 10 February, in No. 6040/A3/5, and 16 February, in No. 6045/A3/4.

16. See note 15. Also Xinhua, 16 February 1979, in JPRS *Translations on the PRC*, No. 72962, p. 115; PLA Literature No. 4, 1 April 1979, in JPRS, *China Report* No. 74061, p. 35, *People's Daily* Editorial, 25 March 1979, in *BBC*/SWB/FE/6078/A3/4–7.

17. Tretiak, 'China's War', pp. 740–2.

18. For example reports on 27 February 1979, in *BBC*/SWB/FE/6055/A3/10–11.

19. For example Xinhua commentary, 7 March 1979, in *BBC*/SWB/FE/6062/A3/2. Also Huang Hua on 16 March in No. 6070/A3/3; CCPCC message, 25 March, in No. 6078/A3/7–8. Also testimony by the German Ambassador in Beijing, Erwin Wickert, *The Middle Kingdom*, p. 222.

20. See generally Christina Holmes, 'The Soviet Union and China' in Gerald Segal, ed., *The Soviet Union in East Asia* (London: Heinemann, for the Royal Institute of International Affairs, 1983); Seweryn Bialer, 'The Sino-Soviet Conflict' in Donald Zagoria ed., *Soviet Policy in East Asia* (London: Yale University Press, 1982); Herbert Ellison ed., *The Sino-Soviet Conflict* (London: University of Washington Press, 1982).

21. Deng to Carter quoted in Brzezinski, *Power and Policy*, p. 406

22. *Time Magazine*, 5 February 1979, p. 16.

23. For Chinese comment on Soviet power as a case of China's actions see Deng on 31 January in Brzezinski, *Power and Policy* p. 410, Carter, *Keeping Faith* p. 204;

Gurtov, 'China Invades'; Deng on 5 January, in *BBC*/SWB/FE/6009/A3/3, *People's Daily* Commentary, 10 January 1979, in No. 6013/A3/3; *People's Daily* Editorial, 18 February in No. 6046/A3/5.

24. *Liberation Army Daily*, 26 March 1979, in *BBC*/SWB/FE/6078/A3/11.

25. Yang Yong in *Liberation Army Daily* reprinted in *Guangming Daily*, 22 January 1983, in *FBIS*-CHI-83-024-K11–15.

26. AFP 20 February 1979, in *BBC*/SWB/FE/6049/A3/12–13. Jencks, 'China's War' pp. 805–6; Chen, 'China's War' pp. 243–6.

27. Jencks, *Ibid*, pp. 806–7 for an excellent survey.

28. NCNA, 17 March, in *BBC*/SWB/FE/6072/A//6–7; NCNA, 3 March, in No. 6058/A3/1; NCNA, 25 February, in No. 6053/A3/1; PLA Literature No. 4, 1 April 1979, in JPRS, *China Report* No. 74061 pp. 35–40; Xinhua, 28 February, in JPRS, *Translations on the PRC* No. 72972 pp. 88–9; *Jiehfang Daily*, 2 March, in No. 73159 pp. 28–9; and *Beijing Radio* on 16 April in No. 73381 pp. 95–6.

29. Yee, 'Border War', p. 22.

30. Jencks, 'China's War', p. 809; Chen, 'China's War' pp. 246–52.

31. Jencks, *Ibid*, pp. 809–11.

32. 25 March CCPCC message in *BBC*/SWB/FE/6078/A3/7–8. The claims of human wave tactics have appeared in previous PLA engagements and were also made in this war. See AFP 24 February in No. 6052/A3/7, and *Hanoi Radio*, 7 March, in No. 6062/A3/3.

33. AFP, 5 March, in *BBC*/SWB/FE/6061/A3/15; Chen, 'China's War' p. 257.

34. Mirsky, 'China's Invasion' pp. 59–60.

35. See *Liberation Army Daily*, 15 January 1983, in *FBIS*-CHI-83?011-K4–5 for reports of changes after the war. Also, Jencks, 'China's War' pp. 812–14.

36. Deng on 26 February 1979, quoted by Kyodo in *BBC*/SWB/FE/6054/A3/2.

37. AFP, 20 February 1979, in *BBC*/SWB/FE/6049/A3/22.

38. Harry Gelman, *The Soviet Far East Buildup and Soviet Risk-Taking Against China*. (Santa Monica, California: The Rand Corp. R-2943 AF-August 1982), Ch. 8.

39. Jencks, 'China's War', p. 804.

40. Tretiak, 'China's War', p. 749.

41. Yee, 'Border War', p. 23.

42. Gelman, *Soviet Far East* p. 89.

43. *Ibid*, and Gerald Segal, 'The Soviet Union and the Great Power Triangle' in Gerald Segal ed., *The China Factor* (London: Croom Helm, 1982), and Douglas Pike, 'The USSR and Vietnam', *Asian Survey*, Vol. 19, No. 12, December 1979. Chen, 'China's War', pp. 251–2.

44. Gelman, *The Soviet Far East*, p. 89.

45. Tretiak, 'China's War', p. 764.

46. Gerald Segal ed., *The Soviet Union in East Asia* (London: Heinemann, for the Royal Institute of International Affairs, 1983).

47. Carter, *Keeping Faith*, pp. 194–99; Vance, *Hard Choices* and Brzezinski, *Power and Policy*, pp. 197–230 make plain the leading US role in timing.

48. Note the 16 December PRC announcement of US–China relations and the Ministry of Foreign Affairs protest at the establishment of the Heng Samrin led Kampuchean coalition on the same day. *BBC*/SWB/FE/5997/A3/1 and C/1.

49. Tretiak, 'China's War' pp. 743–6.

50. Brzezinski, *Power and Policy*, pp. 403–15 makes plain the extent of divisions in the administration.

51. *Ibid*, and Tretiak, 'China's War' pp. 754–63.

52. Tretiak, 'China's War', p. 754.

53. The Indian Foreign Minister had completed his official visits but was still scheduled to stay on in China for a few more days. *BBC*/SWB/FE/6045/A3/1.
54. Jencks, 'China's War', pp. 805–6.
55. Gerald, Segal, 'The PLA and Chinese Foreign Policy Decision-Making', *International Affairs*, Summer 1981, pp. 463–4.
56. Gerald Segal, 'China's Strategic Posture and the Great Power Triangle', in *Pacific Affairs*, Vol. 53, No. 4, Winter 1980–1. Also Chen, 'China's War'.
57. 8 March 1979, in *BBC*/SWB/FE/6062/A3/2. Also *Liberation Army Daily*, 30 March, in No. 6083/A3/1–2.
58. 18 December 1978, in *BBC*/SWB/FE/6007/BII/7–9.
59. *BBC*/SWB/FE/6023/BII/4–6.
60. *Liberation Army Daily*, 26 March 1979, in *BBC*/SWB/FE/6078/A3/12.
61. *Liberation Army Daily*, 15 January 1983, in *FBIS*-CHI-83-011-K4-5. The shift away from the infantry to more modern weapons pre-dated the war. *Liberation Army Daily*, 18 December 1978, in *BBC*/SWB/FE/6007/BII/7–8.
62. *BBC*/SWB/FE/6046/A3/18. *Liberation Army Daily*, 20 February 1979, and AFP 21 February in *BBC*/SWB/FE/6050/A3/8–11.
63. *BBC*/SWB/FE/6060/BII/1–3.
64. Carter, *Keeping Faith* p. 198; Brzezinski, *Power and Policy*, p. 230; Also Yee, 'Border War' pp. 19–20.
65. *Liberation Army Daily*, 30 March 1979, in *BBC*/SWB/FE/6083/A3/1–2. Tretiak, 'China's War', pp. 751–2, 757–8.
66. Ronald Mitchell, 'Chinese Defence Spending in Transition', in *China Under the Four Modernizations*, Part I (Washington: JEC, August 1982).
67. Ellis Joffe and Gerald Segal, 'The Chinese Army and Professionalism', *Problems of Communism*, Vol. 27, No. 6, Nov–Dec. 1978. Also Yeh Jianying, 1 November 1978, in *BBC*/SWB/FE/5960/BII/1–3; *Liberation Army Daily*, 14 January 1979, in No. 6021/A3/4–5.
68. Gerald Segal and William Tow, eds., *Chinese Defence Policy* (London: Macmillan, 1984).
69. Tretiak, 'China's War', pp. 757–8.
70. Brzezinski, *Power and Policy*, p. 216.
71. 30 March 1979, in *BBC*/SWB/FE/6083/A3/1–2. For a related debate on relations with the United States see for example *Workers' Daily*, 20 April 1979, in No. 6101/BII/1–2. Generally on the debate after 1979 see Gerald Segal, 'China's Security Debate', *Survival*, Vol. 24, No. 2, March/April, 1982.
72. Cited in Hung, 'Sino-Vietnamese Conflict', p. 1050.

13

Conclusion

Conclusions usually try to tie together analyses so as to provide a coherent picture of the subject. However, in the case of China's use of force in its foreign policy, it seems that we will end up with more in the way of loose ends than some neat synthesis. For those expecting some kind of coherent Chinese strategy to emerge from consideration of these case studies, this study can only disappoint. In the end, there were too many differences and changes in Chinese policy to make such generalization possible. Nevertheless, there is some point in returning to the original ten major research questions set out in the introduction, so as to point with greater precision to the changing and pragmatic dimensions of Chinese strategy. On some questions it is possible to outline a few underlying regularities of Chinese behaviour, but on most there is seen to be more diversity than unity.

The Role of Geography

To what extent has China's geography determined the way in which the military instrument was used? In the first place, the very diversity of China's geographic problems sets the background for the diversity of China's reaction to foreign policy problems. China's geographic vastness, encompassing everything from mountain frontiers to open and vulnerable plains, obviously makes it impossible to plan according to any single military strategy. Thus regionalism in defence planning has geographic roots, but this very regional diversity makes it difficult to suggest any over-arching strategy suited to the defence of all China.

Regularities in Chinese defence policy can be more easily found in that dominating characteristic of China, its vast population. The enduring poverty of China and the immense expense of military modernization, derived in large part from the massive population, means that China will necessarily place greater stress on manpower than on equipment. The massive population is a source of Chinese power, as it is for the superpowers, but in China's case it is also an enduring source of weakness.

China's population problem leads to other enduring characteristics of China's defence policy. First, China's relative denigration of threats of nuclear war is well-founded on the belief that China must be invaded to be defeated. Nuclear weapons are destructive for any society, but China is less vulnerable in many respects than either of the superpowers. It is also less vulnerable to general invasion because of the same factor. Thus the notion of people's war as an over-arching defence strategy continues to be valid, especially if it is taken to mean that to defeat China it is necessary to win the hearts and minds of its one billion citizens. (See below)

China's huge population also means that there is likely to be an enduring bias towards using men instead of machines in war. The Korean war, and the Sino-Vietnamese war, separated as they were by nearly thirty years of revolution in military technology, were still conducted largely in the same way. If there is to be movement away from China's reliance on man-over-weapons in war, it will be a protracted process.

A further dimension of China's population, the scattered minority peoples along China's borders, seems to have hardly figured in Chinese defence policy. It is true that the Tibet operation was crucially concerned with pacifying such a minority group, but in both the Sino-Soviet and Sino-Vietnamese conflicts, where other minority populations straddled the frontier, the causes and conduct of the war had more to do with broader bilateral disputes. While aspects of physical geography (outlined above) may suggest regionalism may be an important defence problem for China, in terms of human geography such regionalism has so far not proved to be a problem.

What we called core China—the geographic, demographic and industrial heartland—has only proved to be an important concept in discussing threats of general invasion to China. As already suggested, the features of this core in large measure lends validity to people's war and deters invasion. But outside the core, in the underpopulated borderlands, China continues to face potential security threats, although none have so far materialized. The threat to partition-off these distant parts of China remains only a real possibility along the

Sino-Soviet (and Mongolian) frontier, but it has not figured in any crisis examined in this study. From the past thirty-five years experience, China is less vulnerable than the worst-case planners would have us believe.

So far the discussion of geography has emphasized broad, strategic aspects, but geography has had some impact on less important levels. The geographical context of some of China's recent conflicts has proved important in how China conducted military operations. Certainly the difficult terrain of Tibet and the Sino-Indian war both determined the kind of campaign China could wage, and in the latter case gave China decided advantages over its opponent. Similarly in the Taiwan and Xisha cases, the problems of force projection, determined by China's weakness in naval power, set obvious limits on what China could achieve. A great deal of the nature of these crises can only be understood if the basic geographic problems are understood.

So far, the naval dimension has not loomed large in China's use of force, despite obvious geographic realities of a long coast line that suggests that China can be almost as much as a naval as a continental power. The two Taiwan crises and the Xisha operation suggest no obvious trend towards naval concerns, but they do suggest that China will neglect its naval power at its peril. In the future, it would not be surprising to see China making more of the naval dimension in its foreign policy, and the limited past practice suggests it is willing to use this power offensively if it has the chance.

Finally, the climate aspect of geography deserves a brief mention. The limits imposed by the variations in Chinese climate have not determined the outbreak of any conflict, but they have affected the timing of several. The need to wait for cold weather and the formation of packed ice in order to fight at Zhenbao, or the need to avoid monsoon conditions in the 1979 Sino-Vietnamese war all set certain limits on how combat could be conducted. While it is true that it 'also rains on the enemy', offensive operations are made more difficult if the climate is harsh.

In sum, in certain broad strategic aspects, and a few minor cases of crisis management, Chinese geography retains relevance for the use of force in Chinese foreign policy. This is not to say that geographic realities determine Chinese actions, but it is often difficult fully to understand Chinese policy without reference to the geographic dimension. Certainly the continuing relevance of people's war, and the impact it has had on China's approach to strategy and tactics, is derived in large part from geography. Changes may well be under way in China towards greater emphasis on weapons rather than men, and naval rather than continental operations, but the realities of Chinese geography will make the change slow.

The Role of History

To what extent is there historical continuity in the way in which China uses its military instrument in foreign policy? First, it is clear from Chinese history, and the past thirty-five years, practice, that the military in China is subordinate to civilian authority. In none of the crises analysed was the military found to have determined, or even guided, the course of events. It is, however, far more difficult to suggest that this pattern is due to historical tradition. No doubt tradition encouraged this state of affairs, but other factors, such as the role of ideology, (see below) seemed to play a more crucial role.

Second, in all of the crises analysed, the Chinese penchant for stressing man-over-weapons seemed apparent. However, the fact that this trend matched the historical legacy in China, seems to point more to the importance of China's enduring geographic realities. In the era of rapidly changing military technologies, it might have been expected that this man-over-weapons bias might change. But, as has already been pointed out, China's poverty and massive population provides great incentives to continue to denigrate relatively advanced military technology.

When turning to the question of the continuing relevance of Sinocentrism in Chinese policy, the judgement is more difficult. It has already been suggested, in chapter two, that China's peculiar Sinocentric and hierarchical world view was never as coherent as many had thought. But it is even more clear that such a world view is of little help in analysing contemporary Chinese foreign policy. To be sure, China, like almost any other state, is most concerned with its own security. In that respect Sinocentrism still applies. Equally, China like other great powers suffers from ethnocentrism. In that respect as well Sinocentrism still applies.

But Sinocentrism is clearly not relevant to contemporary defence policy if it is taken to mean the refusal to enter into alliances. The Sino-Soviet ties of the 1950s, and the calls in the 1970s for explicit

Sino-Western co-operation are only the most obvious cases in point. More importantly still, if Sinocentrism means a rejection of the state system, then China has clearly abandoned historical traditions. The incessant campaign to gain international recognition, and displace Taiwan in international organizations, illustrated China's desire to be accepted as a leading member of the state system.

It has also been suggested that, even if historical experience is less relevant to these major dimensions of Chinese policy, it is important in certain narrower aspects. It has been suggested that there is a continuing tradition to emphasize surprise and deception in military strategy. China has from time to time used deception, for example in the outbreak of the Korean war. But in most cases the requirements of effective crisis management have led to precisely the opposite Chinese policy. Effective communication in crisis reduces the opportunities for deception, and China has often tried to be effective in communicating to opponents in order to manage crises.

Second, there is the 'great wall' notion that China believes in passive and static defence at the gates. Obviously, Maoist military thought provides much evidence for precisely the opposite, urging the fluidity and activity of people's war in its guerrilla phase. In fact, neither policy was implemented consistently. In Korea, China fought beyond its gates and at times fought a positional war. In the 1962 war with India it fought beyond its gates in a largely fluid war. In the Vietnam war it also fought beyond its gates but in small numbers. The specific nature of the conflict, and above all changing military objectives, determined the nature of Chinese strategy. No single tradition holds.

Neither is there necessarily a bias against fighting a naval war. The two Taiwan crises and the Xisha incident indicate that China can and will fight at sea where it can. The main limit to such operations seem to be the availability of forces, not the bias against a maritime strategy. In sum, historical traditions governing the use of force do at times match present day practice, but in no case do they determine contemporary policy. Modern Chinese strategy seems overwhelmingly a result of pragmatic reactions to changing factors in any given crisis.

The Role of Ideology

The Chinese communist revolution was not merely for the purpose of achieving power, but for achieving power in order to implement certain ideas. To what extent have these ideas shaped the way in which China has used military force in its foreign policy? First, Mao and his colleagues believed firmly that, although the revolution was made by force and that political power grows out of the barrel of a gun, this force must be subordinate to a set of ideals, as embodied in the Party. The Party therefore must control the gun. This has indeed been the case in the past thirty-five years of Chinese foreign policy, although the Party and Army have not always been unified. What is crucial is that the PLA has not dictated the way in which armed force was used, although it no doubt had some impact in the decision-making process. The need to accept Party control means that in the final analysis, although decision making may be complex, the role of the PLA is kept firmly limited.

Second, Mao's revolution was premised on the notion that men rather than weapons were a more crucial source of power. This meant that in making revolution, and indeed in winning any pro-tracted struggle, the hearts and minds of the people had to be won over. This was a struggle of ideas more than gunpowder. This enduring reality of Maoist ideology is obviously derived from realities of Chinese geography already outlined, but it has also entered the communist doctrine as an ideological principle.

However, the superiority of man over weapons was not unquali-fied when it came to armed struggles less comprehensive than revolutionary war. In the various crises, from Korea to Vietnam, the role of weapons was acknowledged by Mao and others as being crucial. The role of man also remained central. The Chinese were urged to pursue a 'just' policy, because only a policy accepted by the people and the PLA could produce the necessary motivation among the population and the armed forces. However, the judgement on just what constituted a 'just' war was acknowledged as a difficult one and one that was hard to bring to bear in limited war. Thus the relevance of man over weapons was not unqualified, even for Mao.

Third, Maoist ideology, as indeed Soviet ideology, suggests the need to further the cause of world revolution. China, like the Soviet Union, has had different views on how much aid should be given to this supposed historical process, but both never repudiated it as an ultimate goal. China's intervention in the Korean and Vietnam wars, to support friendly communist regimes, was both for ideological as well as geopolitical reasons. The Tibet, Xisha and first Taiwan

Straits crises were based on the desire to spread and consolidate the Chinese revolution. Military aid to revolutionary movements and radical foreign regimes was also part of the general support for revolution. To be sure there have been different phases of such support, as China more or less felt that local states should make revolution on their own, but the basic revolutionary objective remained.

While these general dimensions of ideology do continue to be relevant in helping to determine Chinese military actions, it becomes much less clear that China operates under any more specific ideological guidelines in military strategy. These issues will be developed below, but suffice it to say that it is very difficult to suggest that Mao left behind any specific over-arching military strategy. As has been suggested, people's war generally refers to a war in keeping with the large, poor, populous nature of China, but does not necessarily dictate that such a war must always be waged as a fluid guerrilla war, where the enemy is lured in deep. There is evidence that Chinese strategists were far more pragmatic, both in theory and practice, in the past thirty-five years. People's war under modern conditions is neither a new idea, nor does it represent any fundamental break with so-called Maoist strategy. In fact there were several, changing, Maoist strategies.

In sum, ideology, like geography, retains some important relevance for Chinese defence policy. Neither in themselves determine Chinese policy, but an understanding of their principles does contribute to a full picture of Chinese actions. The enduring nature of Party control, the relative emphasis on men-over-weapons, and the continuing relevance of revolutionary change, are all important. But beyond these principles, ideology is not a guide to military action. There is no judge more equitable than the cannon, says a maxim of nineteenth century European strategy, and the reference was not to ideological canon. The study of military thought in communist states makes crucial distinctions between military science which represents certain enduring laws, and military art which by necessity is flexible and adaptive to change. People's war is a so-called scientific principle, but prescribes no definite art of waging war.

The Role of Institutions

Social scientists now seem agreed that it is necessary to take into account the role of institutions in foreign policy making. But what role do these bureaucracies play in the country that invented bureaucracies—China? On balance, rather like historical factors, institutions need to be understood, but seem to have very little direct impact on Chinese policy.

The most crucial institutional divide is of course that between Party and military. As has already been suggested, there is little question that Party control has been retained on foreign policy issues. In order fully to understand the nature of Chinese policy it is important to appreciate Party policy. However, the fundamental flaw in the simple Party/Army view is to suggest that either the Party or the army was a unified institution with a single institutional point of view.

While Party and Army may vie for influence over such basic questions as resource allocation and the weight to be accorded to professional skills, once there is basic agreement on these problems, other divisions in both bodies become apparent. Conflicts between the different services, among different branches of military industry, and between centre and region are all well documented. Similarly, splits within the Party on domestic and foreign policies are equally evident. But this bewildering pattern of cross-cutting cleavages is precisely what makes the institutional analysis approach so fruitless.

This is not to say there is no point in appreciating the extent of inter or intra-institutional conflict. On the contrary, the constant reference to such cleavages is meant to make it plain that institutional factors do play a role. However, the role is rarely consistent from one crisis to another, and certainly produces no coherent pattern of policy.

There are, however, two lines of institutional power that are worth dwelling on at greater length. First, there is an evident bias towards the ground forces in the Chinese military. This flows naturally from the huge Chinese population and the poverty of the economy. Since modern equipment cannot be purchased for the world's largest standing army on an adequate basis, the ground force bias has included a tendency to stress men-over-weapons. Such a bias does not necessarily mean that professionalism in the PLA must be ignored, for there have been times in the past thirty-five years where the inadequacy of military equipment was in part balanced by stress on greater professionalism. That certainly appears to be the case in today's PLA.

Despite the centrality of ground forces, there is still no clear pattern of the predominance of this service over any other in foreign policy decision-making. This is no doubt true for many reasons, including the institutional cleavages already outlined. Most notably, different regional interests of once-powerful regional commanders no doubt made it difficult to formulate a 'ground force' view. But the most central reason is the retention by the Party of overall control.

China's nuclear weapons, and their control by central civilian authority, also point in the same direction of Party dominance. Nuclear weapons obviously do not loom as large for China as they do for the superpowers, but they do provide yet another institutional cleavage that undermines military influence. Nuclear weapons under civilian control, provide the Party with a relatively low-cost option for certain aspects of Chinese deterrence. But when it comes to limited crises, nuclear weapons are only of secondary importance. Nuclear weapons have only figured directly in one crisis for China since 1949, (Zhenbao, 1969) but remained not too far in the background when China confronted the US over the Taiwan Straits and Korea. On balance, nuclear weapons are crucial for China's overall security calculation, but have not figured in many of the immediate crises China has faced in the past thirty-five years.

In sum, institutional analysis is important in understanding the use of force by China in that it reinforces conclusions derived from more important factors. This is most true of the Party/Army division. It is also important to appreciate that institutional determinants of policy do exist, but they are mostly too complex and changing to suggest any coherent pattern of influence. It is central to understand these institutional lines of power, even if they can only be applied on a case by case analysis of crises. As the PLA modernizes and its institutions acquire more clout, as has happened in the Soviet military, it is possible that the analysis of institutional factors in Chinese defence policy will become more important. But for the time being, like the historical dimension, the institutional dimension of defence policy is of lesser importance.

Chinese Objectives

It has been suggested in other studies that China pursues consistent, and largely defensive objectives, in its use of force in foreign policy. Neither judgement was substantiated in the analysis of nine case studies undertaken in the preceding chapters. In fact, it was found not only that Chinese objectives changed from one crisis to another, but they often changed during one crisis in response to changes in internal, external, or battlefield events. Each crisis had different causes, a different course, and naturally different outcomes. Thus it is not possible to understand Chinese actions either through use of a ladder of escalation, or of some coherent calculus of deterrence. In fact, there seemed to be four major types of Chinese actions in which seven distinct types of objectives were pursued.

On a scale of defensive to offensive action, the seven objectives can be seen as follows.[1] First, the use of compellence against a perceived threat to China's territory. The only case of this action was in the 1962 Sino-Indian war. Second, deterrence of a threat to China's territory. The only clear case of action taken to obtain this objective was to counter Soviet threats from March to October 1969. Third, compellence against a threat to one of China's neighbours. China's decision to intervene in the Korean war is the most clear-cut example of such action. Fourth, deterrence of a threat to one of China's neighbours. This took place during the early stages of the Korean war, prior to Chinese intervention, and most clearly during the Vietnam war, 1964–6. Fifth, a probe of intentions. This fairly neutral, but none the less offensive, policy of testing the waters before further action was most notably pursued by China during the 1958 Taiwan crisis. Sixth, attack for the purposes of teaching a lesson. China pursued this objective not only during the Sino-Vietnamese war in 1979, but also in the final stages of the 1962 Sino-Indian war. Seventh, attack for the purposes of obtaining territory. This, the most offensive form of action, appeared both as a result of success in crises begun for more defensive reasons for example Korea, or Taiwan in 1954, and as a result of intentionally offensive campaigns such as that against Tibet and the Xisha Islands in 1974.

But these seven objectives do not appear on any simple ladder of escalation. In fact, China has pursued several of these goals in combination with one another, so that there have been at least four major types of actions in the past thirty-five years. First, China begins with the need to deter a threat and then acts out a strategy of compellence if deterrence fails. Having once achieved these defensive objectives, China attempts to end the crisis. Surprisingly there has only been one such clear-cut defensive use of force by China—its intervention in the Vietnam war.

Second, there is the opportunistic model wherein China begins by deterrence of a threat and follows up with compellence. But then, when faced with military success, China seizes the opportunity either to teach the enemy a lesson, or to take territory. Three such cases have taken place since 1949. In 1950, China entered the Korean war for defensive reasons but then sought to eliminate South Korea and therefore make gains when the military tide turned in its favour. When these gains were frustrated, China then reverted to the objective of deterrence. In 1954 China entered the Taiwan Straits crisis for defensive motives, but soon found it could make gains by seizing some offshore islands. In 1962, after deterring and taking action against Indian threats to China, Beijing so routed India that it found it could teach the Indians a lesson before withdrawing from captured Indian territory.

Third, there is the more offensive model. China begins gingerly with a probe, or even misses out this stage, and moves rapidly on to try to teach the opponent a lesson or seize territory. Four cases of this type of action have taken place since 1949. In the Tibet operation of 1950, China's initial probes were an attempt to achieve a peaceful take-over, but when the diplomatic phase produced no results, China seized Tibet. In the 1958 Taiwan Straits case China's probe of intentions was followed by a blockade in order to induce the fall of some offshore islands, and/or teach the US a lesson after the Middle East crisis of that year. As it turned out, China was frustrated by US power and achieved neither objective. In 1974, China's seizure of the Xisha Islands was achieved with virtually no probe of the opponent's intentions. In 1979 China's attack on Vietnam was preceded by a probe, but was intended to teach a lesson rather than seize territory. China failed even in this limited objective.

Fourth, the backfire model, is in many respects the opposite of the opportunist model. Here China begins with offensive purposes, but in the face of superior force finds itself needing to take defensive action. Only one case of this sort of military action has taken place. In 1969, following an attempt to teach the Soviet Union a lesson, China found itself under serious pressure from the Soviet Union.

This breakdown of objectives and patterns of Chinese actions is not intended to suggest that China acts any more or less offensively than any other great power. It is, however, intended to make clear that Chinese actions are at times aggressive, as might be expected from what remains a revolutionary power with great-power aspirations. It is also intended to make clear that China acts pragmatically, seizing opportunities where it finds them. The notion that it has an unchanging calculus or logic of policy underestimates the degree if pragmatism in Chinese defence policy.

Nor has China's military instrument been especially effective. China clearly obtained its objectives in Tibet, the Vietnam war, and the Xisha Islands. In two of those cases Chinese objectives were blatantly offensive. In two cases, Taiwan 1954 and India 1962, China gained more than it started out to obtain. In one case, Korea, China gained what it originally desired, but its objectives had been raised during the course of combat. In three other cases China clearly failed to obtain its goals. In Taiwan 1958, Zhenbao 1969, and the Sino-Vietnam war of 1979, China not only failed to teach a lesson, but certainly in one case, Zhenbao, seemed to be taught a lesson itself.

Chinese success or failure seemed primarily dependent on the balance between China's own strength and determination against that of its oppenent. China's relative strength—PLA power—was evident in Tibet, Taiwan 1954, India, and the Xisha crisis. China's determination was crucial in the Korean and Vietnam wars. Chinese failures in 1958, and 1979 were all primarily due to the enemy's superior military power and determination. Thus there is no pattern determining success or failure. In the end, each case must be assessed on an individual basis.

Patterns of Crisis Management

As has already been suggested, Chinese behaviour during foreign policy crises is anything but consistent. Therefore there are few patterns of crisis management to be identified. To be sure, a process of escalation and de-escalation in crises can be identified, but that is no different from saying 'what goes up, must come down'. The notion that crises inevitably pass through a common and in this case an especially Chinese method of crisis management is patently untrue. As already outlined, China pursues various different objectives and there are at least four different models of crisis behaviour. The course of Chinese crisis management is thus pragmatic, and changing—in fact like any other great power facing a number of internal and external constraints on policy.

Nor is it possible to suggest that Chinese crisis management is any better than that of other great powers. As has already been outlined, problems in China's behaviour stem from changing objectives from one crisis to another, and changing objectives during crises. The shift from defensive to offensive and then back to defensive objectives in the Korean war is as good an example as any of China's different approaches to crisis management.

There are however added reasons why China has consistently had problems in managing crises. These problems, as with the one already mentioned, are not especially Chinese problems, but rather seem to be common to most managers of crises. For example, Chinese communciation in crisis has often been less than consistent. China does not necessarily pursue a graduated policy of deterrence declarations. Certainly, in the offensive operations as in the Xisha and Sino-Vietnamese cases there was no gradual escalation of Chinese statements. In the Indian and Vietnam wars, Chinese statements were often inconsistent. In the 1958 Taiwan crisis it was obvious that China often did not mean what it said, thereby undermining the credibility of its communciations. Obviously where there were breakdowns in communication there was often more than one culprit, for example in the Korean war. But China is rarely blameless in this process of mutual incomprehension. Perhaps there has been too much emphasis in some previous analyses on the need to understand China better, when somewhat more equal attention should be paid to China's failure to understand its opponents. The Korea and Zhenbao clashes are prime examples of cases where war, and certainly high tension, might have been avoided if *China* as well as its opponent, had had a better understanding of the enemy's objectives.

To a certain extent, Chinese crisis management might have been improved if China had been simply stronger militarily. Part of China's problem has been the attempt to compensate for military weakness with political acumen. In Taiwan in 1958, China had to back down because it lacked the power to enforce its blockade. The shift from political to military operations left the United States uncertain as to subsequent Chinese actions. In the 1969 Zhenbao crisis and the 1979 Sino-Vietnamese war, China attempted a complex political effort to teach an opponent a lesson when China lacked sufficient military clout to do so. China has always made much of its pretension to mean what it says, but the meaning tends to be lost when China is unable to fulfill its threats. In such cases communication becomes incredible, and crises are poorly managed. Once again this is not to suggest that China is any worse at handling crises than any great power, but merely that it makes mistakes, and fails from time to time.

Chinese crisis management is therefore highly context-dependent. Mao's dictum 'despise the enemy strategically, but take him seriously tactically' is in fact a classic of pragmatic crisis management. China therefore can seek gains where it feels they are possible, and retreat when necessary. Short-term objectives can be sacrificed in the hope of long-term fulfillment. What determines specific action is a complex web of local battlefield conditions, and internal and external pressures.

It is also clear that crisis management takes place in stages. Thus objectives change, sometimes without the participants being fully aware of the process. In the 1969 Sino-Soviet clash, China found itself on the defensive but was loath to recognize that it had lost control of the crisis. Similarly in the 1958 Taiwan Straits crisis, China found the pace and nature of the crisis determined by others, and Chinese objectives had to change accordingly. These stages were often not fully understood as they happened, but in retrospect they point to the way in which crises can change their nature fairly swiftly.

Finally, it is plain that the nine crises rarely solved anything in themselves. Only in the Tibet and Xisha cases, where China was the outright winner, did the use of force more or less resolve the problem. But Tibet did erupt in revolt in 1959 and the Xisha Islands are only part of a much larger Chinese territorial claim. In three other crises, Chinese military operations seemed to make things worse rather than better. In the Sino-Indian war China's teaching of lessons surely left a much deeper wound in ties with Delhi than existed before. In the 1969 Sino-Soviet clash China's tweaking of the Russian bear's tail led to a far more serious deterioration of relations than could have been initially expected by the Chinese. The 1979 punishment of Vietnam certainly set back any slim hopes of a degree of *rapprochement* between the two states. In the other six cases the military instrument was seen as useful by China, albeit not uniformly so. Crisis management therefore has its uses, but it is rarely a way of resolving a problem. It is often less a sign of skill, and more an indication of desperation.

In sum, it is obviously necessary to study the way in which China has managed crises, but it should be clear that China is no more successful or straightforward in its conduct of policy than any other power. This is not an argument for throwing up one's hands and ceasing to study Chinese actions, but rather a recognition of the complexity of the problem. Indeed the complexity requires even greater analysis, albeit not of a kind that seeks to impose neat frameworks that do not fit a more messy reality.

Military Strategy

Despite the critical tone already adopted concerning the ability to identify patterns of crisis mangement, this study does not share MacNamara's belief that 'there is no such thing as strategy, only crisis management'. In fact, it could be argued that crisis management is so pragmatic that 'there is no such thing as crisis management, only common sense'. Strategy, on the other hand, is something grander, at least in theory. According to Liddell Hart, via Clausewitz, strategy is 'the art of distributing and applying military means to fulfil ends of policy'.[2] Strategy is therefore more concerned with what communists call military science, and defines fairly constant factors governing war. To what extent can such a Chinese strategy be identified from the past thirty-five years of the use of the Chinese military instrument?

First, there is the enduring validity of people's war. As has already been outlined, people's war is taken in its broadest context to mean a war that is conducted in keeping with local conditions. In the Chinese context (people's war is not necessarily only Chinese) people's war is derived from the realities of China, a massive territory, and even larger population, and a relatively poor peasant economy. Thus in the conception of people's war, combat is waged by placing greater stress on man than weapons. This does not mean that weapons are not important, and they cannot be updated (for people's war under modern conditions), but that China's large numbers of people are a more important asset than for other states.

This emphasis on the people, is also relevant in terms of broader aspects of defence. The defence of China is seen to be determined by the fact that an invader must control the one billion Chinese people in order to win. Nuclear threats are not seen as likely to achieve such victory. Neither are offshore powers who show they have no intention to fight on dry land. In order to defeat China, people's war suggests it must be invaded, and the people won over. Thus the defence of China is felt to be guaranteed by the facts of China's geography, and people's war is merely the theoretical statement of these realities.

People's war as a theory of war does not necessarily dictate specific military tactics. As already pointed out in chapter three, the tactics of the revolutionary war were suited to those conditions, but Mao never claimed they were valid for all types of wars. To make such an assertion was to confuse military science and military art. Therefore to speak of people's war under modern conditions, as has been done from time to time for close to twenty years in China, means merely the need to take into account modern conditions that affect even China. Chinese conditions change, and change is built into the doctrine of people's war by the injunction to suit local conditions. Like communist ideology, people's war doctrine is flexible enough to cope with change, for a military doctrine, like an ideology, that does not take into account change will surely die.

People's war has taken on additional glosses as it has been adapted to suit the needs of the Chinese Communist Party. For example, the Maoist/Leninist notion of a vanguard party gives pride of place to a military power harnessed to the wishes of the Party. For both Mao and Lenin, revolution was not a dinner party. Force was crucial, but the 'Party must control the gun', for force is only valid if directed for revolutionary ends. Thus China's people's war is directed by the CCP, and so it has been for more than thirty-five years. The military as an institution is always in principle subordinate to the civilian authority, a principle in keeping with waging a people's war. Military élites have a tendency otherwise to lose touch with the people.

Beyond these basic dimensions of people's war, it is difficult to suggest there is *a* Chinese strategy. Several propositions have been suggested as comprising this strategy, but none is universally valid. For example, surprise may have figured more prominently in Chinese military history than in the history of other states, but there is little evidence that it is more used by the PLA than by other armies. As has already been suggested above, surprise often conflicts with the need for effective communication in crisis. China uses surprise where it can, but it is not a substitute for military power. Chinese victories in the past thirty-five years have been more due to superior power than to effective surprise.

Second, there is said to be a Chinese bias in favour of fluid defence, one that allows the enemy to advance deep into Chinese territory so as to swallow up the invading force in a 'sea of people's war'. Thus according to this view China will not defend static positions such as frontiers, or fight beyond its gates. This view is fatally flawed in a number of ways. First, as already suggested, people's war is not so rigidly defensive or passive. Swallowing an enemy is advocated for certain conditions, but not all. People's war is more flexible than such a narrow definition suggests. Second, China has clearly fought beyond its frontiers when its leaders saw fit. In Korea and Vietnam where defence was seen as best conducted on other people's territory, China waged war beyond its gates. Similarly, when military conditions warranted it, China has fought wars of fixed lines, for example in the later phase of the Korean war. What is more, China has fought offensive campaigns which take the battle to the enemy rather than waiting for the enemy to strike first. These different types of operations were not ruled out by Mao and other strategists, even during the revolutionary war, and point to the fact that Maoist strategy was always more flexible. Mao recognized that conditions of war change, and the transformation from leader of a guerrilla army to a commander of a state with fixed frontiers necessarily required an adaptation of strategy. With a flexible and broad definition of people's war, these modern conditions posed no problems for Chinese strategists. The debates over strategy turned not on the question of whether people's war could be adapted, but rather on what was the nature of the threat. If the threat was defined as a general invasion of China, then the strategy of the revolutionary war was more applicable. But if the threat was seen as more local, or indeed if there was no threat but rather opportunity for gain, then a variation of strategy could be countenanced.

There are, however, two aspects of Chinese strategy that have remained more or less constant in the past thirty-five years. Naturally, both flow out of the basics of people's war already mentioned—China's large size, population, and poverty. First, there has been a bias towards ground combat, with air and sea forces relatively neglected. Airpower was used to any effect only in the Korean and Xisha operations. Naval power figured in the three offshore conflicts, but only in a major way in the Xisha operation.

China's continental as opposed to maritime bias has long been recognized. It stems from past practice, and from past experience of invasions from land neighbours. But most crucially, the bias stems from China's lack of power and resources to project forces to any distance. This lacuna is derived from economic weakness and lack of military modernization. As modernization is achieved, there is reason to believe this land bias may shift in some degree. But until then, the ground forces will remain the heart of Chinese defence policy.

The high cost of equipping a modern land army was an important motive for China obtaining nuclear weapons. Although China's nuclear weapons strategy cannot be developed in detail here,[3] it is important to point out some of the more distinctive aspects of Chinese thinking about nuclear weapons. First, Chinese thought on this subject flows naturally from China's over-arching people's war doctrine. That is to say, China argues that nuclear weapons cannot defeat it. Thus they are paper tigers. That these weapons can wreak devastation on China is no longer disputed (although Mao did dispute these facts from time to time). The Chinese argument is simply that to be excessively fearful of the utility of nuclear weapons, is to overstate their importance.

Therefore China sees the necessity for a nuclear deterrent, but less for defence against a general threat to China, and more for possible use in a limited war, where the weapons might be used to frighten an enemy. Thus China needs some weapons, at various ranges, to deter various ranges of threats, but so far sees no need for massive numbers in each category. This amounts to minimum deterrence in numbers, but not in range of weapons. The range of possible nuclear threats has no doubt been acutely felt in China. Leaving aside vague American threats in Korea or the Taiwan Straits, China has been on the receiving end of explicit Soviet nuclear threats in 1969. No other power has been so openly threatened. China's response was deterrence, but not the sort of deterrence pursued by the superpowers.

China's variation of minimum deterrence does however bear some resemblance to deterrence Soviet-style. The Soviet Union unlike the United States, believes in deterrence more by denial than by punishment. China holds that the threat to deny the enemy victory rather than merely to inflict punishment is the heart of deterrence. In order to carry out that threat, China, like the Soviet Union, requires three tiers of forces: one for passive defence (shelters) one for active defence (air defence) and one offensive capability to take the attack to the enemy. In this third tier, as already pointed out, China seeks to have ranged offensive forces like the superpowers, but without massive numbers in each category.

This brief resumé of Chinese nuclear strategy makes it clear that Beijing does have a distinctive view of the role of nuclear weapons in modern strategy. The notion of deterrence by denial with minimum ranged forces is derived essentially from the realities of Chinese demographic and economic power. China's relative denigration of nuclear forces has also meant that China's leaders have not used or threatened the use of their nuclear weapons in any crisis. China genuinely does not seem to see the utility of such weapons except for deterrence. Nor has China encouraged its allies to go nuclear. Pakistan, an ally facing the joint enemy in India (which has nuclear capability) has apparently not benefited from Chinese know-how to encourage proliferation of nuclear weapons.

In sum, military strategy can take several forms. For Moltke, it was merely the non-strategy of expedients.

All consecutive acts of war are not execution of a premeditated plan, but spontaneous actions, directed by military tactic...Strategy is a system of *ad hoc* expedients:...it is the application of knowledge to practical life, the development of an original idea in accordance with continually changing circumstances. It is the art of action under the pressure of the most difficult conditions.[4]

For others, at the opposite extreme, strategy is seen as the unchanging code of conduct inflexibly applied to all conflict. But there is a centre ground, for if the strategy is seen as tolerating some change, then China can be said to have retained a fairly consistent belief in the strategy of people's war. People's war as the guiding notion of Chinese military science suggests the importance of three dimensions in the way which in China uses its military instrument. First, the waging of war requires popular support. Second, the war should be fought in keeping with Chinese conditions, taking into consideration the poverty and peasant-based nature of China. Third, the war is directed by the CCP with firm control over the PLA. These criteria are not inflexible, for like any enduring principle of ideology, they need to adapt to inevitable change.

Military Tactics

In as much as it was difficult to find unchanging aspects of Chinese military strategy, it is not surprising that it is even more difficult to isolate components of Chinese tactics. A few enduring tactics result from the people's war dimension of strategy, but by and large tactics are too subject to changing conditions of war to last very long without being altered.

On balance, China does seem to rely fairly heavily on well-trained and ill-equipped troops for combat. Soldiers therefore favour close combat where technology counts for less. But such tactics need to be qualified, for in four cases since 1949, China has fought even less well-equipped forces. In the Tibet, Taiwan in 1954, India, and Xisha cases, the Chinese were the better equipped force. This is not to say that Chinese forces had changed their tactics, but just that in relative terms the nature of the tactics did not seem special as the enemy was fighting in a similar fashion. In four other conflicts, the Chinese did take on better equipped forces, but in only two cases, Taiwan in 1958, and Zhenbao in 1969 did the Chinese come off second best. In Korea and Vietnam China largely achieved its objectives. In the Sino-Vietnamese war China fought a less well-equipped force and still failed to achieve its objectives. Thus it seems that although some aspects of China's low technology approach to war seem distinctive, these are not a useful guide as to which conflicts China is likely to win.

Second, how dependent are Chinese tactics on mobility? Certainly, in guerrilla war, mobility was seen as crucial, But it seems less clear that this is a characteristic of Chinese tactics after 1949. To begin with, past Chinese mobility was by and large on foot, whereas modern mobility, for example in combined arms operations, is by vehicle or air. Thus China's type of mobility may be of a very limited kind. What is more, it seems that Chinese forces placed special emphasis on mobility in only two conflicts since 1949: Tibet and the Sino-Indian war. In both cases, China's type of foot-mobility could be brought to bear in difficult geographic conditions. In all other cases mobility either was not a factor on either side, or China was out-manoeuvred, as in the 1958 Taiwan Straits case. It is true that recent Chinese discussion of new tactics places new emphasis on mobility, especially in the context of combined arms operations, but the very notion of these type of tactics is not especially Chinese, and is seen as a change from the Chinese past.

Chinese troops do seem to rely on enormous fire-power and human wave tactics to help achieve tactical breakthroughs. In the Korean war under Soviet guidance, in the two Taiwan Straits crises and in the 1979 Vietnam venture, artillery was used heavily. However, this tactic is not specifically Chinese. In fact it was learned from the Soviet Union, and retained after the Sino-Soviet split, even though it put greater emphasis on weapons-over-men, and fixed positions over mobility. Clearly the Soviet influence in Chinese tactics lived on well after the split.

Finally, there is the question of human wave tactics. It has been suggested, mostly by China's enemies, that China achieves tactical breakthroughs by a callous disregard for human life. By flinging wave after wave of cannon fodder against enemy positions, Chinese troops can make local gains. This accusation has figured prominently in almost every conflict in which China has fought. It seems to have been true from time to time in almost all these cases, but not as a general feature of strategy. PLA tactics did use its main resource, people, from time to time to achieve key breakthroughs. The personal heroism of such attackers of course borders on fanatacism, but then most medals for heroism are awarded for doing what most would in other circumstances think unthinkable. On balance, human-wave tactics shows no more disregard for life than exhibited, say, by World War I generals.

In sum, Chinese tactics as a special feature of combat do not exist. There are tendencies of combat, such as the more lavish use of men than weapons, but the use of such tactics is far from uniform, or indeed unusual in comparison to many of China's opponents. China has shown itself to be pragmatic in tactics, for example in the Korean war when the final arrival of Soviet aid allowed China to shift from men to weapons, and from mobile to static war. Tactics, even more than strategy, change during war and reflect new conditions. The recent moves towards combined arms operations in the PLA is not startling, and is in keeping with past practice that allowed for other great changes in tactics.

The Role of Outside Powers

The myths of Sino-centrism, not to mention official Chinese propaganda, would have one believe that China needs to take little heed of outside powers, and certainly needs no alliances when it uses military force. However, while China does try to act as independently as possible, it does interact with other powers, and finds it necessary to compromise in seeking friends.

is already been suggested in the discussion of Chinese
es, the course of Chinese military actions is determined by
in domestic and foreign policy, as well as battlefield conditions. In China's consideration of outside forces, it pays special
attention to 'the correlation of forces'. This Marxist–Leninist
concept is also a pragmatic consideration of power politics—who is
with us and who is against us. China's calculation of risk seriously
considers not only the depth of China's concern, but the extent to
which outside powers will stand in China's way. It seems clear that,
especially as China sees its own interests as less crucial and the
interests of others as stronger, China takes into consideration outside
powers in a more serious manner. In the Korean and Vietnam wars,
where China perceived massive potential threats, it chose to act
largely alone, although in Korea it did eventually garner Soviet aid.
In the Taiwan, Tibet, Xisha and Sino-Vietnamese conflicts, China
acted on its own, but clearly took great care to consider the views of
outside forces.

It is therefore not surprising that China does not shun the concept
of alliances. While China has no formal multilateral alliance commit-
ments, (unlike the other superpowers) in the wider definition of the
term,[5] China does see the value of alliance. China signed a bilateral
alliance with the Soviet Union which had a defence component and
then called upon its terms in Korea and the second Taiwan crisis. In
China's eyes, Moscow's failure to live up to the principles of this
alliance was a problem in the Sino-Indian war.

China has also played the senior role in other alliances, for
example in a reportedly formal way with North Korea; in an explicit
but informal way with Vietnam in the 1960s; and in a less clear, but
no doubt important way with other Asian states, such as Pakistan
and more recently Thailand. China's proclamations of unity 'like
lips and teeth' is certainly a form of alliance. Finally, in the 1970s,
China's call for the 'unity' of anti-hegemonist powers against the
Soviet Union, was another form of alliance. The search for at least
tacit United States support in the 1979 Sino-Vietnamese war was
evidence of how seriously China took even this loose sense of
alliance.

Obviously there is the other side to the alliance coin as well.
China has shown willingness to go it alone without alliances,
especially where it thinks the risks can be controlled, or if the price
of alliance is too high. The Sino-Indian war and the Xisha operations

are examples of both. This is not to say that China kow-tows to foreigners, for when Mao said in 1949 that 'China had stood up', he properly pointed to the depth of feeling about past foreign abuse of China. But independence is a relative concept, even for China, and even in its most isolated periods since 1949 it never closed its eyes to the realities of world power or the 'correlation of forces'. That China formed alliances, formal and tacit, shows no more Chinese weakness than does the formation of Nato or the Warsaw Pact indicate superpower frailty. What it does show is that China is like other great powers, and does seek alliances where it has a use for, and can find them, in order to nudge the correlation of forces along to a better balance.

The process of forming alliances is not an abandonment of ideological principle. Certainly for the Soviet Union, despite the compromises that alliances even with weaker allies inevitably requires, such bonds indicate ideological strength. For China, the formation of alliances can be in keeping with the broad ideological goal of the triumph of socialism. However, the very flexibility of the ideology, setting millennial goals without setting out a road map to reach the destination, allows for alliance flexibility. If the Soviet Union is judged to have abandoned true socialism as China saw it in the early 1960s, then China is free to struggle against Moscow. Especially if the Soviet Union is seen to pose a threat to true socialism in China, then it might even be permissible to ally with the United States in the short term. The concept of the United Front is flexible,[6] as it depends on an assessment of the primary contradiction. In the 1950s the United States was seen as the main 'contradiction' but in the 1970s China viewed the Soviet Union as the primary threat. The 1980s looks like seeing a return to a variation on the Chinese 1960s view of two main contradictions in the two superpowers. Alliance formation is thus in keeping with a flexible ideology. This has in fact been the basis of China's changing views of the superpowers, and the Chinese habit of forming an alliance of sorts with one superpower or the other. It does show that for China, alliances are not necessarily a sacrifice of independence, and are therefore a useful dimension to the use of military force in foreign policy.

The Role of Domestic Politics

As has already been outlined, the use of military force is affected by the role of foreign pressures and the changing military fortunes on the battlefield. The third dimension, and of equal importance, is the domestic dimension, which in China as in other states, has a direct impact on the conduct of foreign policy.

It is striking that in almost every case of China's use of force in foreign policy, there has been domestic turmoil of some sort. In six cases: Tibet, Korea, Taiwan in 1958, Vietnam, Zhenbao, and Xisha, the unrest has been of a significant nature. This offers fertile ground for those who would see Chinese foreign policy as a reflection of domestic politics, whether it be defensive (China feels threatened from inside and out) or offensive (China covers up internal unrest by foreign ventures). Neither theory is sufficient. While domestic unrest must be considered in understanding Chinese foreign policy, it rarely produces such neat explanations.

If the domestic unrest is scrutinized more carefully, there seems to be a real foreign policy link in only two cases. In Korea, China's calculation of the risks posed by US power were undoubtedly skewed by the recent experience of defeating a US backed rival, the Guomindong, for power, and the still shaky state of the communist revolution. In the Vietnam war, China's reaction was the opposite, but equally linked to foreign policy. Mao's calculation of the need for a Cultural Revolution stemmed in part from a reaction to what Mao saw as revisionism in the Soviet Union. Thus, when faced with a perceived US threat in Vietnam, China both refused Soviet calls for 'United Action' but also refused to be drawn into large-scale foreign ventures that entailed risks that would deflect China from the Cultural Revolution. In these two cases the link between foreign and domestic policy is evident, but such a link was only one of several determinants of policy.

There is little evidence to support the opposing notion that China uses force in foreign policy to deflect internal dissent. The serious internal problems may have led China to act decisively in Tibet and Korea, as China openly stated its concern with the vulnerable state of its revolution. In 1958, the unrest created in China by the Great Leap Forward was manifest, but China clearly refrained from using the Taiwan incidents as a tool to divert attention from failures in domestic economic policy. In the mid-1960s, China purposely kept the Vietnam tensions as low as possible, so that it could concentrate on the domestic issue of the Cultural Revolution. If anything, in this case, foreign policy was used as an excuse to carry on domestic rectification. In 1969, the unrest which accompanied the end of the Cultural Revolution, and Lin Biao's burgeoning power may have made China feel more sensitive to a Soviet threat, but there is no evidence of any attempt to cover up these domestic problems by foreign ventures.

In each case, these domestic debates were complex. The cleavages of power were varied and often changed during the same crisis. As has already been pointed out, there are no neat and coherently consistent lines of factional argument in one, let alone several crises. For example, civilian control over the military was consistently maintained, but this is not to suggest that either group was uniform in its views. Debates took place within the civilian leadership, most notably in the 1958 Taiwan period and the mid-1960s Vietnam war period. At the same time, military men were often divided amongst themselves, whether it be along lines of inter-service disputes or region versus centre. Obviously it is necessary to analyse these divisions of opinion in order to understand how the military instrument was used, but there has been no pattern of, say, one group supporting foreign policy adventures or another favouring alliance with the Soviet Union. That factional politics takes place in China is indisputable. That such politics often touch on or coincide with foreign policy issues is equally unchallengeable. But that there is any model for such activites is to seek to simplify a far more complex reality.

Military Power in Foreign Policy

Obviously it is not possible to do justice to the evidence gathered in the preceding few hundred pages, but it is useful to try to restate some of the more basic principles that it is hoped have emerged from this study. Two phrases seem to recur most often—'Chinese conditions' and 'strategy of pragmatism'.

To the extent that there are some patterns in the use of the Chinese military instrument in foreign policy, they stem from the nature of China's large size, huge population and relative poverty. Some of these characteristics are shared with other states, but none have the same combination of elements. None share either the specific nature of Chinese ideology or institutions which were in part shaped by Chinese culture and history. Thus the notion of people's war is neither surprising for China, nor applicable far beyond its borders.

However, people's war is to be implemented, 'under modern conditions'. Yet modern conditions by their nature change, and that introduces the concept of pragmatism and expediency in policy. There has been too much of a tendency to see China as pursuing a specific logic or calculus of policy. This narrow conceptualization is derived in no small measure from China's own habit of explaining its defence policy in confident and coherent theoretical terms. But whether it be the model of Sino-Soviet alliance, or the 'theory of the three worlds', all such conceptualizations have found their way into the rubbish bin of history.

Now there is a new pragmatism and flexibility in Chinese foreign and domestic policy. Since the death of Mao China has felt more free to state clearly,

In order to have a correct understanding of...present-day international political phenomena (we must) start from reality and not from abstractions...Relations between countries or nations...are interconnected and extremely complicated. We can hardly form correct judgements on international political phenomena and make a correct differentiation of the political forces of the world if we adopt an idealistic or metaphysical approach and make abstract, isolated observations...Therefore, we can never lay down any hard and fast formula for differentiating the world's political forces....[7]

Comrade Mao Zedong's basic principles for directing wars are still applicable under today's objective conditions, but they must be applied flexibly in the light of actual conditions...theories should be a kind of observation, not rigid rules.[8]

It is hoped that the analysis in the preceding pages has been in keeping with this new spirit of 'seeking truth from facts'. That is not to say that this book has abandoned proper consideration of China's needs and problems, nor has it abandoned critical assessment of China's failures. China now seems to recognize a more complex reality, both at home and abroad, both in economic and in military policy. It would be a shame if foreign observers stuck to outmoded models when the Chinese themselves have become more pragmatic. This study has tried to explain Chinese defence policy as simply as possible, but not so simply that it misunderstands the more complex reality.

NOTES

1. Obviously notions of offensive and defensive action contain an element of value judgement. For example, the view that compellence of a threat to a neighbour is more offensive than mere deterrence of a threat to China, assumes that any action beyond China's territory is inherently more aggressive. It is a contentious judgement. This seven tier scheme is merely intended to highlight differences in objectives, not necessarily establish a code of 'just' conduct.
2. On the problems in defence strategy apart from those outlined in the introduction see Lawrence Freedman, *The Evolution of Nuclear Strategy* (London: Macmillan, 1981) pp. xvii–xviii.
3. Gerald Segal, 'China's Nuclear Posture for the 1980s', *Survival*, Vol. 23, No. 1, Jan/Feb. 1981, 'Strategy and Ethnic-chic', *International Affairs*, Vol. 60, No. 1, Winter 1983–4; 'Nuclear Forces' in Gerald Segal and William Tow, eds., *Chinese Defence Policy* (London: Macmillan, 1984).
4. Hajo Holborn, 'Moltke and Schlieffen, The Prussian-German School' in Edward Mead Earle ed., *Makers of Modern Strategy* (Princeton: Princeton University Press, 1961).
5. Robert Simmons, *The Strained Alliance* (New York: The Free Press, 1975) for the different notions of alliance.
6. David Armstrong, *Revolutionary Diplomacy* (Berkeley: University of California Press, 1977).
7. *People's Daily*, 1 November 1977, in *Peking Review* 4 November 1977, pp. 11–12. It is interesting that this quote appeared in an article ostensibly supporting the theory of the three worlds. The implicit undermining of the theory explains why the theory was abandoned soon after.
8. Su Yu to the PLA Military Academy, 19 January 1979, quoting in part from Clausewitz, *BBC/SWB/FE/6031/BII/5–6*.

Index